Transportation and Energy:
Strategies for a Sustainable Transportation System

ACEEE Books on Energy Policy and Energy Efficiency

Series Editor: Carl Blumstein

Using Consensus Building to Improve Utility Regulation

Transportation and Global Climate Change

Regulatory Incentives for Demand-Side Management

Energy-Efficiency and the Environment: Forging the Link

Efficient Electricity Use: A Development Strategy for Brazil

State of the Art of Energy Efficiency: Future Directions

Energy-Efficient Motor Systems:
A Handbook on Technology, Program and Policy Opportunities

Residential Indoor Air Quality and Energy Efficiency

Electric Utility Planning and Regulation

Energy Efficiency: Perspectives on Individual Behavior

Energy Efficiency in Buildings: Progress and Promise

ACEEE also publishes numerous reports on a variety of topics
addressing energy policy and energy efficiency.
For a catalog of publications, write:
ACEEE 2140 Shattuck Avenue, Suite 202,
Berkeley, California 94704.

Transportation and Energy:
Strategies for a Sustainable Transportation System

edited by
DANIEL SPERLING AND
SUSAN A. SHAHEEN

American Council for an Energy-Efficient Economy
Washington, D.C. and Berkeley, California
1995

Transportation and Energy:
Strategies for a Sustainable Transportation System

Published by the American Council for an Energy-Efficient Economy,
1001 Connecticut Avenue, N.W., Suite 801, Washington, D.C. 20036
and 2140 Shattuck Avenue, Suite 202, Berkeley, California 94704

Cover art copyright © 1995 M.C. Escher Heirs/Cordon Art—Baarn—Holland. All rights reserved.

Cover design by Chuck Myers
Printed in the United States of America by Edwards Brothers, Inc.

Library of Congress Cataloging-in-Publication Data

Transportation and energy: strategies for a sustainable transportation
    system/edited by Daniel Sperling and Susan A. Shaheen.
        p.323   23 cm.
    Papers from a conference held in August 1993 at the Asilomar Conference
Center, Pacific Grove, Calif.
    Includes bibliographical references and index.
    ISBN 0-918249-20-1: $28.00
    1. Transportation—United States—Planning—Congresses.
    2. Transportation—Environmental aspects—United States—Congresses.
    3. Environmental policy—United States—Congresses.   I. Sperling, Daniel,
    1951 –.   II. Shaheen, Susan A., 1966 –.
    HE206.2.T677 1995–03–95
    388'.068—dc20   95-13975
                                                                              CIP

 Printed on recycled paper.

Acknowledgments

The 1993 Asilomar Conference on Strategies for Sustainable Transportation was organized by the Institute of Transportation Studies–Davis (ITS) in conjunction with the Transportation Research Board (TRB) of the National Research Council, with leadership from the TRB Committee on Alternative Transportation Fuels and the TRB Committee on Energy Conservation and Transportation Demand. Conference sponsors were the U.S. Department of Energy, Office of Policy, Planning, and Program Evaluation; the U.S. Environmental Protection Agency, Office of Policy, Planning, and Evaluation; and the U.S. Department of Transportation, Federal Highway Administration. Co-sponsors included the American Council for an Energy-Efficient Economy (ACEEE), the Center for Transportation Research of Argonne National Laboratory, and the Center for Transportation Analysis of Oak Ridge National Laboratory. Organizational support was provided by Susie O'Bryant and Carol Earls of ITS–Davis. The sponsorship and support of each of these organizations is gratefully acknowledged.

ITS–Davis compiled these proceedings in conjunction with ACEEE. We would like to extend special thanks to the following individuals who assisted in preparing these proceedings and in making the conference a success: David Greene, for co-directing the conference, and the steering committee members, John DeCicco, Larry Johnson, David Kulp, Barry McNutt, and Wil Schroeer. We also thank Glee Murray, ACEEE's director of publications, and Mary Anne Stewart, copyeditor, for their assistance in editing and managing the book's publication.

The opinions expressed by authors within this book are those of the authors and do not necessarily represent the opinions of the editors or sponsoring institutions of the conference.

v

Preface

Widespread concern about energy efficiency, environmental quality, traffic congestion, and inequities between social classes have led to renewed scrutiny of our transportation systems. Is the auto-highway model as we know it anachronistic? Is a new model needed? Must behavior and attitudes shift? Should entirely new technologies be developed and deployed? These questions underlie the call for what is becoming known as "sustainable" transportation.

The concept of sustainability became a major issue internationally with the issuance of the Bruntland Commission Report, which resulted from the 1987 World Commission on Environmental Development. Although the agricultural community had explored the topic of sustainability at least a decade before the World Commission gathered in 1987, the Bruntland Report figures prominently as the keystone document on sustainability, establishing it as a global issue. That report has faced much criticism because it identified many issues relevant to sustainability, including equity, international trade, and technology development. Since 1987, many individuals from academia and various professional fields—including the transportation and energy communities—have struggled to define the concept of sustainability.

In August 1993, representatives from government, universities, industry, national laboratories, environmental advocacy groups, and private consulting firms from across the country gathered at the Asilomar Conference Center in Pacific Grove, California, to discuss strategies for a more sustainable transportation system. Over the course of three days, members of these diverse groups examined transportation and energy policies and emerging technologies. Conference presenters and participants explored a variety of strategies for analyzing and achieving more sustainable transportation planning, including: (1) the need for a paradigm shift in our current transportation and energy worldview, (2) policies for reducing travel demand, (3) travel forecasting models, (4) high-occupancy-vehicle alternatives, (5) alternatives to freight transportation, (6) alternative-fuel vehicles and the zero emission vehicle (ZEV) mandate, and (7) the role of social costs.

This volume contains many of the papers that were presented at the 1993 Asilomar conference. It is not, however, a complete compilation of conference presentations. Rather, it includes selected papers that elucidate new policies, strategies, and analytical models that aid the search for more sustainable transportation. All of the papers included in this book have been reviewed, revised, and expanded since the 1993 conference. Overall, this volume contains thirteen chapters that are organized into four separate sections.

Part I:
Toward a Sustainable Transportation Future for the United States

Part I of this book consists of an introductory chapter, "Sustainable Transportation: What Do We Mean and How Do We Get There?" by Deborah Gordon. It defines sustainable transportation, focusing on the United States, and offers recommendations for achieving this end. Arguing that the general goal of sustainable transportation is widely shared, but that the specifics of how to do so are not, Gordon examines three competing visions and solutions.

The first of these visions centers on changing people, the second on developing technology, and the third on changing prices. While at first glance these visions may appear to be distinct from one another, Gordon argues that the ultimate solution to the world's transportation problems is likely to require interconnecting all three visions. In her conclusion, Gordon suggests that shorter-term solutions are likely to focus on pricing and educational policies, that mid-term solutions will be premised on technology, and longer-term solutions will focus on changed land use patterns and lifestyles.

Part II:
Mobility, Growth, and System Change

Part II addresses large-scale system changes. In Chapter 2, "Land Use and Transportation Alternatives," Robert A. Johnston and Raju Ceerla explore the effect of pricing policies on land use and travel demand. The authors review case studies and modeling analyses of the effects of auto pricing and land use policies on travel and then describe modeling methods they used in studying the Sacramento, California, region. They contrast their findings with earlier studies and suggest modeling improvements that may help to better capture policy impacts on travel demand.

In Chapter 3, "Future Directions in Travel Forecasting," Frederick W. Ducca and Kenneth M. Vaughn focus on future directions for travel forecasting. They point out that today's state-of-the-practice travel demand models are not well suited to analyzing the types of transportation investments and policies being contemplated in the 1990s. The authors explore new demand modeling approaches amenable to professional use that more accurately forecast effects of policies and investments on auto ownership, peak spreading, and overall travel patterns. They suggest that future models will: (1) operate at the household level, (2) use a Geographical Information System (GIS) platform, (3) include both revealed and stated preference data, (4) reflect time of day, (5) interrelate regional travel demand and traffic operations models, and (6) address relationships between long-term land use decisions and daily travel decisions.

Chapter 4, "Strategies for Goods Movement in a Sustainable Transportation System," by Laurence O'Rourke and Michael F. Lawrence, focuses on the efficient movement of goods. The authors examine the relative efficiency and environmental impact of different modes of freight transportation in a multimodal context. They explore the potential environmental and energy security benefits associated with shifting between modes and the barriers to doing so. Recent developments in heavy-duty truck fuel efficiency and alternative-fuel use are examined.

Part III:
Energy and Vehicle Alternatives

Part III includes several chapters that address opportunities to introduce more benign vehicles and fuels. In Chapter 5, "Hypercars: The Next Industrial Revolution," Amory B. Lovins examines ultralight hybrid-electric vehicle technology. He argues that vehicles can be made so efficient and inexpensive that government mandates will not be needed to bring them to market. These new vehicles would represent a leap forward to a completely new design.

According to Lovins, ultralight hypercars could be extremely efficient because they would (1) cut the overall weight of a typical vehicle by three to four times through the use of advanced materials, primarily synthetic composites; (2) reduce aerodynamic drag by two to six times; (3) cut tire and road energy losses by three to five times through the combination of better tires and less weight; and (4) operate the internal combustion engine at near-constant speed by matching it with an electricity storage device. Because the composite materials used to construct these superefficient vehicles could absorb far more energy per pound than traditional metal, they could be equally as safe as today's steel cars.

According to Lovins, the hypercar, even when run on conventional fuels, would be cleaner than a pure electric battery-powered vehicle because the emissions from an electricity-generating power plant to charge the battery would be greater than the emissions produced by the hypercar's tailpipe. Consequently, hypercars could be even cleaner than ZEVs.

Chapter 6, "Alternative Fuels and Greenhouse Gas Emission Policy," by Laurie Michaelis, presents the results of a study carried out at the International Energy Agency (IEA). This chapter draws on IEA's analysis of the life-cycle energy use and greenhouse gas emissions of a range of alternative transportation fuels. Michaelis discusses the performance and market potential of each these alternative fuels and policies for reducing greenhouse gas emissions.

In Chapter 7, "Emission Reductions of Alternative-Fuel Vehicles: Implications for Vehicle and Fuel Price Subsidies," Michael Quanlu Wang analyzes the cost-effectiveness of vehicle and fuel pricing strategies for controlling emissions from alternative-fuel vehicles. Emission control cost-effectiveness was estimated for ten alternative-fuel-vehicle (AFV) types. Wang found that compressed natural gas vehicles were the most cost-effective and E85 flexible-fuel vehicles the least effective if air pollutant emission reductions were the *only* goal. However, these results were highly sensitive to changes in vehicle and fuel costs, AFV emissions reductions, and baseline gasoline vehicle emissions. When the three parameters remained uniform across AFV types, the vehicle rankings remained essentially unchanged. In contrast, when Wang altered the three parameters, the rankings changed dramatically. Ranked on the basis of their emissions reductions, vehicles fueled with reformulated gasoline had the lowest per-vehicle value, and electric vehicles had the highest value.

In Chapter 8, "A Social Cost Analysis of Alternative Fuels for Light Vehicles," Mark Fulmer and Stephen Bernow examine a broader set of costs and benefits. In their study, the authors analyzed natural gas, electricity, methanol, and gasoline fuels for two different scenarios—the "near term" and "longer term"—to reflect an evolution in technologies and environmental requirements over time. In each scenario, the authors assigned values to environmental impacts, focusing on air pollution. They distinguished between areas that are severely polluted and those that are less so. Because other externalities, such as congestion and energy security, are not included in this study, the social cost analysis should be considered partial.

In the near term, the authors found that light-duty vehicles fueled by gasoline would likely have the lowest direct and social costs in both environmental settings. In the longer term, the authors found that electric light-duty vehicles would potentially replace gasoline-powered vehicles as the lowest-social-cost option in both environmental settings. The authors concluded that any number of different, yet plausible, sets of assumptions in this study could have changed the results so that any of the tested fuels could have been considered "least cost."

Part IV:
Beyond Command and Control

Part IV examines the use of market-based and technology-forcing regulatory approaches. Chapter 9, "A Consumer Surplus Analysis of Market-Based Demand Management Policies in Southern California," by Michael Cameron, has a dual objective. The first is to demonstrate that the implementation of market-based demand management policies, such as congestion pricing, would reduce urban traffic congestion and mobile-source air pollution. His second objective is methodological: to present a consumer surplus model for conducting transportation policy analysis. Among the findings Cameron presents is an estimate that a fee of $0.95 per vehicle-mile (roughly equivalent to a gasoline tax of $1.25) would increase the net transportation benefits of Southern California's surface transportation system by 10 percent: from about $30 billion to $33 billion per year.

Chapter 10, "Steering with Prices: Fuel and Vehicle Taxation as Market Incentives for Higher Fuel Economy," by John M. DeCicco and Deborah Gordon, examines the likely effectiveness of pricing policies as a way to reduce light-vehicle fuel consumption in the United States. The authors analyze a gas guzzler tax, other taxes or registration fees based on vehicle fuel consumption rates, and feebates (whereby rebates are provided to purchasers of vehicles with lower than average fuel consumption). They provide evidence that the primary response to an increase in fuel price is more fuel-conserving vehicles, not less driving.

DeCicco and Gordon estimate that light-vehicle fuel consumption in the year 2010 could be held to 1990 levels by increasing retail gasoline prices two- to threefold or implementing feebates that average 5 to 10 percent of the total vehicle price. They conclude that vehicle pricing approaches, such as feebates, have a greater potential for controlling light-vehicle fuel consumption than do gasoline taxes. In closing, the authors note that the development of an effective and equitable vehicle pricing policy requires the active participation of automakers and that the effectiveness of new policies will hinge on product development and marketing strategies of the auto manufacturers.

Chapter 11, "Taxation Policies Affecting Automobile Characteristics and Use in Western Europe, Japan, and the United States 1970–1990," by Lee Schipper and Gunnar Eriksson, examines a variety of pricing strategies to restrain fuel and automobile use. The authors come to conclusions different from those of Gordon and DeCicco. Analyzing data from Organisation for Economic Cooperation and Development (OECD) countries, Schipper and Eriksson conclude that "taxation schemes aimed directly at fuel (fuel taxes) or driving (kilometer taxes) will have a more profound impact on fuel use than those aimed primarily at new-car purchases."

Chapter 12, "Technology, Economics, and the ZEV Mandate: A Vehicle Manufacturer's Perspective," by Dean A. Drake, addresses electric vehicles and the zero-emission vehicle mandate. Drake points out that the free market has favored gasoline-powered vehicles over electric vehicles and claims that there is little evidence to suggest that electric vehicles will ever occupy more than a market niche. He argues that the appropriateness of the ZEV mandate should be reexamined if electric vehicles will require continuous subsidies. Drake believes that the ZEV mandate is the wrong policy instrument to encourage the development of electric vehicles.

Chapter 13, "How Government and Industry Can Cooperate to Promote Fuel Conservation: An Industry Perspective," by Paul McCarthy, begins with a brief overview of cooperative research efforts related to improving vehicle fuel efficiency. He describes the emerging precompetitive cooperation among the Big Three and the active participation of federal laboratories in developing automotive technology as unprecedented but points out that significant barriers to effective cooperation remain. Some of these barriers are institutional, reflecting the differing constraints and objectives of government and industry. The author explores from an industry perspective the constraints faced by automakers in responding to new regulatory initiatives. After reviewing barriers, he takes a broader view of policy issues by exploring some options and tradeoffs associated with efforts to conserve fuel. McCarthy makes a case for rethinking cooperation between government and industry in balancing public and private goals and stresses the use of benefit-cost analysis tools in helping government and industry determine what are reasonable expectations to place on each other.

Final Comments

One of the primary objectives of the conference organizers was to offer a wide range of research results and views on how to create more sustainable transportation systems. The success of the conference in fulfilling this objective is reflected in the divergence of views and research represented in this volume. This divergence stems from several phenomena: the large but uncertain benefits and costs of new technologies, the limited understanding of travel and purchase behavior, and the large number of interests at stake. It is not surprising that decision makers will find it difficult to agree on a definition of sustainable transportation, much less the best approach to achieving it.

A benefit of the 1993 Asilomar conference is that it brought decision makers and researchers together in a relaxing setting to continue the process of untangling facts, values, and beliefs. This book is part of a more formal process aimed at the same goal—that of determining what is known, what is unknown, and what is unknowable.

Contents

Transportation and Energy:

Strategies for a Sustainable Transportation System

Chapter One

Sustainable Transportation: What Do We Mean and How Do We Get There?

DEBORAH GORDON

It is frequently asserted that our current transportation system is not sustainable and that we need to make changes to remedy this situation. I have often made similar statements myself. The problem with such a broad statement, of course, is that it avoids the central question: What is "sustainable transportation" and how do we get there?

Sustainable transportation, it seems to me, is one of those slippery concepts like a "sound economy" or a "good school system." All of us are for it, but no one is certain exactly what anyone else means by it.

Defining what we mean by sustainable transportation is nevertheless important because the stakes are so high. Transportation is inextricably linked not only to our private well-being but to a host of societal problems. Some of the social costs of transportation include air pollution, lost productivity due to traffic congestion, death and disability resulting from traffic accidents, military costs to secure oil imports, water pollution caused by spilled petroleum, and global warming. As hard as it is to quantify these externalities, few would disagree that they exist and must be addressed. If we fail to make improvements in the transportation sector, we will each pay these costs increasingly with our time, health, and welfare. Moreover, the decisions that we make today affect not only us, but future generations to come.

To make matters more complicated, the transportation system comprises a complex network of economic activities whose many players have varied—and sometimes conflicting—interests. Some of these activities include infrastructure construction, vehicle manufacture, fossil fuel production, vehicle use (passenger and freight), vehicle disposal, and transportation-related land use development. Taken together, these transportation activities make up 20 percent of the U.S. gross national product and employ one out of every ten Americans. Given the scope of individual and societal investment, changes to the transportation sector will come slowly over time.

Defining "Sustainable Transportation"

Underlying the debate over the meaning of sustainable transportation, I believe, are three competing visions of the nature of our transportation problems and their solutions. The first of these visions centers on changing people and the way they live, the second on changing technology, and the third on changing prices.

Changing People

The first vision starts from the premise that what we need to do is to change people and the way they live. The overarching societal goal here is to reduce the need for transportation in the first place. This view is premised on the belief that automobile vehicle-miles of travel (VMT) are a destructive ecological force. According to Senator John Chafee (R-RI) (1992), for example, we must permanently change our transportation habits if we are going to maintain our mobility and preserve the environment that sustains us. It is no longer enough to manage demand; we must reduce demand.

Accordingly, all needs—work, shopping, personal services, and other social and recreational activities—would be met close to where we live, within a comfortable walking distance, thereby alleviating motorized transportation demand. This arrangement is termed "access by proximity." Clearly this view of sustainable transportation must be accompanied by a very different land use pattern characterized by compact, multifunctional, pedestrian- and bicycle-oriented urban development. Some who subscribe to this vision take it a step further and would restrict car use in urban areas or ban cars altogether.

Changing Technology

The goal of the second vision of sustainability, which I term "changing technology," is to employ appropriate technologies to reduce the impact of transportation on society. Rather than focusing on behavior directly, this view is premised on providing for relatively constant transportation demand at a lower ecological impact. For example, according to John Gibbons (1992), White House science policy advisor and former director of the Congressional Office of Technology Assessment, ample evidence suggests that technological improvements alone can make substantial contributions to sustainability.

The goal here is to relieve transportation's burden on society while maintaining individual mobility and preserving our current lifestyles. Policies consistent with this vision include cleaner, alternative-fueled vehicles; enhanced vehicle fuel economy; ultralight composite, nonfossil-fueled cars; demand-responsive public transit and ridesharing; telecommunications; and a host of other evolving advanced transportation technologies.

Changing Prices

The third vision of sustainability assumes that what we need to do is to get the prices right and let the market solve our transportation problems. The goal of this vision is to modify transportation demand through the use of market forces to enhance overall systemwide transportation efficiency. Social costs must be fully accounted for if we expect consumers to make choices that have societal benefits. Underpricing transportation services has resulted in their overconsumption and a misallocation of resources. Russell Train (1992), chairman of the World Wildlife Fund, argues that the most efficient way to achieve environmental progress toward sustainability is to harness market forces. The role of public policy in this framework is to send the right signals to the economy and make the marketplace work for, instead of against, environmental protection.

A comprehensive means of achieving this goal would be to develop a least-social-cost planning approach to transportation decision making. Other pricing options would employ taxes, subsidies, feebates, user fees, and marginal cost pricing to internalize transportation-related externalities and provide individuals with economic information that results in environmentally beneficial mobility choices. Moreover, the revenues generated would be invested into those transportation services that have the lowest ecological impact on society.

3

In the environmental community as well as within industry and government, these three visions are often portrayed as competing. One reason that the debate is so heated is that these views implicate core beliefs on difficult philosophic questions, including the desirability of capitalism as an economic system, the potential for scientific progress, and even one's conception of human nature. As the debate rages on, socially beneficial change is put on hold.

The great irony of this debate is, of course, that although at first these visions may appear to be competing, the ultimate solutions to our transportation problems are likely to rely on all of them and their inherent interconnections. What, after all, is the point of setting prices closer to economic costs unless we think consumers will make more socially efficient choices? Why force the market to develop new technologies unless we expect people actually to use them effectively? And finally, why attempt to mandate behavioral changes unless we believe that we have the technological, economic, and political capacity to help people find more socially efficient transportation arrangements?

Policies That Move Us Toward Sustainable Transportation

If we are serious about achieving sustainable transportation, we need policies that impose the true costs of transportation on different modes, bring to market technologies that reduce transportation impacts, and provide information for people to make better choices. We need to change the incentives facing individuals and thereby individual behavior so that entire communities will demand transportation and land use improvements. Clearly, the most effective policies are those that affect all three visions of sustainability.

I do not mean to imply that tensions between different policy solutions do not exist, for they clearly do. One example of such conflict is evident in the current debate on intelligent transportation systems (ITS) (also known as intelligent vehicle highway systems, or IVHS). This technology is being developed to address concerns about highway capacity, but if ITS is used to effectively double lane-miles of roadway, the environment is likely to suffer in the long run. Clearly, in an era of fiscal constraints, solving our transportation-related problems will be even harder. All future transportation investments must provide enhanced accessibility along with reduced social impacts. Environmental quality, energy efficiency, and aesthetics deserve as much attention in the transportation policy debate as personal freedom, convenience, and safety.

4

Whether it is to commute to work, to bring children to day care, or to buy a quart of milk, there must be options other than driving alone if the transportation system is to be ecologically sustainable. These options must be delivered through rational pricing strategies, appropriate technology investments, improved user information, and redefined development patterns.

Sustainable transportation policies must overcome several hurdles. First, on the margin, the cost to drive a car is too low in comparison to its fixed costs. Given that 80 percent of the total cost to own and operate a car is fixed—that is, remains the same whether the car remains in the garage or is used to the maximum extent possible—Americans are acting rationally when they use their cars to provide nearly all of their transportation needs.

Second, most motorists believe they have paid for the roads through gasoline taxes. This is a myth. But the government has been willing to maintain a system of highly subsidized automobile use that maintains this misperception. Our road-based transportation system is highly underpriced with respect to the total cost of providing transportation services. System user fees cover only a portion of the maintenance, repair, and law enforcement costs associated with roads and do not contribute even a penny to the social costs that arise.

Finally, through lack of coordination on land use, transportation, and environmental policy goals, most U.S. cities have followed an auto-oriented development pattern resulting in the least sustainable transportation use. Desired destinations are spread out, chiefly through sprawled land use, and a network of roads requires individuals to drive their own vehicles to fulfill their desired daily needs. The Intermodal Surface Transportation and Efficiency Act (ISTEA) of 1991 is the first federal attempt to initiate and encourage some coordination between land use, transportation, and environmental objectives, but it is too early to determine how successful these efforts will be.

Because transportation is considered by many to be a "public good," the government has historically been required to take a lead role as a transportation policymaker. The U.S. policy adopted in 1956—to make its biggest transportation investment in a facility most suited for cars and trucks, namely in highways—has achieved its intended goals, but they have come with a price. For too long the negative side effects of our transportation system—pollution, excessive oil use, injury, diminished aesthetics, and congestion—have been overlooked.

But setting transportation policy is not, nor should it be, the responsibility of government alone. More than most issues, transportation policy directly affects, often on a daily basis, the welfare of individuals and institutions throughout society, from consumers to corporations. As a result, transportation policy, to be effective, must take into account the range of interests at stake and must encourage wide public participation.

Clearly no single policy can solve our transportation problems. Rather, a comprehensive solution will require an array of creative policies drawing from each of the sustainable transportation visions outlined above: changing behavior, changing technology, and changing prices.

Pricing Policies

Transportation systems and services must be priced to result in the optimal allocation of resources. This entails including external social costs into the pricing of all goods. Taxation, subsidization, user fees, and other economic policies can be used to induce behavior rather than mandate it. This principle should be applied broadly throughout the transportation sector, including vehicle manufacturing, infrastructure construction, fuel production, vehicle operations, vehicle disposal, and land use development.

Some of the more promising pricing policies that have been proposed include:

1. *Taxes:* Increasing state and regional fuel taxes and dedicating revenues generated to single-occupant-vehicle (SOV) transportation alternatives.

2. *Subsidies:* Increasing public transportation subsidies to maintain and expand system service while keeping fares down.

3. *User fees:* Establishing user fees in the form of pay-as-you-drive insurance and variable-road-pricing programs to increase the marginal cost of driving. Any revenues generated by road pricing would be invested into alternatives to SOV modes of transportation.

4. *Allowances:* Instituting cash allowances for individuals who forego driving and relinquish their parking spaces. Program funds would come from parking fees.

5. *Variable interest rates:* Establishing variable interest rates on home mortgages according to household commute distances. Less driving would yield lower house payments.

6. *Buyback programs:* Initiating buyback programs, such as vehicle scrappage programs that buy back the dirtiest and least efficient cars and trucks from consumers. Scrapped vehicles can be repaired, if possible, or removed permanently from use.

7. *Feebates:* Adopting a system of feebates directed at either consumers or manufacturers. Such financial incentives would reward purchasers or producers of clean, fuel-efficient vehicles and penalize purchasers or producers of dirty, inefficient vehicles. Examples of programs previously introduced or adopted include California's DRIVE+ and EV Development Incentive Programs, and Maryland's Gas Guzzler Feebate Program.

8. *Least-social-cost planning framework:* The successful application of least-cost integrated resource planning by utilities has generated much interest in developing a similar framework for transportation decision making. Under this new paradigm, decision makers would look toward integration of the full range of available options to truly gauge the best use of scarce transportation investment dollars while factoring in externalities. Instead of focusing on transportation supply, planners would concentrate on providing transportation services.

Developing a least-social-cost planning framework for transportation is complex because of the many social, political, environmental, and financial factors that are difficult to quantify accurately. To institute this type of planning process, economic tools would need to be developed to compare all transportation alternatives across a full range of social and private criteria. Although decision makers are discussing such an integrated transportation planning framework, to date it has not been applied.

Technology Policies

Technology plays a vital role in making different transportation options convenient and in providing necessary information to users and suppliers. Moreover, technology is often employed to reduce environmental damage without reducing utility. Again, technology policies should be broadly applied throughout the entire transportation sector. However, when technology works to reduce the private or social costs of transportation, policymakers must be careful that unintended consequences do not substantially erode the intended benefits—for example, through rebound effects and induced latent demand.

The potential of transportation technologies is essentially limitless. But not all advanced transportation technologies result in environmental benefits. Some of the more promising technological policies from a sustainable perspective include:

1. *Investing in low-tech transportation alternatives, such as bicycle and pedestrian services.* These technologies include innovative human-

powered vehicles (which can be assisted electrically); battery-powered shopping carts for neighborhood shopping; infrastructure designs for safe pedestrian passage and safe use and storage of bicycles; and covered solar-powered pedestrian and bicycle malls.

2. *Developing ITS technologies for public transit and ridesharing vehicles.* Telecommunications links to home or office could provide real-time information to transit users. Rather than wasting time waiting, transit users would gain convenience and be assured of the system's reliability. Telecommunications could also be used to establish a demand-responsive transit system in which the user could place a standing order for public transit on a daily basis. Hand-held interactive computers could be used to connect SOV drivers with available passengers. A security check of both the passenger's and driver's accounts would enhance safety, and a financial transfer between accounts could induce such ridesharing arrangements.

3. *Developing resource-efficient transportation technologies that minimize waste by-products.* Such technologies include enhanced vehicle efficiency; zero-emission vehicles; ultralight composite, non-fossil-fueled cars; telecommuting; telework centers; teleconferencing; rubber-modified asphalt pavement to recycle waste tires; efficient technologies and recycling programs in vehicle manufacturing processes; and steel-wheel high-speed rail to compete with short-distance air travel.

Land Use Policies

America's land use is oriented completely around the automobile. Some 60,000 square miles (an area about the size of Georgia) are dedicated to automobile infrastructure. It should not be surprising, therefore, that 98 percent of U.S. transportation needs are met by cars and trucks. Our current land use patterns—especially those of sprawled metropolitan areas, where 75 percent of all Americans now live—challenge the use of alternative modes of transportation. Without land use reforms, it is unlikely that pricing and technology strategies will deliver their full effectiveness for change in the long term.

Examples of land use policies that would result in a more sustainable transportation sector include:

1. *Designing urban villages* characterized by "European-style" development, which combines medium- and high-density housing with diverse commercial facilities in a car-free environment.

2. *Employing mixed-use development around transit*—especially rail

transit—including residential, commercial, industrial, and recreational developments.

3. *Instituting traffic calming* in urban and suburban areas to create more pedestrian- and bicycle-friendly environments.

4. *Reconfiguring zoning ordinances* to encourage development supportive of alternative transportation modes.

5. *Adopting land use investment strategies,* such as land acquisition programs, and *financial strategies,* such as development fees and land banking, to encourage non-auto-oriented development.

6. *Instituting regulatory strategies,* such as conservation zoning and development timing permitting, to oversee the urban development process.

7. *Revisiting parking requirements* in urban and suburban areas. In many cases these ordinances are antiquated and require the unnecessary paving of parking lots.

Behavioral and Educational Policies

Changing people and the way they use transportation may require behavioral and educational policies. Such policies can range from dissemination of information to requests for voluntary action to actual restrictions on types of vehicle used. We already employ many restrictive behavioral policies in the transportation sector, such as speed limits and laws restricting drunk driving. Cities in other countries—for example, Mexico City—take these policies a step further by imposing mandatory restrictions on daily vehicle use. Clearly this is a sensitive subject in the United States because policymakers recognize that motorists and voters are one and the same, and behavioral policies affecting personal transportation are not usually very popular. Nevertheless, educational policies can be extremely effective, as evidenced by the success of recycling programs in recent years.

Behavioral and educational policies that could result in a more sustainable transportation sector include:

1. *Promoting voluntary "no-drive" days* based on license plate numbers. This policy could be triggered by high-pollution days or congestion problems.

2. *Increasing the distribution of the EPA Gas Mileage Guide* to new-vehicle purchasers and including emissions information for cleaner vehicle models in the guide.

3. *Launching statewide promotional campaigns* for transit and high-occupancy-vehicle programs, advertising the benefits of such behavioral changes to the public.

4. *Using the media to encourage shifts in travel behavior.* TV can educate an entire community about socially beneficial transportation options and provide moral suasion that leads to behavior changes.

5. *Providing training for the general public* on techniques to reduce motor vehicle emissions, energy use, and accidents, as well as training on safe bicycling techniques.

6. *Educating children* before they are old enough to use a car. Materials on the societal impacts of our transportation choices can be incorporated into primary and secondary school curriculums in programs similar to those on recycling, which has become a popular subject to teach younger children.

Conclusion

The overarching societal goal for transportation is to articulate a vision of our transportation future—a future that both enhances choice and protects natural ecosystems—and to adopt specific strategies to achieve that vision. Developing a sustainable transportation future seems at first blush a reasonable societal goal, but most of us have a hard time articulating what sustainable transportation really means.

I have argued that sustainable transportation entails elements of several visions. These visions include changing people and the way they live, changing prices, and changing technology. Each of these, in turn, will contribute to a transportation sector that has fewer problems attributed to it.

Given the range of players involved and what is at stake, consensus will be difficult to achieve on precisely what the transportation sector of tomorrow should look like. Individuals must choose how to get around while minimizing inconvenience and cost; planners must design transportation improvements and arrange for their funding; transportation industries must market products and services that contribute to their profitability; and policymakers must pass innovative transportation laws while maintaining their public support. Such complexity means that solutions will come slowly over time.

There is no simple solution to our transportation problems. We need transportation policies that will reinforce the societal goals we all establish. One way to arrive at such policies may be through an integrated, least-social-cost decision-making framework. Comprehensive policymaking, however, is difficult to achieve, especially in a sector with so many different stakeholders acting independently of one another. Thus, individual transportation policy solutions are more likely to be adopted in piecemeal fashion. Shorter-term solutions may focus on pricing and educational policies, midterm solutions on technology, and longer-term solutions on land use patterns.

As for the very long term, it is difficult to predict which policies will be most beneficial and effective. Certainly we need a transportation sector in which there are good alternatives to single-occupant cars and one in which consumers, producers, and other transportation actors have incentives to behave in socially efficient ways. But what we need most of all is a continuing commitment to search for new and better answers and, more importantly, to acknowledge and learn from our mistakes.

References

Chafee, John H. 1992. "Driving Home a New Transportation Policy." *EPA Journal* 18 (4): 21–23.

Gibbons, John. 1992. "Moving Beyond the 'Tech Fix.'" *EPA Journal* 18 (4): 29–31.

Train, Russell E. 1992. "A Call for Sustainability." *EPA Journal* 18 (4): 7–10.

Chapter Two

Land Use and Transportation Alternatives

ROBERT A. JOHNSTON AND RAJU CEERLA

It is claimed that many metropolitan regions in the United States will not be able to meet the federal Clean Air Act requirements for emissions reductions unless they can substantially reduce travel (U.S. OTA 1988). Improved "smog" inspection procedures and cleaner engines will not be adequate to meet the new standards in many urban regions, given present technologies and the short time-lines in the act.

Several types of modest travel demand management (TDM) measures are being deployed throughout the nation. Generally speaking, these measures will decrease vehicle-miles traveled (VMT) by only a few percentage points over the next ten years, a reduction that will not balance VMT growth in most regions (e.g., see Bay Area 1991; Bae 1993). There are, however, two types of TDMs, largely untried in the United States, that offer the possibility of greater reductions in trips and VMT: travel pricing measures and land use measures that support transit, walking, and bicycling.

Background

Many general overviews of transportation demand predict increased travel in developed countries in the future because of

13

higher incomes allowing increased levels of activity per person. These researchers also predict a continuation of the shift to more energy-intensive modes. Even though each mode is becoming less energy-intensive because of technological improvements, the increases in VMT and the switch to autos and airplanes for passengers, and to trucks for freight, is causing an increase in energy use in transportation per capita (Schipper, Steiner, and Meyers 1993). Vehicle growth exceeds population growth, especially in developing nations, and these nations will contribute much greater shares of pollutants and greenhouse gases in the future (Walsh 1993).

In the United States, the fact that travel costs have gone down, especially out-of-pocket costs, has increased travel, even in recent years when per-worker incomes have fallen slightly. Shelter costs have risen as a proportion of income, and therefore households have traded longer commutes for cheaper housing in the suburbs. In addition, basic employment is no longer dependent on rail facilities and therefore is also decentralizing.

All of these trends have caused concern, and attention recently has focused on TDM measures, which are required by the federal Clean Air Act in addition to its requirements for substantial reductions in mobile emissions in many urban regions.

Literature Review

Land use policies and travel pricing policies are largely untried in the United States. For this reason, both empirical studies and simulation research will be reviewed.

Land Use Policies

The two main types of land use measures for TDM are jobs/housing balance and density increases near to transit facilities.

The general opinion is that jobs/housing balance (land use mix) will not reduce motorized trips and VMT much because theoretically one expects workers to search for jobs within a certain (say, 30-minute) commute radius, not a shorter one, and therefore they end up with 25-minute average commutes because the bulk of the jobs are in the outer area of their circular search pattern.

A comparative study using models from several urban regions in developed countries to test the same TDM policies found that jobs/housing balance alone reduced VMT by only a few percentage points because of this phenomenon (Webster, Bly, and Paulley 1988). However, a southern California agency simulating a regional jobs/

housing balance policy found that it could reduce VMT by 11 percent and vehicle-hours of delay (VHD) by 63 percent over 20 years (SCAG 1988a). Unfortunately, the modeling was apparently done incorrectly, without the feedback of assigned travel times to the trip distribution modeling step (SCAG 1988b). Such an omission could be expected to cause the overprojection of changes in VMT and, especially, in VHD. Moreover, research by Giuliano (1992) showed that actual commute distances in southern California were shorter for workers who *worked* in areas with poor jobs/housing balances. Thus the large reduction in VMT found by SCAG probably is largely an artifact of the model or of its operation.

Analysis of San Francisco Bay Area data for selected suburban work zones established that the availability of housing *in a workplace zone* slightly decreased commute travel distance and increased the share of commute trips by foot and bicycle. However, analysis of the same data for the entire region at the district level showed no relation between jobs/housing ratio in the district of travelers' *residences* and total daily VMT per capita (Harvey and Deakin 1990). A simulation by a Bay Area agency demonstrated that increasing jobs/housing balance in areas near transit stations decreased emissions per capita slightly (projections corrected by us for identical regional population totals). The scenario also increased densities in these areas, and therefore the effects of the two policies cannot be separated (ABAG 1990; MTC 1990c).

An empirical study in Toronto found that an increase in residential units in the downtown area reduced commute trips to the center by 240 trips per work day per 100 units built (Nowland and Stewart 1991). The infill residential developments from 1975 to 1988 reduced one-way peak-hour demand by about 3,000 auto trips and by about 7,800 transit trips, thereby saving considerable public monies that would have been needed for expanding transport supply.

An empirical study in the San Diego region found that jobs/housing balance at the zone of *residence* correlated with shorter commute trips (explained 3.3 percent of variation) (SANDAG 1991).

Our interpretation of this evidence is that jobs/housing balance may help under very congested conditions for roadways in the future if densities are sufficient to permit walking and bicycling and are clustered near good-quality transit services. One must remember, however, that if regions increase rail transit availability (urban and commuter rail), workers can live farther away from their jobs (Wachs 1989).

We note here that standard regional travel models typically have no accessibility variables in the trip generation and trip distribution steps and do not represent nonmotorized modes (walking and bicycling) at all, and they therefore underrepresent the effects of land use TDM policies. The total effect of these limitations is unclear.

The evidence is much more positive and complete concerning density increase as a TDM. An international literature review found some consensus that a system of many medium-sized cities with moderate densities or linear cities with moderately high densities would use less energy in transportation (Cope, Hills, and James 1984). A recent review of cross-sectional data from 32 cities from around the world showed that higher densities greatly reduced VMT per capita (Newman and Kenworthy 1989). That study has been disputed on the basis of the quality of both the travel data and the definitions of the regions' boundaries.

An analysis of metropolitan land use data in the United States demonstrated that population level increased gasoline consumption when density and clustering were controlled for (Keyes 1982). That study also found, however, that relatively high densities and relatively high levels of clustering reduced gasoline consumption, whereas a concentration of jobs in the urban center increased consumption, presumably because of longer commutes. The author showed the need to carefully specify the measures of density and clustering used in the analyses (generally regression models).

A recent international study using urban transportation and land use models from several urban areas to simulate the effects of a set of TDM policies found a fairly good consensus that higher *residential* densities reduce VMT per capita. Land use policies, however, were found to be hardly effective unless accompanied by travel pricing policies and improved transit and walking/bicycling facilities. Reducing sprawl at the edge with urban growth boundaries also was seen to reduce VMT in conjunction with pricing and transit improvements (Webster, Bly, and Paulley 1988).

A recent report by the California Air Resources Board (CARB) reviewed the literature showing that higher residential and employment densities, especially if located near rail stations, generate higher mode shares for transit and cited Toronto as an example of good land use planning, with its policies for infill development, density increases near rail stations, and jobs/housing balance, including in the urban center (CARB 1993). CARB staff estimated possible regional VMT reductions of 4 to 11 percent as a result of land use changes and an additional 5 to 10 percent from improved transit and ridesharing.

Several regional simulations of density policies carried out in the United States agree that such policies are effective to some extent. A study of the Seattle region found that the concentration of growth into several major centers would reduce VMT about 4 percent over 30 years, but there was no clear winning scenario in terms of emissions, even including a dispersed-growth scenario. It appeared that the concentration of travel in the centers left the peripheral areas less congested, and therefore people traveled farther in these areas (Watterson 1991). This study is noteworthy because the travel models were run properly equilibrated and land use models were also run, so travel–land use interactions were captured. We note that a tighter urban growth boundary might have reduced VMT and emissions slightly more in the growth centers scenario, especially if road expansions were limited in the outer areas.

A simulation in Montgomery County, Maryland, showed that density increases near rail stations and bus lines, combined with auto pricing policies and the expansion of passenger rail service, would reduce single-occupant commute trips substantially (Replogle 1990). The modeling was sophisticated, using land use variables in the equations for peaking factors and mode choice.

A 20-year simulation in the Portland, Oregon, region found that substantial increases in densities near light-rail stations and near feeder and express bus lines, combined with free transit, all within the western quadrant of the region only, would reduce regionwide VMT by 14 percent while leaving VHD unchanged when compared with a scenario with an outer circumferential freeway (Cambridge 1992). These models included walking and bicycling modes and incorporated land use variables in an auto ownership step.

A review of several regional simulation studies in the United States found that higher densities near transit would reduce auto travel and energy consumption about 20 percent over 20 years. The Washington, D.C., regional study reviewed found that sprawled growth could use twice as much energy in travel as would dense centers with good transit service. Wedges and corridors, a less drastic scenario, reduced travel energy use by 16 percent (Keyes 1976).

Another review of simulation studies in the United States concluded that higher density near transit lines could reduce travel by up to 20 percent regionally (Sewell and Foster 1980). A review of studies in several countries found that improved transit service could reduce auto ownership by 5 to 10 percent and that households with fewer autos had lower VMT (Colman et al. 1992).

An empirical study of five San Francisco Bay Area communities found that doubling residential density reduced VMT per household and per capita 20 to 30 percent, a finding corroborated by data from other urban regions around the world (NRDC 1991). A simulation in the Bay Area concluded that increasing residential density and jobs/housing balance near to passenger rail stations produced slightly lower levels of emissions per capita (calculated by us) and lower emissions in areas adjacent to the region. No feedback of assigned travel times to trip distribution was done, and therefore the results may be slightly biased (ABAG 1990; MTC 1990c).

An analysis of Bay Area data showed that increased residential density decreased VMT per capita. Unfortunately, the densest areas also were served by rapid rail transit, and thus the two effects cannot be disentangled. Examination of the districts with such transit service, however, still shows a strong relationship between density and VMT. Districts with poor transit service also show this same slope, but more weakly (Harvey and Deakin 1990).

To conclude regarding land use policies, jobs/housing balance (land use mix) seems not to be very effective as a policy approach, unless as part of a density policy. Density increases near transit lines seem to be effective in reducing VMT, emissions, and energy use, particularly in conjunction with travel pricing, not building more freeways, and major improvements to transit, especially exclusive guideway transit.

Pricing Policies

An international comparison performed with travel and land use models testing the same TDM policies found in general that auto costs had to rise by 300 percent to reduce VMT by about 33 percent (Webster, Bly, and Paulley 1988). If accompanied by density increases near transit, better transit speeds, and worse auto travel speeds, pricing was seen to be much more effective. Since the work trip is so unresponsive to price increases (demand is inelastic), good transit service to work centers was found to be needed. It was also found that large parking charges must be regionwide or, better yet, nationwide to deter firms and households from moving from existing employment centers to the suburbs or from one urban region to another. Increasing auto operation costs per se was seen to increase transit travel to work in the various regions, especially if good radial service (to the urban center) was simulated. This policy also increased walking to local retail centers. Increasing auto purchase costs was also found to work well since autos seem to be used for about the same amount of VMT annually in various countries, regardless of household incomes and location (Webster, Bly, and Paulley 1988).

Road and travel pricing have been advocated by economists for decades. One recent review of the literature shows the large welfare savings possible from road charges but concludes that these policies are infeasible politically and therefore recommends efficient levels of parking pricing, efficient truck weight fees, transit subsidies, and bus-only and carpool lanes (Morrison 1986). Another recent review finds that congestion is not inefficient and that economic efficiency requires carpool or bus-only lanes to speed up local and express bus transit, more rail transit, and toll roads as well as free roads, all in order to improve competition among modes (Starkie 1986). We do not address whether transit operators can increase service fast enough to meet the large demand increases that would occur if significant road pricing were used. Regions will have to adopt road pricing gradually and also make many transit improvements up front—that is, before the road pricing takes effect. The travel pricing demonstration projects being started in the United States recognize this problem.

A comprehensive review of congestion charging mechanisms for roadways found that indirect charges—such as parking charges, fuel taxes, area licensing, and vehicle purchase and license taxes—are not economically efficient in reducing congestion and travel costs. Peak-period road pricing was recommended, supplemented by parking taxes. Automatic vehicle identification (AVI) was found to make tolling in motion less costly than tollbooths (Hau 1992). Another recent analysis also recommends peak-period road pricing and parking pricing to relieve congestion (Downs 1992). The above studies (Morrison, Starkie, Hau, Downs) are conceptual economic evaluations accompanied by limited empirical evidence and must be carefully interpreted for the purposes of reducing travel, emissions, and energy use since their objective is usually economic efficiency.

A review of congestion charges in Europe (Jones 1992) states that roadway and downtown cordon tolls are being investigated in Greece, Sweden, the United Kingdom, and the Netherlands. One conclusion of interest is that peak-period road tolls are more likely to spread peaks and suppress trips than to cause a switch in mode in low-density urban regions with poor transit service. If densities are high, good transit service is available, and road charges are high, mode switching is predicted to be the prevalent response. Carpooling would rise only when pools were exempted from tolls. Support for tolls would increase substantially if the avowed purposes of the tolls were to include safety and environmental quality. This analysis was mainly conceptual.

Mogridge (1986) issued a proviso for very large cities with well-developed transit systems. He argued that tolling road travel or parking would not reduce auto travel much because of unmet demand for auto travel by transit users. Charging autos would simply shift wealthier travelers to auto and less wealthy ones to transit;

mode shares and speeds would not significantly change. This equilibrium situation exists only where transit travel times are roughly equal to auto travel times, a situation present only in very large urban areas. Mogridge was arguing from modeling experience in London.

Empirical studies show that the effects of pricing auto travel vary greatly according to the quality of the alternative modes available and the nature of the charging scheme. May (1992) reviewed the evidence, which includes the Singapore downtown A.M. cordon charge of $2.50, which reduced morning downtown-bound traffic about 44 percent, and the Bergen, Oslo, and Trondheim toll rings, which charge from $.80 to $1.60 per trip all day and reduced traffic only a few percentage points.

A simulation of area pricing for downtown London projected a 45 percent decrease in traffic with a $2.50 charge (May 1992). An interesting finding of another London simulation study showed that expanding commuter rail itself would not reduce auto commuting significantly, whereas road pricing together with rail improvements could reduce auto commuting by up to 20 percent, and even 30 percent if rail fares were reduced (May 1992).

A simulation of auto pricing policies in southern California found that VMT could be reduced by about 12 percent and pollutants by about 20 percent with a peak-period road congestion charge of $.15 per mile, employee parking charges of $3.00 per day, retail and office parking charges of $.60 per hour, emissions fees averaging $110.00 per year per vehicle, and deregulated (cheaper, better) transit services (which accounted for about 2 percentage points of the reductions) (Cameron 1991). A rather good set of travel demand models was used for this evaluation.

Empirical studies of large employer sites show 20 to 30 percent reductions in commute trips to the sites when employees pay fully for their parking (Willson and Shoup 1990). Shoup (1992) argues that eliminating employee parking subsidies will create growth in urban centers and other employment centers; increase infill development on small, "leftover" parcels; and reduce transit ridership peaks. All of these changes would increase the efficiency of transit and transportation in general.

A regionwide simulation in the Bay Area found that eliminating parking subsidies to workers would reduce commute trips 25 to 50 percent, with the high values in the densest centers (MTC 1990b). Another Bay Area study showed that pricing measures could reduce VMT by 15 percent in five years. The policies were parking charges as per the southern California study, smog fees averaging $125.00 per year per vehicle, a fuel tax of $2.00 per gallon, and unspecified congestion pricing (MTC 1990a).

The conclusion regarding pricing is that it is effective, except in very large urban areas with excellent transit service, where pricing auto use at peak periods per se may not reduce VMT because of pent-up demand for auto travel. However, spending toll revenues on transit improvements (not considered by Mogridge) could reduce VMT and emissions by making transit more competitive. To be effective, pricing measures must be accompanied by substantial improvements in transit service.

Conclusions Regarding Land Use and Pricing Policies

In terms of identifying potentially useful policies, these studies indicate that generally

1. density per se is more important than land use mix per se.

2. density near transit seems to be even more effective.

3. mix (jobs/housing balance) can be effective only if nonauto modes are available (walking, bicycling, transit).

4. auto pricing greatly improves the effectiveness of density and mix policies.

5. distance-based road pricing may be needed to reduce travel on the edges of urban regions.

6. auto pricing (travel, parking, fuels, emissions) is ineffective in most regions unless accompanied by transit improvements and density increases near transit.

7. vehicle purchase taxes can be effective.

8. parking charges can be effective.

9. downtown cordon charges can be effective.

In terms of travel pricing, we consider only peak-period and all-day road pricing in this study, not downtown cordon charges. Relying on previous studies, we expect that peak-period road charges would reduce peak-period travel and congestion and could reduce ozone precursor emissions—nitrogen oxides (NO_x) and total organic gases (TOG)—and energy consumption. In cases of high congestion, however, tolls could increase travel by increasing throughput at, say, speeds of 30 to 40 mph. We would expect carbon monoxide (CO) hotspots to be reduced, depending on local situations. Cordon charges, levied upon entering the downtown, would be more effective in reducing CO. Such charges are being studied by large European cities. We do not consider cordon pricing because of its poor reception in the United States and because very high-quality transit service is needed to make it effective. Perhaps it could follow the policies we consider here.

We do not consider the equity effects of tolls in this phase of our research. We note, however, that several studies have shown that tolls can benefit all income groups (Small 1983; Small, Winston, and Evans 1989). A recent paper develops a program for spending the revenues that would be generated by the southern California pricing policies suggested by Cameron (1991) and shows that all commuters would benefit financially because of posited tax rebates and transit improvements (Small 1992).

We cannot simulate vehicle purchase taxes or annual registration and emissions fees with the present model set. We do test parking pricing, however, since it has been found effective, and we test a fuel tax.

By way of integrating the discussions of pricing and land use measures, we note that cold starts account for the majority of mobile hydrocarbon and CO emissions in most large urban areas and that therefore the short trip should be a focus of TDMs. Improved transit provision and peak-period auto pricing may reduce work trips if land uses are concentrated around transit lines. Parking pricing can be very effective as a TDM, especially if transit service is adequate to meet demand. Nonwork trips can be shifted from the auto to walking, bicycling, or transit if land use mix and density are sufficient and if sidewalks, bicycle lanes, and adequate transit service are provided. Only exclusive guideway transit (rail, busway) can compete favorably with autos in most urban regions.

Controlling growth at the edge of the urban region may not be very effective as a TDM measure, according to one set of studies reviewed. We think that all-day (distance-based) travel pricing may make this policy effective, however.

We conclude that all of these policies should be simulated in an attempt to project changes in VMT, emissions, and energy consumption. We test policies separately and together, since the studies show the need for mutual reinforcement among increased density and mix near transit, improved transit service, and auto pricing. The following evaluation should be viewed as heuristic, not determining. Also, we do not consider political feasibility. Simulation studies, as well as empirical ones, can affect politics, and thus in the long run we may not have to be bound by present attitudes.

Methods

Because modeling methods affect results and we operated our models in an unconventional fashion, we describe the methods used in some detail.

Travel Demand Modeling

We will attempt to distinguish between the travel modeling done using regional agency methods and changes made by us.

Description of the Modeled Area

The study area was that of the Sacramento Regional Transit (RT) Systems Planning Study of 1990. All base-year freeway and highway system characteristics represent conditions existing for the year 1989. The no-build 2010 alternative represents the land use growth after 1989 without any new major transportation facilities.

Network Characteristics

No changes were made to the 1990 Systems Planning Study transit network. The transit network developed was based on conditions and lines existing for the year 1989 (base year). The transit network included transit lines operated by agencies other than Sacramento RT and also included separate A.M. peak-period and off-peak-period transit networks (Parsons 1990). Separate methods were used for the purpose of proper mode split during the peak and nonpeak periods. Zonal walk-to-transit accessibility measures were also included in the Systems Planning Study.

Land Use and Socioeconomic Data

We used the Sacramento Area Council of Governments (SACOG) base-year (1989) and projected-year (2010) land use files for all runs except those in which we tested land use policies. In those cases, we describe the changes that we made.

Trip Generation

In the Systems Planning Study, the trip generation model was based on the 1968 Sacramento Area Transportation Study that was developed from a 1968 household survey data set. Changes were made to the production rates according to rates for similar urban regions. The trip production rates were then recalibrated (though without using any new household trip data) to reflect 1989 land use and travel

23

conditions. A new set of trip attraction rates was estimated using trip rates in the 1976–1980 statewide travel survey. Commercial trucks were not modeled.

Trip Distribution

The trip distribution process uses the trip production and attraction data developed in the trip generation stage to distribute trips to the 812 zones according to a standard gravity model (Comsis 1991).

The travel impedance matrix is the zone-to-zone travel times determined in a step prior to trip distribution. It is calculated as the shortest time path for links along a path between any two zones and accumulating the travel time of the links along the path.

The travel impedance matrix was generated initially using free-flow speeds; a feedback process was then employed by us using speeds from assignment. Because this protocol departs from the Systems Planning Study methods, the feedback process is explained below. In the RT Systems Planning Study and in our analysis, intrazonal travel times were generated by estimating the average travel time to adjacent traffic analysis zones. Terminal times were added to each zone-to-zone travel time to represent access time to automobiles.

In the trip distribution model, the friction factors represent the likelihood of travel between zones based upon the impedance (time cost, in this model) between the zones. The friction factors used in the Systems Planning Study were based on those used in the Seattle region, which was assumed to have characteristics similar to those in the Sacramento region. The Seattle friction factors were for daily travel, as the Sacramento model is a daily travel model. Five sets of friction factors were developed, one for each trip purpose. The same friction factors were used for both the 1989 base year and the 2010 future-year forecasts.

Mode Choice

New mode choice models were developed for the 1989 Systems Planning Study based on the 1989 RT ridership and on-board surveys. Mode choice models were developed for two sets of trip purposes, home-based work trips and nonwork trips.

The home-based work trip mode choice model is a multinomial logit model that predicts mode shares for walk to transit, drive to transit, drive alone, two-plus-person auto, and three-plus-person auto. Most of the coefficients of the mode choice model were obtained from comparative studies of other models from other large urban areas in the United States. Insofar as these other models were discrete choice, household-based utility models, such transference is arguably acceptable. Midrange values from models of other urban areas were used for the level-of-service coefficients (Parsons 1990).

The home-based work trip mode choice model was further stratified into car ownership categories. The characteristics of the model were maintained in our modeling processes for the various alternatives. Changes were made only in the auto operating cost estimation process, in which additional variables to reflect roadway and fuel pricing were introduced.

The nonwork trip mode split estimation process involves factoring applied to the home-based work trip transit shares. These factors were applied to each zone-to-zone interchange that had transit service during the off-peak period and were factored for origin-destination distances, auto ownership, and trip purpose.

Traffic Assignment

In the MINUTP systems software, traffic assignment is done by reading trip files, building paths for those trips, assigning the trips to the links in the paths (accumulating link volumes), and, when all trips have been processed, adjusting the link travel times based on congestion and repeating the entire process for the specified number of iterations. The number of iterations that had been used in the Systems Planning Study was five, and this number was maintained in our study.

Peak-hour modeling is performed using A.M. peak-hour directional trip percentages derived from the San Francisco Bay region for each trip purpose and assigning the trips. These travel times are then used for calculating mode choice for all daily work trips.

The mode choice model has been structured to read two sets of travel times, one for single-occupant trips and the other for high-occupancy vehicle (HOV) trips. The model assigns travel time based on capacity-constrained peak-hour assignment to each occupancy alternative and computes the mode shares, recognizing the HOV time savings.

Transit Modeling

The transit module has the capability to form transit networks, develop zone-to-zone paths along transit networks, extract level-of-service matrices along transit paths, and assign trips to transit paths (Comsis 1991). The transit network generates sets of transit links that have travel times, distance, a valid mode indicator and parallel links for various modes, transit speeds, and transit time slices for each

25

zone-to-zone path. The bus links are represented by the highway links in the base network, whereas for light-rail transit (LRT), separate links are coded. Transit assignment is not capacity constrained.

Overall Model Operation Methods

In the Systems Planning Study, speeds and travel times were estimated for all peak-hour and daily trips in the assignment step. A loop was used to feed these congested speeds and times back into mode choice. This process provided new peak and daily speeds and travel times based on the first estimation. This feedback loop can be repeated a number of times until the speeds and times do not change significantly (equilibrated values). This partial feedback protocol corrects mode choice for the effects of congestion but does not correct trip lengths (in the trip distribution step) for these effects. This is a serious flaw when modeling for the purpose of projecting travel and emissions because trip length is a main determinant of VMT and VMT also determines link speeds. VMT by speed class is a main determinant of emissions.

Therefore, for our modeling, we also fed assigned travel times back to the trip distribution step. The assigned peak-hour speeds were fed back to the trip distribution step, where new origin-destination (O-D) tables were created for work trips. The daily average speeds were fed back to the trip distribution step to recalculate O-D tables for the nonwork trips. Modeling texts agree that such feedback is desirable. The Environmental Protection Agency adopted regulations at the end of 1993 that require feedback to trip distribution for air quality conformity analyses done from 1995 on.

Our Feedback Procedure Using MINUTP

The first model run involves the use of uncongested speeds in the trip distribution step, from which a set of O-D tables is estimated for all zone pairs. The new speeds and travel times obtained at the end of the modeling process (after assignment) can be very different from those used at the beginning of the model process. Several iterations need to be done to obtain equilibrated speeds. The feedback process is very computationally time-consuming, and thus five iterations are done by us; the average (arithmetic mean) of the five plus the initial run is considered as the equilibrated set of values.

Feedback to mode choice is retained; thus distribution, mode choice, and assignment use the same travel times for work trips and nonwork trips. We graphed regional VMT for the six runs of the 2010 no-build scenario to verify that the output oscillated because of the negative feedback of VMT on speed. We found that VMT did oscillate in a dampening fashion, as expected. Our runs plotted VMT as a set of converging points; that is, the model iterations were leading toward equilibrium. We also inspected the VMT X speed class data that were fed into the emissions models to see if they also followed regular patterns and did not vary wildly. The VMT for the 5–10 mph, 10–15 mph, and 15–20 mph classes varied regularly, inversely to total VMT, and dampened. The VMT for the speed classes for 50–55 mph, 55–60 mph, and 60–65 mph varied regularly with total VMT and dampened. Both of these results were as expected. We checked the VMT in these speed classes because emissions per mile are much higher in them than in the intermediate classes and we wanted to verify that our emissions projections were not affected by some artifact of the modeling.

We did not recalibrate the full feedback model for several reasons. First, the 1989 base-year VMT fell by only 5 percent, not a large change compared with that of typical calibration tests (within 10 percent for regional VMT and larger ranges for facility types). Second, the model was already calibrated using friction factors for daily travel in Seattle, a larger region with worse congestion. Third, we checked our projected volumes against the base-year counts and found that they were 96 percent of the downtown cordon counts. The outer screenline projections were 91 percent of the counts in the aggregate. Fourth, adjustment of the friction factors in trip distribution (or even trip generation rates) would not change the rank orderings of our projections. Gravity trip distribution models are not behavioral and thus are not policy-sensitive or theoretically robust. They are merely phenomenological/descriptive ways of extrapolating past behavior. Fifth, traffic counts in this region, and in most others, are likely to be inaccurate because of poor sampling.

Model Travel Data Outputs

Model parameters were calculated using the adjusted loaded daily road network. Parameters calculated were as follows:

- total network vehicle-miles traveled (VMT)
- total vehicle-hours traveled throughout the network (VHT)
- vehicle-hours of delay on the whole network (VHD)
- lane-miles of congestion (LOS E and LOS F)
- average network speed

The model also estimates the person-trips by trip purpose and vehicle trips by mode.

Strengths and Weaknesses of the Models

This set of models is representative of those in use in many medium-sized urban regions; therefore, our simulations should be taken to represent what would happen if agencies with similar models performed these tests. The borrowed friction factors and logit coefficients make this model set somewhat abstract—that is, not necessarily accurate for this region—but, we would argue, useful for policy evaluation in general. There is a logit model for work trips that includes walking access and driving access to transit, and the model set was refereed by the federal transit agency under the previous rules for rail alternatives analysis. Other strengths include separate HOV modes and network, allowing us to evaluate HOV scenarios, and small zones in the downtown, which permit fairly accurate estimates of walk-to-transit shares. Also, no K-factors were used in the calibration of the trip distribution step.

On the other hand, many weaknesses require one to treat our projections with care. The factoring for peak-hour trips and the application of those travel times to all work trips probably exaggerates the transit share for work trips and perhaps for all trips. With full feedback, work trips are overshortened and nonwork trips undershortened, but the total effect is unknown. The factoring of nonwork mode shares from the work trip logit model shares is crude, even though corrected for O-D distance, auto ownership, and trip purpose. There is no auto ownership model and no peak spreading routine. Also, link capacities are approximate and output link speeds inaccurate, problems common to past models. The model set was not validated on average speeds by road class. The lack of feedback of assigned speeds, or of any other accessibility measure, to trip generation and auto ownership, even in our "full feedback" runs, leads to the underprojection of VMT reductions due to congestion. The lack of travel cost variables in all the model steps except mode choice leads to the underprojection of the effects of pricing in reducing VMT. There are insufficient demographic variables in trip generation. Age and income affect auto ownership and trip generation, as well as mode choice. There is no land allocation model, and thus the effects of major transit and pricing policies in reducing auto travel are underprojected. In addition, there are the problems common to all cross-sectional models.

Policy Alternatives Modeled

We compared our TDM scenario to the conventional alternatives being implemented in the region in order to indicate real policy impacts.

Preexisting (Official) Alternatives

Several alternatives from the Systems Planning Study were examined in our study and their travel characteristics compared. No changes were made to any input data unless otherwise indicated here. The following alternatives were already developed but were rerun by us with full feedback:

1. *1989 base year.*

2. *2010 no-build.* Modeled with year 2010 predicted land use data without any major transportation facility improvements. The land use allocations conformed to the federal and state totals projected for the region. The allocations among jurisdictions were determined, however, through political negotiation with the regional agency. The effects of transport improvements on land use patterns were not considered in this process or in the modeling.

3. *HOV lanes.* A 93-lane-mile system of existing and proposed new HOV lanes on the inner freeways by the year 2010.

4. *Light-rail transit (LRT).* Alternative 8 of the Systems Planning Study.

Our Land Use and Pricing TDM Alternatives

The transit-oriented development (TOD) alternatives and the pricing alternatives were both based on the LRT alternative. For the TOD alternatives, the land use (housing and employment) and zone characteristics (transit accessibility index) datasets were changed. For the pricing alternative, the zone characteristics (zonal parking costs) dataset was altered. All other zonal input datasets were maintained.

The modeling process for the pricing scenarios was based on three travel cost increases. The auto operating cost was increased by $.03 per mile to reflect an increase in gasoline taxes of $2.00 per gallon. Since the long-run elasticity of demand for travel with respect to fuel costs is low, about −0.3, because of a shift to higher-miles-per-gallon vehicles, we entered a (static, short-term) fuel tax of $.60 per gallon. This procedure, then, simulates the reduction in fuel consumption due to reduced auto mode choice properly with the (too-high) fleet miles per gallon (mpg) assumed by the California Air Resources Board, based on lower fuel price assumptions than would occur. Fleet mileage was assumed at 20 mpg, and thus the per-mile cost increase is $.03. In terms of the effects on VMT and the other travel indicators themselves, the fuel tax entered should be seen as $.60 per gallon.

The congestion pricing was placed at $.25 per mile for arterials and $.50 per mile for freeways and applied to home-to-work trips on all links with failing level-of-service (LOS E and F) to (poorly) approximate peak-period trips. The model is for daily trips and does not directly project peak trips. Parking costs were increased to $5.00 per day in the downtown, $3.00 per day at other major employment centers, and $2.00 per day at all other places. Parking costs are entered into the land use zone files but are read into the mode choice equations as applied to each O-D pair.

After performing runs with this ambitious pricing scenario, including the peak-period congestion tolls, we found that travel (VMT) increased because the shift to HOV mode speeded up travel and lengthened trips. The HOV mode also attracted riders from transit. So we defined a second, all-day pricing scheme (applied to all trips) for comparative purposes. This charge was $.30 per mile on all roadways. We also included the same parking and fuel charges.

The prices in these two scenarios are near levels that are economically efficient in large urban areas. Lee (1992), for example, shows that efficient (long-run) peak tolls for average U.S. urban highways in urban regions range from $.26 to $.95 per vehicle-mile, whereas average (peak and nonpeak) tolls would be about $.15 per vehicle-mile. This figure includes only roadway capital costs. Aschauer (1990, in Decorla-Souza and Kane 1992) estimated average peak-period costs in the Chicago region at about $.41 per mile and nonrecovered nonpeak costs at about $.05 per vehicle-mile. Other studies reviewed by them estimate peak-period tolls at $.20 to $.40 per vehicle-mile (Decorla-Souza and Kane 1992). Small (1992) estimates that peak tolls that are efficient in the short run (efficient use) and the long run (efficient capacity) for the Bay Area are $.05 to $.37 per vehicle-mile, higher in the central areas.

To those tolls must be added subsidies and external costs, to be economically efficient. A recent unpublished review estimates these costs at about $.20 per mile (CEC 1993). These estimates are much debated, and conservative estimates range down to $.02 per mile (Decorla-Souza and Kane 1992). However, the lower-end estimates omit difficult-to-quantify costs, such as defense of oil fields and unreimbursed local road services. All of the studies leave out the effects of excessive auto travel on land use, which increases sprawl, walk times, and urban service costs. Many of these subsidy and external costs are for all travel, not just peak travel.

The TOD alternatives involved the use of the official LRT network, but with considerable changes to the 2010 land use data. Land use intensification was simulated around existing and proposed light-rail stations.

All employment and household growth for the year 2010 from the surrounding rural edges was shifted into the TOD zones. About half of the employment growth from the areas adjacent to the corridors was also shifted into the TOD zones to maintain a reasonable jobs/housing balance in the TOD zones. Two-thirds of housing growth from the zones adjacent to the corridors was moved into these zones. Only 25 percent of the housing growth in the zones adjacent to the Natomas corridor was shifted to the TOD zones of its corridor to maintain a reasonable housing density in those TOD zones. Because of the high density of housing and employment along the Roseville corridor, only half of the growth in zones adjacent to that corridor was shifted. The shifting of households and employment was done keeping in mind the growth restrictions in some of the TOD zones involving flooding problems and because of the 65-decibel noise boundary around Mather Air Force Base.

A quarter-mile radius was used to identify the TODs surrounding the stations, and all land use zones falling mostly within this perimeter were used. The transit accessibility indexes for these zones were converted to 100 percent to reflect total accessibility of all households and employment to transit. The shifted households were then distributed among the car ownership stratifications to maintain the control totals for each car ownership category and for total trips in the region. Once the housing units and jobs were moved into the TOD zones, they were then shifted between TOD zones along each corridor to maintain reasonable jobs/housing balances and densities.

Approximately 70 percent of single-family housing growth and about 65 percent of multifamily housing growth were shifted into the TOD zones from the other zones, and from within these totals, approximately 7 percent of the single-family and 6 percent of the multifamily housing growth were shifted into the downtown area. Approximately 78 percent of retail employment growth and 73 percent of nonretail employment growth were shifted from all other zones to the TOD zones. No retail or nonretail employment was shifted into the downtown area to improve jobs/housing balance there.

No shifts were made in Davis because this TOD was already quite dense and the surrounding zones were also dense. For all TOD zones, a density cap of around eight households per acre and 10 retail plus 30 nonretail employees per acre was used as a guideline in shifting the land uses. No changes were made in the special generators and gateway trips included in the land use data.

This land use scenario is very ambitious. Intensification near light-rail stations, however, has been the cornerstone of the revised Sacramento County land use plan and is also strongly favored by the RT district. A modest intensification scenario was also evaluated by the regional transportation agency (Sacramento Area Council of Governments—SACOG) in the late 1980s, but without proper model feedback. Our scenario goes beyond these earlier ones in comprehensiveness (all stations), densities, and jobs/housing balance. In the Portland, Oregon, study of land use intensification, 65 percent of new residential units and 78 percent of new employees were moved to their rail station TODs and along feeder and express bus lines (Cambridge 1992). This intensification was simulated only in one county, which occupies the western quadrant of the region.

The Emissions Model

To minimize controversy, we used the official California emissions models with all setups done according to past studies in our region.

Emission Factors

Mobile emission rates for the region were estimated using the California Air Resources Board's BURDEN and EMFAC7EPSCF2 computer models for calculating airborne emissions (CARB 1991, 1992). We used the fleet emission factors for Sacramento County, which comprises about 85 percent of the fleet in the region. The output from these models was then converted for use in Caltrans's PC-DTIM, a travel impact emissions model (Caltrans 1993).

EMFAC7E produces emission factors for three exhaust emission processes and four evaporative emission processes. It also produces fuel consumption rates for 13 vehicle class/technology combinations. Emission and fuel consumption rates were estimated both for the base-year vehicle models (we used 1990) and for future-year (2010) vehicle models.

The emission factors were estimated from the following emission processes:

Exhaust Emission Factors	Evaporative Emission Factors
Running	Diurnal
Cold start	Hot soak
Hot start	Running losses
	Standing losses

EMFAC7E calculates emission factors for a range of dew points by default. Dew point was set at 30°F for conformity with the emissions studies done by the regional agency. Ranges of speed and temperature can be specified for different emission factor runs depending on the temporal requirement of the transportation model. In our case, a temperature range of 62° to 110°F at 10° intervals was selected for the summer inventory. This temperature range also conforms to the emissions studies done by SACOG for the run temperature (for running exhaust) and starting temperature (for both hot and cold starts). A speed range of 0 to 65 mph in 5 mph increments was used for emission factor generation. The emission factors generated from EMFAC were then converted for input to PC-DTIM.

Direct Travel Impact Model (PC-DTIM)

PC-DTIM calculates air pollutant emission estimates for on-road mobile sources based on detailed information regarding each link (roadway segment) for each hour of the day. Thus this program can be used on the output from most travel demand systems models, such as MINUTP, to generate mobile emissions. In our case, the organic air pollutants consisted of TOG from tailpipes, evaporative emissions (EVAs), CO, NO_x, exhaust particulate of nitrogen (PMEX), and particulate matter due to tire wear (PMTW).

Transportation Model Outputs for PC-DTIM

Transportation model outputs could be directly generated from MINUTP models for the PC-DTIM program to calculate daily emissions. PC-DTIM requires a trip table consisting of volumes of trip productions and attractions in both directions and hourly link capacity. It also requires detailed information on the network in terms of link speed, link distance, node coordinates, and facility type, as well as information on intrazonal volume by trip type, trip end volumes for both attractions and productions by trip type, and the corresponding node coordinates and zones.

Hence the MINUTP model needs to generate an intrazonal file, a terminal volume file, and a link description file containing the above information. For each iteration of the feedback-to-trip distribution, these files were generated separately. The separate transportation model files were then used to generate hourly and total daily mobile emission estimates. The separate estimates for six runs were then averaged to obtain the converged mobile emissions. This process was repeated for each alternative.

Steps Involved in MINUTP

1. Person-trips by purpose are converted to person-trips by purpose by vehicle occupancy (drive alone and shared ride)

2. Person-trips by purpose by vehicle occupancy are then converted from production/attraction to O-D format.

3. Person-trips by purpose by vehicle occupancy in O-D format are then converted to vehicle trips.

4. Vehicle trips by purpose by vehicle occupancy that are in separate tables are combined into one table.

5. The daily vehicle trip table for home-based work, home-based other, non-home-based, and through trips is then used to generate the intrazonal trip file and terminal volume file for PC-DTIM.

6. The daily vehicle trip table is then used to assign trip volumes onto links and, when all trips have been processed, adjusts the link travel times based on congestion. In this case, assignment is also done separately by trip purpose to generate link volumes by trip purpose and in percentage format.

7. Step 6 provides a new loaded network with link volumes in percentage format by trip purpose that is then used to generate the link file containing the link data and volumes for PC-DTIM.

Findings and Discussion

Because of the complexity of our results, the travel demand results will be discussed before the emissions results.

Travel Demand

The three TOD scenarios have the lowest VMT and vehicle-hours traveled (VHT) (Table 2-1). LRT plus all-day road pricing ($.30 per vehicle-mile) has the lowest vehicle-hours of delay (VHD). The two LRT with pricing alternatives have low VMT and vehicle-hours.

Peak-period road pricing reduced transit travel by pushing many auto drivers into HOVs. Flat pricing ($.30) did not have this outcome in general. Interestingly, however, LRT + $.30 produced higher transit ridership than TOD + $.30. It appears that the surface street congestion caused by the higher densities in the TODs made drive to transit fall off somewhat more than walk to transit. But the fact that both types of transit trips fell indicates that because the TODs are near to freeways, it became easier to travel by auto in the TOD scenarios, even with all-day pricing, because of the time savings due to the clustering near to the freeways.

The LRT scenario has a lower VMT than does LRT + pricing because pricing reduces peak-period trips and congestion; auto travel is

Table 2-1

Summary of Daily Travel Results

Scenario	VMT[a] (millions)	VHT[b] (thousands)	VHD[c] (thousands)	Transit (trips)	HOVTs[d] (millions)
No-build	49.28	1,198	349.9	74,910	1.33
HOV[e]	51.09	1,225	320.3	117,310	1.33
HOV + pricing	49.56	1,187	289.7	86,088	1.50
LRT[f]	48.97	1,188	387.0	126,557	1.32
LRT + pricing	49.25	1,178	273.5	92,287	1.50
LRT + $.30	48.14	1,152	249.3	243,949	1.39
TOD[g]	46.81	1,136	334.0	151,149	1.32
TOD + pricing	45.66	1,106	301.1	104,107	1.49
TOD + $.30	45.83	1,112	306.7	162,629	1.34
Ranges from no build	7.0%	7.2%	21.8%	117.1%	12.8%

[a]VMT = vehicle-miles of travel.
[b]VHT = vehicle-hours of travel.
[c]VHD = vehicle-hours of delay.
[d]HOVTs = HOV trips.
[e]HOV = high-occupancy vehicle.
[f]LRT = light-rail transit.
[g]TOD = transit-oriented development.

therefore faster, and as a result these trips are longer. These findings demonstrate that some pricing measures will reduce VMT, whereas others, such as peak-period tolls, are likely to reduce congestion and increase VMT. Most agencies think that they can reduce congestion and VMT at the same time. Accomplishing both may be difficult or impossible.

The no-build scenario has lower VMT than does the HOV scenario, a counterintuitive finding for most agencies. This is because the HOV alternative adds HOV lanes to most of the inner freeways, thereby taking many cars off of the mixed-flow lanes, reducing congestion for single-occupant autos, increasing speeds and trip lengths, and reducing transit ridership.

To account for the slight differences across the alternatives in person-trips, which is due to rounding in the many MINUTP calculation steps, we factored up the TOD VMT to take into account its smaller total person-trips (× 1.00404). The resultant corrected VMT, 47.00, does not change our findings.

We also need to ask if the models used are capable of fully simulating the effects of the TDM policies tested. The effects of fuel taxes and parking charges are fairly well represented in terms of mode choice. Such increases in cost would also affect auto ownership by households, and this behavior is not modeled. Large price increases would also affect trip lengths by shortening them somewhat, but this behavior is also not simulated. These model weaknesses will produce projections that underestimate the reductions in VMT due to fuel and parking pricing. Peak-hour pricing is very imperfectly represented because the model is a daily travel model with factoring used for peak-hour assignments. In the peak-period pricing scenarios, we charged per-mile tolls for home-based work trips, and this convention moves travelers into HOVs. This method probably represents the effects of the tolls fairly well. However, the nonwork trip mode shares are factored off the work trip mode shares, and thus the model may overrepresent total HOV and transit trips. It is unclear if VMT is overprojected or underprojected when all three pricing policies are simulated together. The flat toll of $.30 per mile is probably simulated more accurately than the peak tolls. The trip generation and mode choice model steps have no land use variables in them, and thus land use density and mix affects only trip distribution. Mode choice is affected by the increase in households within short walk-access times to rail stations, but not by other land use variables, such as mix. There is no auto ownership step, which would take into account the effects of mixed land uses on reducing auto ownership. The VMT reductions from the land use policies are underprojected by the model.

Comparison with Previous
Travel Demand Studies

Our results are broadly compatible with those of the studies reviewed above. Our LRT + pricing and LRT + $.30 scenarios reduced VMT compared with that in the HOV scenario, but less than did similar packages of policies evaluated in the Bay Area and in southern California (4 to 6 percent versus about 10 percent). Reasons may include the following: we modeled a $2.00-per-gallon fuel tax as only $.60 to account for the low long-run elasticity of demand for miles traveled (–0.3); our region has poor transit service compared with that of the Bay Area and parts of southern California; our freeways are uncongested compared with those of the other two areas; and our model is daily with factoring for the peak hour, rather than separately calibrated for peak and nonpeak traffic, as is the case in the other two regions.

Our land use policies had an effect roughly similar to those reviewed above. We projected very optimistic levels of density and mix in our TODs, levels that would not easily be achieved. The Portland, Oregon, study showed a 14 percent reduction in VMT for the region. Their employee parking pricing was $3.00, about the same as ours, but it applied only to work trips and only in the western sector. Transit was free to all work destinations in the western area, however. Given that no auto travel or fuel pricing measures were simulated and that the polices were applied only in a large portion of the region, the Portland VMT reductions are larger than ours. This difference is probably because their models are more sensitive to congestion, land use changes, and pricing.

Emissions Results

Emissions are largely a result of trips, especially those with cold starts (which are a fixed percentage of all trips in this modeling), and of VMT, especially VMT under 15 mph and over 50 mph. We ran the summer inventory emissions, which are higher than the winter inventory emissions for all pollutants except CO. The scenarios with low emissions are those with low VMT, low total vehicle-hours, and low vehicle-hours of delay (Table 2-2).

The lowest energy (fuel) use is for the three land use (TOD) scenarios, with LRT next best. The two LRT + pricing scenarios have higher fuel consumption than do other scenarios even though they have lower VMT and VHT and lower lane-miles of congestion. We cannot explain this phenomenon and so cannot defend these projections. All model calculations cannot be reported with these official state models.

Table 2-2

Daily Emissions and Fuel Use

Scenario	TOG[a] (tons)	CO[b] (tons)	NO$_x$[c] (tons)	Fuel (tons)
No-build	19.53	306.35	45.72	2.25
HOV[d]	18.73	305.17	48.19	2.26
HOV + pricing	18.63	302.83	47.67	2.24
LRT[e]	17.54	280.65	42.79	2.01
LRT + pricing	17.37	274.96	41.79	2.30
LRT + $.30	17.32	273.52	41.53	2.30
TOD[f]	17.31	276.73	41.67	1.95
TOD + pricing	17.26	275.17	41.60	1.95
TOD + $.30	17.22	274.37	41.44	1.94

[a]TOG = total organic gases.
[b]CO = carbon monoxide.
[c]NO$_x$ = nitrogen oxides.
[d]HOV = high-occupancy vehicle.
[e]LRT = light-rail transit.
[f]TOD = transit-oriented development.

Evaporative emissions are unchanged across the alternatives, and therefore we will not discuss them. CO, the winter hotspot pollutant, cannot be reliably evaluated on a regional basis since the violations typically occur locally at large intersections and parking areas and sometimes in urban street canyons. TOG and NO_x, the ozone precursors, are somewhat correlated in this analysis because they both rise for very low and for high vehicle speeds. TOG, however, is much more of a problem at very low speeds (under 15 mph), and NO_x rises more rapidly at high speeds (above 50 mph), which accounts for some of the differences in the rankings. CO also rises sharply at very low speeds. TOG and NO_x also have different emission rates for cold and hot starts.

The TOD alternatives have the lowest emissions of TOG and NO_x (and CO). The no-build scenario has the highest TOG and CO, but HOV has the highest NO_x. Of the two policies actually officially considered in the region, LRT is superior to HOV for all pollutants, especially for NO_x. Apparently the new HOV lanes permit travel at high speeds, which increases NO_x, compared with not adding freeway lanes in the LRT scenario. The TOD scenario without pricing is almost as good as with pricing, and certainly easier to implement. Likewise, LRT without pricing is almost as good as with pricing, and easier politically.

We consider the emissions projections to be very approximate, however, because of the rather inaccurate speeds output by the travel demand models, which are not calibrated on average link speeds or on average facility speeds. This inaccuracy is a problem common to most travel models in the past. However, studies such as this performed in other regions may result in significant differences in emissions rankings. The new California emissions models (with EMFAC7F emission factors), linked to travel demand models that produce better speed projections than in the past, will result in more reliable rankings.

Conclusions

In this research, we reviewed the literature on land use policies and on auto pricing in order to identify promising policies to test in the Sacramento region. We tested the specific policy sets with a four-step travel demand model and fed this travel data into the California emissions models.

Our results show that it is difficult to reduce both congestion and emissions. The scenarios with the lowest VHD (LRT + pricing, LRT + $.30) did not have the lowest VMT and emissions. This phenomenon presents a problem to transportation agencies, most of which are attempting to reduce congestion and meet air quality standards, often by building new HOV lanes on freeways.

Building new HOV lanes in this region appears to be worse than no-build on VMT and NO_x, but better on TOG and about the same on CO and energy. NO_x reductions must be shown in ozone nonattainment regions, compared with the no-build case, however. Building new HOV lanes does not seem a wise policy, especially since it competes with LRT for funding. Take-a-lane HOV with pricing, studied by us in another project, has lower VMT but higher emissions and should be studied further. There are many successful take-a-lane HOV projects in the United States. LRT is substantially better than HOV on travel reduction, all emissions, and fuel use. It is probably a safe policy, and the TOD policy improves it.

The TOD scenarios generally are the lowest in VMT, emissions, and energy use. Lower densities and different mixes of employment and housing need to be investigated. Also, better access to rail stations for drive-to-transit travelers needs to be provided, with extra road lanes in the peak direction (pull the parking), or circulator shuttlebuses need to be simulated to overcome the local congestion in the TOD zones.

We found that peak-period road pricing plus fuel and parking pricing increased VMT, compared with LRT alone, because it increased two-plus-person auto use enough to speed up travel and draw a substantial number of people off transit. Peak-period pricing should be studied more carefully. It reduces emissions slightly when used with LRT or with TODs, but it decreases transit trips when used with LRT, compared with LRT alone. Peak-period pricing reduces congestion enough to attract auto travelers back onto the road. Other policies, or better-designed land use and pricing policies, may work better. Perhaps pricing should be phased in to keep road congestion at needed levels.

The clearest conclusion, however, is that models such as the ones used here are incapable of providing projections in which one can be confident that differences of a few percentage points are meaningful. Even though the results seem reasonable if treated as sensitivity tests, policymakers interested in absolute levels of pollutant emissions, or even in relative rankings across hotly debated alternatives, cannot feel comfortable with models that omit several classes of behavior entirely. Unfortunately, many agencies have models with similar weaknesses.

The accurate evaluation of new freeway capacity versus TDM options is particularly important for this region for three reasons: (1) a system of new HOV lanes is an adopted policy; (2) this region has the highest percentage of VOCs (TOG) from mobile sources of any region in the United States; and (3) the region is under a court order from a lawsuit under the federal Clean Air Act, which requires it to do better planning and analysis. The regional agency has recently developed a much better set of travel models for all of these reasons.

We will replicate these tests with the new regional model set in 1994. That set will include a new auto ownership model, walking and bicycling modes, separate peak and off-peak models, peak spreading, better link capacity data and postmodel checks to improve speed projections, logit models for all trip purposes, intersection delays, and composite (multiple-mode) impedances. Work trip distribution will be in a logit formulation, as a joint mode-destination choice model. Assigned speeds will be fed back to nonwork trip distribution. Accessibility variables are included in the logit auto ownership step. Land use variables are included in auto ownership and in mode choice, making the models more sensitive to land use policies. All models have been estimated on a 1990 household travel survey. In addition, the agency will implement a land allocation model (DRAM/EMPAL). Also, we will use the new California EMFAC7F emission factors, which have higher emission rates for very low and for high speeds. The addition of standing evaporative losses to TOG will show the importance of reducing vehicle ownership.

References

Aschauer, D. 1990. *Economic Impact of Illinois Tollway Improvements on the Regional Economy*. Staff report. Illinois State Toll Highway Authority. November.

Association of Bay Area Governments (ABAG). 1990. *Increasing Transit Ridership and the Efficiency of Land Use While Maximizing Economic Potential*. Working Paper 90-2. Oakland, Calif. October.

Bae, C. 1993. "Air Quality and Travel Behavior: Untying the Knot." *Journal of the American Planning Association* 59 (1): 65–75.

Bay Area Air Quality Management District. 1991. *Bay Area '91 Clean Air Plan*. Vol. 1. San Francisco. October.

California Air Resources Board (CARB). 1991. *Methodology to Calculate Emission Factors for On-Road Motor Vehicles*. Sacramento. July.

———. 1992. *Supplement to Methodology to Calculate Emission Factors for On-Road Motor Vehicles, July 1991*. Sacramento. June.

———. 1993. *The Linkage Between Land Use, Transportation, and Air Quality*. Sacramento: Office of Air Quality and Transportation Planning. March.

California Energy Commission (CEC). 1993. *Background Information for the Transportation Cost Workshop.* Energy Technology Development Division, Technology Evaluation Office. April 8.

Caltrans. 1993. *User's Guide to the PC Version of the Direct Travel Impact Model.* Release 93.1. Sacramento. February.

Cambridge Systematics, Inc. 1992. *The LUTRAQ Alternative: Analysis of Alternatives, an Interim Report.* Boston. October.

Cameron, Michael. 1991. *Transportation Efficiency: Tackling Southern California's Air Pollution and Congestion.* Los Angeles: Environmental Defense Fund. March.

Colman, Steven B., John P. Long, John C. Lewis, and Steve Tracy. 1992. "Back to the Future: Trip Generation Characteristics of Transit Oriented Developments." Paper presented at the Institute of Transportation Engineers International Conference, Transportation Engineering in a New Era, Monterey, Calif., March.

Comsis Corporation. 1991. *MINUTP Technical User Manual.* Silver Springs, Md. January.

Cope, David R., Peter Hills, and Peter James. 1984. *Energy Policy and Land-Use Planning.* New York: Pergamon Press.

Decorla-Souza, Patrick, and Anthony Kane. 1992. "Peak Period Tolls: Precepts and Prospects." *Transportation* 19 (4): 293–311.

Downs, Anthony. 1992. *Stuck in Traffic: Coping with Peak-Hour Congestion.* Washington, D.C.: Brookings Institution.

Giuliano, Genevieve. 1992. *Is Jobs/Housing Balance a Transportation Issue?* Reprint No. 133. Berkeley: University of California, Transportation Center.

Harvey, Greig, and Elizabeth Deakin. 1990. "Mobility and Emissions in the San Francisco Bay Area: Draft Working Paper." Prepared for the Metropolitan Transportation Commission. Oakland, Calif. April.

Hau, Timothy D. 1987. "Using a Hicksian Approach to Cost-Benefit Analysis in Discrete Choice: An Empirical Analysis of a Transportation Corridor Simulation Model." *Transportation Research* 21B (5): 339–357.

———. 1992. *Congestion Charging Mechanisms for Roads: An Evaluation of Current Practice.* WPS 1071. Washington, D.C.: World Bank. December.

Jones, Peter. 1992. *A Review of Available Evidence on Public Reactions for Road Pricing.* London Transport Unit, Dept. of Transport (2 Mansham St., London SW1P 3EB).

Keyes, Dale L. 1976. "Energy and Land Use: An Instrument of US Conservation Policy?" *Energy Policy* 4 (3): 225–236.

———. 1982. "Energy for Travel: The Influence of Urban Development Patterns." *Transportation Research* 16A (1): 65–70.

Lee, Douglass B. 1992. "A Market-Oriented Transportation and Land Use System: How Different Would It Be?" Paper presented at the conference on Privatization and Deregulation in Passenger Transportation, Tampere, Finland, June, 1991. Cambridge, Mass.: U.S. Department of Transportation, Transportation Systems Center.

May, A.D. 1992. "Road Pricing: An International Perspective." *Transportation* 19 (4): 313–333.

Metropolitan Transportation Commission (MTC). 1990a. *Transportation Control Measures for State Clean Air Plan.* Oakland, Calif. June 27.

———. 1990b. *Final Report: 2005 HOV Program Prioritization, Deliverable #8.* Prepared for the Metropolitan Transportation Commission, Oakland, Calif., by Cambridge Systematics, Inc. August 22.

———. 1990c. "Travel Forecasting Results: Land Use Alternative with Transit Capacity Alternative Networks. Technical Note #6." Memo from Chuck Purvis to file. Metropolitan Transportation Commission, Oakland, Calif. December 28.

Mogridge, Martin J.H. 1986. "Road Pricing: The Right Solution for the Right Problem?" *Transportation Research* 20A (2): 157–167.

Morrison, Steven A. 1986. "A Survey of Road Pricing." *Transportation Research* 20A (2): 87–97.

Natural Resources Defense Council (NRDC) and Sierra Club. 1991. "Explaining Urban Density and Transit Impact on Auto Use." Testimony for the 1990 Conservation Report, California Energy Commission, Sacramento, January 15.

Newman, Peter W.G., and Jeffrey R. Kenworthy. 1989. *Cities and Automobile Dependence: A Sourcebook.* Brookfield, Mass.: Gower Technical.

Nowland, David M., and Greg Stewart. 1991. "Downtown Population Growth and Commuting Trips." *Journal of the American Planning Association* 57 (2): 165–182.

Parsons Brinckerhoff Quade & Douglas, Inc. 1990. "Sacramento Systems Planning Study, Task 4.3/4.5 Travel Model Development, Draft." Report prepared for Sacramento Regional Transit. Sacramento. September.

Replogle, Michael. 1990. "Computer Transportation Models for Land Use Regulation and Master Planning in Montgomery County, Maryland." *Transportation Research Record* 1262: 91–100.

Ruiter, Earl R., and Robert B. Dial. 1979. "Equilibrium Modelling." In *Behavioral Travel Modeling,* edited by David A. Hensher and Peter R. Stopher. London: Croom Helm, Ltd., pp. 207–215.

San Diego Association of Governments (SANDAG). 1991. "The Relationship Between Jobs/Housing Balance and Travel Patterns in the San Diego Region." July.

Schipper, Lee, Ruth Steiner, and Stephen Meyers. 1993. "Trends in Transportation Energy Use, 1970 to 1988: An International Perspective." In *Transportation and Global Climate Change*, edited by David L. Greene and Danilo J. Santini. Washington, D.C.: American Council for an Energy-Efficient Economy, pp. 51–89.

Sewell, W.R. Derrick, and Harold D. Foster. 1980. "Analysis of the United States Experience in Modifying Land Use to Conserve Energy." Working Paper No. 2. Lands Directorate, Environment Canada, Ottawa.

Shoup, Donald C. 1992. "Will Cashing Out Parking Subsidies Change Urban Form?" Paper for University of California at Los Angeles extension course on travel pricing, UCLA Graduate School of Architecture and Urban Planning.

Small, Kenneth A. 1983. "The Incidence of Congestion Tolls on Urban Highways." *Journal of Urban Economics* 13 (1): 90–111.

———. 1992. "Using the Revenues from Congestion Pricing." *Transportation Research* 19A (20): 359–381.

Small, Kenneth A., Clifford Winston, and Carol A. Evans. 1989. *Road Work: A New Highway Pricing and Investment Policy*. Washington, D.C.: Brookings Institution.

Southern California Association of Governments (SCAG). 1988a. "Transportation, Land Use, and Energy Conservation Measures." Draft part of Air Quality Plan. Los Angeles. May.

———. 1988b. "Draft Regional Mobility Plan: Technical Appendices." Los Angeles. October.

Starkie, David. 1986. "Efficient and Politic Congestion Tolls." *Transportation Research* 20A (2): 169–173.

U.S. Office of Technology Assessment (U.S. OTA). 1988. *Urban Ozone and the Clean Air Act*. Washington, D.C. April.

Wachs, Martin. 1989. "Thought Piece on the Jobs/Housing Balance." Paper prepared for the City of Los Angeles Workshop on Jobs/Housing Balance. Los Angeles. October.

Walsh, Michael P. 1993. "Highway Vehicle Activity Trends and Their Implications for Global Warming: The United States in an International Context." In *Transportation and Global Climate Change*, edited by David L. Treene and Danilo J. Santini. Washington, D.C.: American Council for an Energy-Efficient Economy, pp. 1–50.

Watterson, W. Timothy. 1991. "Linked Simulation of Land Use and Transportation Systems: Developments and Experience in the Puget Sound Region." Paper presented at the Transportation Research Board Conference on Transportation and Global Climate Change, Asilomar, Calif. August.

Webster, F.V., P.H. Bly, and N.J. Paulley, eds. 1988. *Urban Land-Use and Transport Interaction: Policies and Models.* Brookfield, Mass.: Avebury.

Willson, Richard W., and Donald C. Shoup. 1990. "Employer-Paid Parking: The Problem and Proposed Solutions." Paper presented at the Association for Commuter Transportation conference, Seattle, Wash. December.

Chapter Three

Future Directions in Travel Forecasting

FREDERICK W. DUCCA AND KENNETH M. VAUGHN

The current travel forecasting process, often referred to as the four-step process, has been in place for over thirty years. Designed during the 1960s, it used the existing understanding of travel behavior and available computing capability to create four models, developed sequentially: trip generation, trip distribution, modal split, and network assignment. The model structure is aggregate in nature, with the planning area divided into a number of homogeneous traffic zones.

In the four steps, (1) trip generation models estimate the number of trips, trip origins, and trip destinations for each zone; (2) trip distribution models assign origin and destination zones to each trip; (3) modal split models calculate the proportion of trips carried by each component of the transportation system—highway, transit, carpooling, etc.; and (4) network assignment models distribute the trips to individual routes between origins and destinations.

This four-step process was highly successful in supporting transportation planning analysis during the 1970s and 1980s. However, two major pieces of legislation, the Clean Air Act Amendments (CAAA) of 1990 and the Intermodal Surface Transportation Efficiency Act (ISTEA) of 1991, have significantly changed the questions asked of the travel forecasting process. In addition to the legislation, changes in behavior have also begun to invalidate some of the underlying assumptions of the process. The overall effect of these changes is to require a fresh look at how travel is forecast and a redesign of forecasting procedures (Ducca 1993; Weiner 1993).

Changing Requirements

With ISTEA, the CAAA, and, in California, the California Clean Air Act (CCAA) of 1988, the current legislative setting calls for more responsiveness in travel demand forecasting models (U.S. DOT 1991; Bryner 1993). In California, it is estimated that most major urban areas will not be able to come into compliance with the new federal and even more stringent state air quality standards without the extensive use of measures aimed at modifying or controlling travel demand (Guensler 1992). Measures of this type are known as transportation control measures (TCMs) or transportation demand management (TDM) measures. Including such programs as congestion and parking pricing, expansion of high-occupancy-vehicle (HOV) lane networks, transit subsidy programs, and employer-based rideshare and vanpool programs, these measures are aimed at affecting individual behaviors to increase vehicle occupancy rates and decrease vehicle-miles of travel (VMT).

The application of advanced technologies to the traffic environment is another emerging area that will have significant impacts on individual driver behavior. If real-time, accurate information on the characteristics of the travel environment can be provided to travelers prior to departure and while en route, will behavior be altered in such a way as to improve the individual accessibility of drivers—or to improve the overall characteristics of the travel environment, resulting in accessibility gains for all drivers—or will the individual benefits of such systems conflict with systemwide improvement goals? In order to accurately model the macro-level effects of advanced traveler information systems (ATIS), one must first analyze and understand the micro-level effects of these systems on individual driver behavior.

CAAA

The Clean Air Act Amendments of 1990 mandate that areas that have not achieved air quality standards must, among other things, establish emissions budgets and estimate the contribution of mobile sources (primarily the automobile) to these budgets. The primary methodology for estimating the contribution of mobile sources to emissions is the traditional four-step planning process combined with the Mobil model series developed by the U.S. Environmental Protection Agency (EPA). Forecasts of air quality must be done every three years until the air quality standards are attained.

In addition to the forecasting requirements, regions in serious nonattainment for carbon monoxide (CO) must develop and implement transportation control measures for the purpose of reducing emissions. To fully analyze the regional impacts of these TCMs and estimate overall regional emissions requires processes that forecast travel over a 24-hour period, that reflect the shift of travel time due to the TCMs, and that forecast cold starts. Current travel forecasting processes cannot fulfill these requirements.

ISTEA

The requirements of the Intermodal Surface Transportation Efficiency Act are consistent with those of the CAAA. Key provisions of the ISTEA that have a direct impact on the forecasting process include requirements to

• analyze environmental and intermodal considerations.

• develop systems to monitor and manage congestion, intermodal facilities, and transit.

• achieve consistency between metropolitan development plans, the long-range land use plan, and the long-range transportation plan.

• analyze strategies that reduce single-occupant-vehicle travel. Included in these strategies are ridesharing, high-occupancy-vehicle lanes, telecommuting, pedestrian programs, congestion pricing, and intelligent transportation systems (ITS) (also known as intelligent vehicle highway systems, or IVHS).

Overall, the ISTEA requires the forecasting process to be more sensitive to both land use and pricing, to possess greater capability for analyzing demand management, and to be capable of analyzing nonmotorized modes of transportation, such as walking and telecommuting. These requirements stretch the ability of existing forecasting procedures to the point where new procedures need to be examined.

Behavioral Changes

During the last 25 years, travel-related behavioral changes have occurred that call into question the ability of current modeling practice to replicate behavior. Some of the more significant changes affecting travel are the rise in auto ownership, trip chaining, peak spreading, and changes in household composition.

The rise in auto ownership in the United States has had a very significant impact on travel. Automobile availability is becoming less and less a factor in trip making or trip mode decisions. Recent surveys have indicated an auto ownership rate of over 1.0 per licensed driver. Effectively, this rate means that a car is available to nearly everyone.

Increasing highway congestion has generated many interrelated behavioral responses. Two of the most prominent are trip chaining and peak spreading. In trip chaining, a driver combines multiple purposes into a chain of trips instead of returning to home or work after each purpose has been accomplished. One of the effects of trip chaining is to make the purposes to be accomplished throughout the chain a determinant in the mode choice procedure along with the service level of the different modes (e.g., if at the end of the work day a stop must be made at a grocery store and several bags of food brought home, it is unlikely that the travel will be done by transit, no matter how convenient the transit service may be between home and work).

Many workers are now starting work earlier or later in order to avoid travel during peak hours. Further, in many areas, auto travel is avoided if possible during peak hours. Traditional modeling processes have focused on peak hours and have not directly analyzed the effect of congestion on travel time shifting or combining trip purposes. The effect of these changes cannot be adequately reflected in current travel forecasting processes.

With increased labor force participation by women, two-worker and single-adult households have grown in numbers to the point where they are the norm rather than the exception. With limited free time available, these households may be more likely to use trip chaining to accomplish non-work-related purposes. Two-worker households also affect the travel forecasting process in that land use decisions may be harder to forecast since accessibility to place of work becomes more complex when more than one work site is involved.

Factors contributing to the travel behavior of a household or an individual change almost continuously. At the macro level, continuing urbanization, evolving consumer technology and products, telecommunications systems, highway and transit improvements, and energy and air quality policies all contribute to urban residents' travel decisions. At the micro level, changes in household attributes (e.g., income, household composition, employment, and license holdings) and variations in daily traffic conditions can lead to residential relocation, car acquisition or disposal, and changes in daily travel patterns (e.g., different travel demands and mode, destination, or routing selections).

A household, or individual, when subjected to a change (at either the macro or micro level), responds over a period of time. One of the reasons for such "response lags" is that information is not always acquired immediately, leading to imperfect information or ignorance. A typical example in mode choice is the time it takes a solo driver to become aware of a new bus line and its characteristics. The person may find the new bus service suitable to the commute trip and switch. However, the process of experimentation and learning that the person must undergo before making the switch will take time, the time interval constituting the response lag (Kitamura and Van der Hoorn 1987).

Other behavioral changes will occur in the future. For example, telecommuting, still in its infancy, may have a significant impact on the work trip, and consequently on other trip making. Also, the application of new technology to the transportation system (e.g., advanced traveler information systems) could have a significant impact on travelers' route, timing, and destination decisions.

Behavioral Dynamics

A thorough understanding of behavioral dynamics is critically important when behavior cannot be represented properly by cross-sectional observation, as when time lags exist between a change in the travel environment and a behavioral change in response. Such time lags can be caused by lack of information; experimentation and learning; the psychological, time, and monetary costs of searching; organized behavior based on planning; perception thresholds; constraints; and apparently irrational preferences for habitual behavior. Such factors may lead to behavioral inertia, resistance to change, and differential speeds of adjustment, which in turn may lead to disproportionate responses to change.

It has been theorized that individuals or households do not respond to individual small changes but make an adjustment for all the changes that have accumulated when a major change, or a "life shock," takes place (Haag 1989). Beach and Potter (1992) describe four revolutions in the understanding of how unaided decisions are made. The early view was that all decisions were regarded as choices that, after extensive evaluation of the available options, resulted from maximization of expected utility. The first revolution was the recognition that evaluation is seldom extensive and is virtually never exhaustive. The second came from the recognition that decision makers have a variety of decision strategies that may be quite different from the maximization of expected utility. The third revolution came from the recognition that choices may occur relatively rarely—that past experience usually provides ways (policies, habits) of dealing with problems. De-

49

cisions are required when these solutions fail, and then the decisions may not merely be choices of the best option from some delineated set of options.

The fourth revolution in the understanding of how decisions are made came from the recognition that decisions occur in steps. The first step consists of screening out unacceptable options, whereas the second step consists of choosing the best option from the survivors. The first step focuses on what is wrong with options, whereas the second step focuses on what is right—two uniquely different approaches (Beach and Potter 1992).

All these dynamic aspects cannot be captured by contemporaneous relationships defined for a cross-section. In fact, they imply the presence of multiple equilibria, which denies any analysis based on cross-sectional relationships. From this viewpoint, the use of cross-sectional data and models for forecasting is a fundamentally flawed approach.

Dynamic Decision Making

The recent acknowledgment of the dynamic nature of travel decisions has led to an increasing awareness of the need to incorporate these dynamic effects into the urban transportation modeling framework. Nowhere in the context of travel is the nature of the decision processes more dynamic than in the area of route selection or route choice. Brehmer (1992) describes the classic dynamic decision-making process, which also serves quite well in describing many travel choice processes:

Dynamic decision making is an ongoing process in which

- a series of decisions is required to reach the goal. That is, to achieve and maintain control is a continuous activity requiring many decisions, each of which can only be understood in the context of the other decisions.

- the decisions are not independent. That is, later decisions are constrained by earlier decisions and, in turn, constrain those that come after them.

- the state of the decision problem changes, both autonomously and as a consequence of the decision maker's actions.

- the decisions have to be made in real time.

Dynamic decisions are decisions in context and in time—meaning that the decision maker must consider the consequences of each decision for future decisions, that he or she is constrained by earlier decisions, and that he or she may sometimes be able to correct problems caused by earlier decisions in later decisions (Brehmer 1992).

It is also probable that a change of small magnitude may not prompt any action, perhaps because of the presence of a threshold in perception. However, small changes, each below the perception threshold, may over time accumulate as a large change. Gradually intensifying highway congestion is a good example. The notion of cumulative effect applies well in this context; it may be hypothesized that the individual responds when the cumulative effect of small changes exceeds a threshold. The threshold value itself may be a function of the speed of accumulation; slow changes may allow the individual to get used to them (thereby the threshold value is raised), whereas rapid accumulation may lead to more prompt reaction. Or it may be the case that "any reaction is delayed until the next `life shock' (changing jobs, life-cycle stage, home location, etc.)" (Clark et al. 1982).

The above discussion of behavioral dynamics offers a way of viewing "habitual" or "routine behavior," "behavioral inertia," or "resistance to change." Namely, the same behavior prevails even after it is no longer optimum following changes in the environment because changing the behavior involves monetary, time, and psychological costs. Delaying reaction until the next life shock may be a way of taking advantage of the economy of scale in behavioral change.

The predicting of the magnitude and timing of behavioral responses to changes in contributing factors demands the use of longitudinal data. The discussion of behavioral dynamics clearly points to the need to observe behavioral units repeatedly over time to accurately predict and forecast behavioral response. Theories of leads and lags, behavioral asymmetry, threshold (minimum noticeable) changes, and presence of multiple equilibria have been recognized in the psychometric and sociometric literature. The primary reason these theories have not been used in travel behavior forecasting is that traditional transportation databases do not offer information that can incorporate these theories into modeling efforts. The field of transportation research has been rather sluggish in responding to the need for dynamic information. However, in the last decade, several panel studies have been conducted or initiated in transportation, and investigations into the dynamic nature of travel behavior have begun. Panel or longitudinal data have been used to study the effects of trip reduction measures (Giuliano et al. 1992), modal choice dynamics (Golob and Meurs 1987), travel demand (Golob and Meurs 1988), and destination choice (Nishii and Kondo 1992). The application of panel data for the dynamic analysis of automobile ownership/transaction/utilization commands

51

the largest body of literature in this area (Kitamura and Van der Hoorn 1987; Golob and Wissen 1989; Hensher and Smith 1990; Meurs 1991).

The adequacy of the conventional cross-sectional approach, which assumes the presence of equilibrium, must be fundamentally questioned. At the same time, further effort must be staged toward the development of dynamic model systems that address travel behavior, not necessarily on the trip-by-trip basis as is done in the conventional model systems, but rather on the basis of changes in activity and travel patterns in their entirety in the most suitable time frame.

Response Capabilities of the Existing Forecasting Process

The existing four-step forecasting process was initially aimed at forecasting the need for new highways and the number of lanes on a highway. Later modifications were made to forecast the effects of transit improvements.

To analyze air quality, the four-step process is combined with the Mobil model series developed by EPA. From the travel forecasting process, Mobil requires as input vehicle-miles traveled (VMT), speed, and the number of cold starts. These variables must be input by grid square and by time of day. The capabilities of the existing process to forecast the required input data vary.

VMT forecasting capabilities are generally good, and models are validated to VMT. Speed estimates do not have the accuracy of VMT estimates, speed being a variable used to make the assignment algorithm converge, not an observed variable. Since time does not explicitly enter into the forecasting process, the speed estimates will be inaccurate.

Cold starts are very difficult to estimate using current procedures. Trips are not chained, and time is not included, so it is not possible to determine either the trip chain or the time interval between trips, a critical element in cold starts.

The four-step process operates on a zone system, which may or may not be related to a grid square data system, which is used in air quality analysis. If the zone system is not related to the grid system, a process must be developed to convert from one to the other.

Needed Improvements

In order to respond to legislative requirements and changing travel patterns, travel model capability must be improved in three general areas: time and trip chaining, speeds, and legislative-specific requirements. These improvements will provide better input to emissions models as well as respond to specific requirements of the ISTEA and CAAA.

Air quality models require travel input by hourly segments over a 24-hour period; thus travel data must be generated continuously over the course of the day. In heavily traveled areas, the effect of congestion on trip departure time must be included, a requirement that ties directly into the need to include trip chaining. The total number of starts, determined by trip chaining, and the time interval between trips, determined by analyzing travel by time of day, both play a critical role in determining the impact of starts on emissions.

As stated earlier, emissions models require speed as an input. In current assignment techniques, the speeds derived are numbers that make the assignment algorithm converge, rather than true speed estimates. Since time is not a factor in the models, and since from basic physics, distance equals speed times time, a basic component to estimate speed is missing.

Two areas that need addressing because of legislative mandates are pricing and demand management. The ISTEA requires that pricing be tested as a tool to relieve congestion. Current processes require pricing to be converted to a value of time and added to link impedance. The current models have potential to refine their sensitivity to pricing, including the effects of pricing on different income groups. However, changes to current models will affect route and mode shifts only. Shifts in the time of day of travel cannot be easily accommodated.

Demand management and congestion management must include such options as telecommuting, walking, and bicycling. Current procedures potentially could analyze these options, but the latter require a widening of the scope of travel forecasting and a better understanding of what constitutes a trip and of the interrelationships of travel. For example, it has been difficult to *quantitatively* define the effect of urban design on travel—i.e., the link between transit and carpool usage and easy access to amenities at the work site—yet it is known that urban design does have an effect. In the validation process of current models, highway and transit trips are the primary elements considered; rarely are walking or bicycle trips part of validation.

Most analysis of demand management has been at the employer level, not at the regional level. Techniques need to be developed to allow regional models to better reflect demand management measures in their forecasts. The issue of forecasting demand management is also tied to the issue of the effectiveness of demand management.

Future Directions in Forecasting

Although modifications can be made to current procedures to deal with these shortcomings individually, taken as a whole, they require that the entire travel forecasting process be reexamined. In order to improve existing models and to design new models to meet current and future needs, the Federal Highway Administration, in cooperation with the Environmental Protection Agency, the Federal Transit Administration, the Department of Transportation, Office of the Secretary, and the Department of Energy, has initiated the Travel Mode Improvement Program (TMIP), a major effort to upgrade and redesign the travel forecasting process (U.S. DOT 1994). On the basis of this effort, some preliminary conclusions can be drawn concerning the next generation of travel forecasting procedures.

Design Characteristics

Although the redesigned model process has not been finalized,[1] it will be characterized by the following basic operating features:

1. The basic decision unit will be the household, and the primary forecast for the household will be of a set of activities. Forecasts of trips will be derived from the need to connect activities.

2. A geographic information system (GIS) platform will allow aggregation of data into zones usable for air quality analysis.

3. Both revealed and stated preference data will be used. Stated preference data will be essential to analyze options for which there is little or no experience, such as peak-hour pricing. Mode choice procedures will be expanded to include additional options, such as telecommuting, walking, or bicycling. For certain types of travel, the option of foregoing the trip will be allowed.

4. The models will be dynamic, responding to time of day, both on the demand side and the network side.

5. The relationship of regional models to traffic operations procedures will be explicitly acknowledged. The computing capability to integrate these procedures is now available.

6. The relative time frames of land use forecasting procedures, daily travel forecasting, and shifting trips en route will be addressed.

---

[1] Research on the modeling approach described herein is just beginning at the time of preparation of this chapter. It is likely that as testing and applications get underway, the final version will vary significantly from the approach described here.

Operating Characteristics

In operation, the system will have two components, a supply component and a demand component. The demand component will generate activities that must be satisfied during the day and will modify these activities in response to network conditions. The supply component will convert activities into trip chains and place trips on the network. Each of these components may perform the following activities:

1. *Activity generation:* This phase will generate a series of activities to be accomplished. An example would be that a person must be at work and optionally at shopping and recreation during the day. Constraints may be imposed on this set of activities, such as stops at day care that must precede and follow work. Implicitly, in generating a set of activities to be met, a chain of trips linking those activities is also generated.

2. *Assignment to network:* This phase will place trips onto the network. Mode choice will be accomplished in this phase and will likely be part of the assignment process—i.e., the pathfinding algorithm will find the minimum path using a combination of highway and transit travel times.

3. *Network operation:* The network will accept trips on a continuous basis—i.e., dynamic assignment. There will be feedback between the four modules allowing activity generation, trip making, and departure time to respond to network conditions.

4. *Activity adjustment:* Activities will be adjusted and modified on the basis of network congestion and other factors. For example, congested network conditions may cause trip departure times to be changed, thereby affecting the entire trip chain and whether purposes at the end of the chain are completed.

Overall, the approach will be a simulation, stepping through the day, or week, in discrete time units. This approach is a significant departure from current methods.

Figure 3-1 provides a flow diagram of this approach. It has the potential to answer many of the policy and air quality questions that current models cannot adequately address, such as trip chaining, travel by time of day, the effect of congestion on trip making and departure time, peak-hour pricing, and innovative demand management measures. The GIS framework will allow the conversion of activities to grid squares for air quality analysis, and the dynamic assignment will provide improved speed and 24-hour travel estimates. This approach, when combined with micro-level assignment techniques, will also

Figure 3-1

Flow Diagram

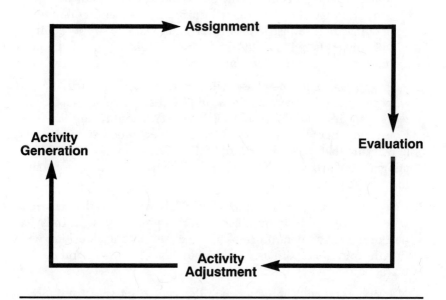

provide the basis of input to the next generation of air quality models, which will involve the drive cycle of the automobile.

Research has begun to develop the tools described here. With adequate funding, their field testing and initial application is three to four years away.

Conclusion

Travel demand models now in widespread use were first developed to plan the routing of new urban "interstate" highways. They performed that task well. New legislative requirements, changing travel behavior, and the shift in emphasis from infrastructure expansion to demand management call for a new approach to demand forecasting. Demand models must respond to the requirements of the Clean Air Act Amendments and the Intermodal Surface Transportation Efficiency Act; must acknowledge increased auto ownership, peak spreading, trip chaining, and changes in household composition and behavioral dynamics; and must accurately assess the effects of various pricing and other demand-oriented strategies. Forecasting procedures must also respond to environmental needs.

Future forecasting procedures will operate at the household level, use a GIS platform, have both revealed and stated preference data, reflect time of day, interrelate regional and traffic operations models, and address the difference in time frame between long-term land use decisions and daily travel decisions.

The forecasting procedure described in this chapter addresses the travel forecasting issue. Using this procedure for air quality analysis will also require the development of an auto ownership model to be integrated into the forecasting procedure. Microsimulation, using the household as the analysis unit and dynamic modeling, is an unproven technology. However, given the changing requirements on modeling and the current state of research, it is an appropriate direction to explore.

Acknowledgments

Significant portions of this chapter are based upon a paper presented by Frederick W. Ducca at the 1993 summer meeting of the Planning and Transportation Research and Computation International Association (PTRC) (Ducca 1993).

References

Beach, R.L., and R.E. Potter. 1992. "The Pre-choice Screening of Options." *ACTA Psychologica, International Journal of Psychonomics* (Amsterdam) 81: 115–126.

Brehmer, B. 1992. "Dynamic Decision Making: Human Control of Complex Systems." *ACTA Psychologica, International Journal of Psychonomics* (Amsterdam) 81: 211–241.

Bryner, G.C. 1993. *Blue Skies, Green Politics: The Clean Air Act of 1990.* Washington, D.C.: Congressional Quarterly Press.

Clark, M., M. Dix, and P. Goodwin. 1982. "Some Issues of Dynamics in Forecasting Travel Behavior: A Discussion Paper." *Transportation* 11: 153–172.

Ducca, Frederick W. 1993. "Improving Travel Forecasting Procedures." Paper presented at the Twenty-first Annual Meeting of the Planning and Transport Research and Computation International Association, Manchester, U.K., September.

Giuliano, G., K. Hwang, and M. Wachs. 1992. "Employee Trip Reduction in Southern California: First-Year Results." Series D; 9201. Graduate School of Architecture and Urban Planning, University of California at Los Angeles.

Golob, T.F., and H. Meurs. 1987. "A Structural Model of Temporal

Change in Multi-Modal Travel Demand." *Transportation Research* 21A: 391–400.

———. 1988. "Development of Structural Equation Models of the Dynamics of Passenger Travel Demand." *Environment and Planning* 20A: 1197–1218.

Golob, T.F., and L.J.G. van Wissen. 1989. "A Joint Household Travel Distance Generation and Car Ownership Model." *Transportation Research* 23B: 471–491.

Guensler, R. 1992. "The Role of Transportation Control Measures in California's Air Pollution Control Strategy." Paper presented at the Air and Waste Management Association International Specialty Conference on PM10 Standards and Non-Traditional Source Control, Scottsdale, Ariz.

Haag, G. 1989. *Dynamic Decision Theory: Applications to Urban and Regional Topics.* Studies in Operational Regional Science. Dordrecht, The Netherlands: Kluwer Academic Publishers.

Hensher, D.A., and N.C. Smith. 1990. "Estimating Automobile Utilization with Panel Data: An Investigation of Alternative Assumptions for the Initial Conditions and Error Covariances." *Transportation Research* 24A (6): 417–426.

Kitamura, R. 1987. "A Panel Analysis of Car Ownership and Mobility." *Proceedings of the Japan Society of Civil Engineers,* No. 383/IV-7, pp. 13–27.

Kitamura, R., and T. Van der Hoorn. 1987. "Regularity and Irreversibility of Weekly Travel Behavior." *Transportation* 14: 227–251.

Meurs, H. 1991. "Panel Data Models of Car Ownership and Mobility." Paper presented at the Sixth International Conference on Travel Behaviour, Quebec, Canada, May 22–24.

Nishii, K., and K. Kondo. 1992. "Dynamic Analysis of Destination Choice Behavior by Visitors to Shopping Complex." Paper presented at the Sixth World Congress on Transport Research, Lyon, France, June 29–July 3.

U.S. Department of Transportation (U.S. DOT). 1991. *Intermodal Surface Transportation and Efficiency Act of 1991: A Summary.* Washington, D.C.: U.S. Department of Transportation.

———. 1994. *New Approaches to Travel Forecasting Models: A Synthesis of Four Research Proposals.* Final Report DOT-T-94-15. Washington D.C.: U.S. Department of Transportation.

Weiner, E. 1993. "Upgrading Travel Demand Forecasting Capabilities." Paper presented at the Fourth National Conference on Transportation Planning Methods and Applications, Daytona Beach, Florida, May.

Chapter Four

Strategies for Goods Movement in a Sustainable Transportation System

LAURENCE O'ROURKE AND MICHAEL F. LAWRENCE

In recent years, the need for greater energy security and a cleaner environment has been the driving force behind the implementation of an increasingly complex web of public policies affecting the transportation industry. The Clean Air Act Amendments (CAAA) of 1990 and the Energy Policy Act have produced a whole new set of public mandates, incentives, and regulations. The need to achieve ever greater efficiencies and environmental improvements has led policymakers to hone regulatory instruments to ever finer purposes. At the same time, legislation such as the Intermodal Surface Transportation Efficiency Act (ISTEA) has also attempted to integrate regulatory efforts within and between different modes of transportation. The spirit of such legislation has acknowledged that the complex economic and environmental impacts of transportation policies can only be understood within a multimodal context. Intelligent public policy not only must attempt to improve energy efficiency and environmental impacts of individual modes of transportation but also must acknowledge that these efforts work within a larger transportation economy. Although much progress has been made in introducing energy-efficient and alternative-fuels technology into the transportation industry, much work remains to be done to achieve freight mode shifts that work toward achieving environmental and energy policy goals.

As a result of recent legislative initiatives, it appears that funding and federal efforts will advance the implementation of alternative-fuel programs. The CAAA of 1990 impose a wide variety of programs on the transportation industry, including a mandate for cleaner diesel engines in trucks and a requirement for reformulated fuel programs in some nonattainment areas. Other recent legislation, including ISTEA and the National Energy Policy Act, also address energy use and transportation policy. The recent flow of funds to alternative-fuel programs has acknowledged the important efficiencies that may be realized with prudent investment in research.

While substantial research has focused on alternative-fuel policy for highway trucks, it is also productive to view alternative fuels and energy efficiency in a multimodal context. An examination of energy use and efficiency in different transportation modes suggests that economic and environmental benefits may be realized by promoting alternative ways to move freight. Movement of freight by more energy-efficient and environmentally sound modes of transportation can reinforce efforts to improve the energy efficiency and environmental soundness of each individual mode.

New technology has substantially improved the fuel efficiency and the environmental soundness of highway truck freight movements. Engineering design, new transportation fuels, and more efficient scheduling and routing of freight movements have all contributed to this development. Some researchers believe that there are substantial energy security and environmental benefits that can also be achieved by encouraging freight mode shifts.

Trends in Freight Movements and Environmental Impact

Although recent trends in freight movement have favored trucks, new technology has the potential to improve other modes of transportation and make them more competitive with the trucking industry. Rail's market share of freight transportation fell during the 1970s but has stabilized over the last decade. Although the railroad industry still dominates transportation in ton-miles moved, it has been pressed by trucking, which has been able to provide more reliable service and faster delivery times.

Although the trucking industry has been successful in increasing its market share of freight movements, it is the least energy-efficient and, in many cases, the most expensive mode of transportation. Compared with pipeline, railroad, and waterborne transportation, trucking

Figure 4-1

Intercity Freight Movement Energy Intensities by Mode

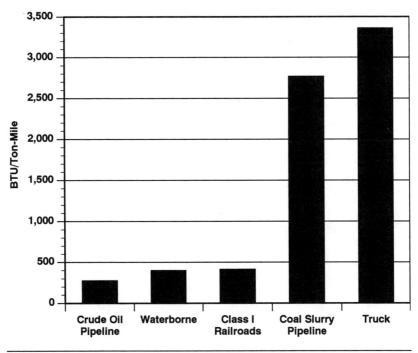

Source: Davis and Strang (1993), p. 2-26.

is the most energy-intensive, consuming more than 3,000 Btu per ton-mile, whereas waterborne and rail transportation both use less than 500 Btu per ton-mile (see Figure 4-1). Water, rail, and pipeline are extremely competitive in cost per ton-mile as well. Rail is usually cheaper for comparable line hauls, with truck transportation costing up to ten times as much as rail per ton-mile.

The investigation of alternative ways to move freight becomes even more imperative when one looks at the environmental impacts of trucking's energy use. A sample California Emission Inventory (see Figures 4-2, 4-3, and 4-4) illustrates that of all the modes of freight transportation, trucking is the worst offender in every emissions category. For PM10, carbon monoxide (CO), and nitrous oxides (NO_x), one can see that the estimated emissions of trucks far outweigh those of all other modes combined.

Figure 4-2

**1987 California PM10 Emission Inventory
for Selected Transportation Modes**

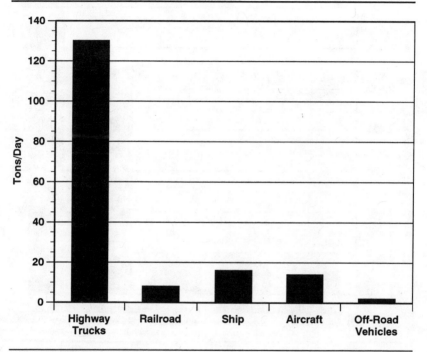

Source: Guensler and Sperling (1991), p. 2.

Feasibility of Freight Mode Shifts

Investigating and encouraging alternative freight modes may have beneficial economic, environmental, and energy security impacts. The extent to which truck traffic can be diverted to other modes is, however, uncertain. Any analysis of freight movements must take into account that transportation and logistical decisions are made in a complex business environment where service, delivery time, and inventory management are important considerations for choice of mode. Price comparisons between modes can also be misleading since the type of freight hauled by each mode often differs. Bulk freight is often hauled by rail or barge, whereas small manufactured items and mixed cargos are often moved by truck. Shorter hauls and smaller cargo loads increase the ton-mile price of truck freight.

The fuel efficiencies of alternative freight movement can only be

Figure 4-3

**1987 California CO Emission Inventory
for Selected Transportation Modes**

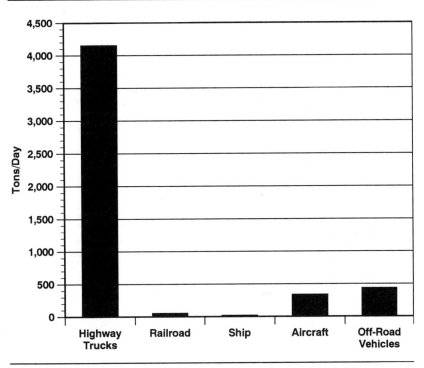

Source: Guensler and Sperling (1991), p. 2.

realized if alternative modes can effectively haul truck freight. Examination of the commodities moved by different modes of transportation shows significant differences in the volume and types of freight hauled by the different modes. Overall, rail moves 26.6 percent of all freight tonnage, whereas trucks move 40.8 percent of domestic freight tonnage. Water and pipeline each move about 16 percent of freight tonnage (see Figure 4-5). However, the relative importance of rail and truck freight movement is reversed when the distance of the freight movement is taken into account. Measuring freight movement by ton-miles makes rail the largest transporter of freight, accounting for about 32 percent of the ton-miles in the freight market, as compared with trucking's 23 percent (see Figure 4-6). Rail movements are thus more fuel-efficient, in part because they tend to be long-haul movements. Long-haul truck freight is therefore one of the best candidates for alternative-mode transportation.

Although good data on truck freight movements are hard to come by, in general, truck freight is characterized by shorter hauls, higher-value products, and smaller-sized loads. Truck freight is more likely to comprise small manufactured items and/or mixed cargos than freight moved by other modes. It is distributed across a wide cross-section of commodity groups. Important among these are such commodities as building materials, processed foods, farm products, mixed cargos, fabricated metal products, furniture, and petroleum. For some of this freight, intermodal competition is possible, but there are limits to competition between trucking and other modes of transportation.

The type of commodities moved by different modes is one limit to freight mode shifts. Rail, pipeline, and water freight movements

Figure 4-4

1987 California NO_x Emission Inventory for Selected Transportation Modes

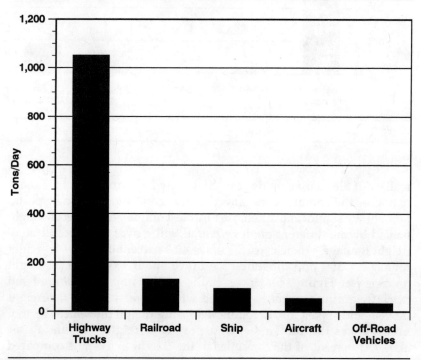

Source: Guensler and Sperling (1991), p. 2.

Figure 4-5

Intercity Tonnage Carried by Mode

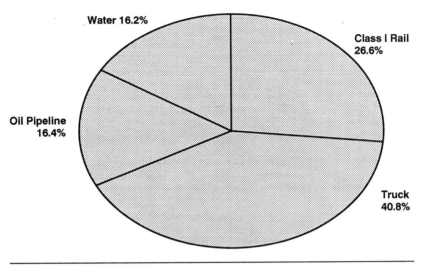

Source: Davis and Strang (1993), p. 2–5.

Figure 4-6

Intercity Ton-Miles Carried by Mode

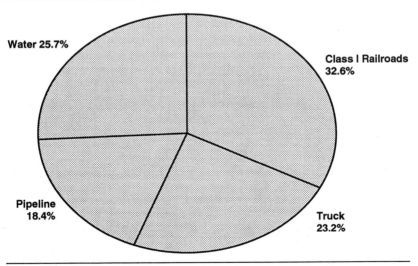

Source: Davis and Strang (1993), p. 2–5.

Figure 4-7

Principal Commodities Carried by Water

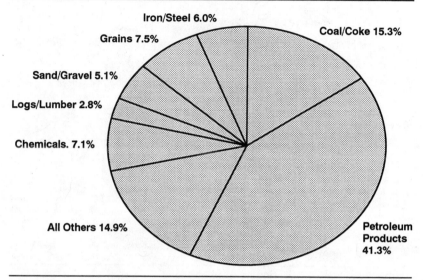

Source: Army Corps of Engineers (1988), p. 12.

achieve a high level of fuel efficiency because they tend to comprise bulk products shipped in high volumes. This is particularly true of waterborne commerce. Over 50 percent of freight moved by water is coal, coke, or petroleum products (Army Corps of Engineers 1988). Figure 4-7 shows a breakdown of waterborne commerce by commodity type.

Railroad freight also falls into a few commodity categories. Rail freight movement is dominated by coal, farm products, truckload-on-flat-car (TOFC), and container-on-flat-car (COFC) movements. If one examines the other primary commodities moved by rail, one finds that most of these other commodity categories are also bulk items. Pulp and paper products, lumber and wood, nonmetallic minerals, and food and kindred products are other major commodity groups moved by rail (see Figure 4-8).

Freight movements in the railroad industry have been influenced by two major trends. First, since 1970, the number of revenue carloads has declined as freight traffic has been captured by other modes. Second, within the industry, rail freight has become more concentrated in only a few commodity categories. For example, between 1974 and 1990, rail freight traffic increased substantially in the coal and "other"

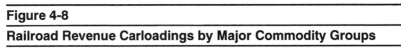

Figure 4-8

Railroad Revenue Carloadings by Major Commodity Groups

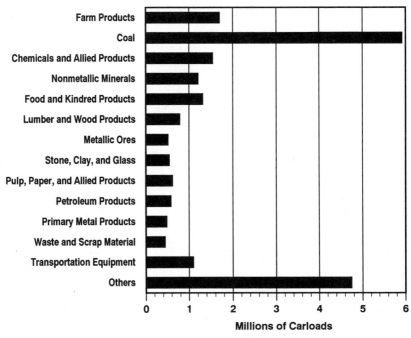

Source: Davis and Strang (1993) p. 6-28.

commodity categories. Rail freight movement of nonmetallic minerals and chemicals also increased, but in every other major commodity category, revenue carloadings fell (see Figure 4-9).

The consolidation of the rail freight market into bulk and long-haul activities is driven by many factors. One factor has been the expansion of intermodal transportation. The increase of COFC and TOFC freight traffic shows up in all of the commodity categories, but particularly the "other" group (see Figure 4-9). Overall, although recent trends in rail commodity shipments would seem to suggest that rail is competitive in an ever smaller segment of the transportation market, developments in intermodal containerized transportation and changing business conditions may minimize the impact of this trend.

Another important factor that must be taken into consideration in assessing the competition between truck and other modes of transportation is the inadequacy of current transportation infrastructure.

67

Figure 4-9

Railroad Revenue Carloadings by Commodity Group (1974 and 1990)

Revenue Carloads Increased in Only Four Freight Groups

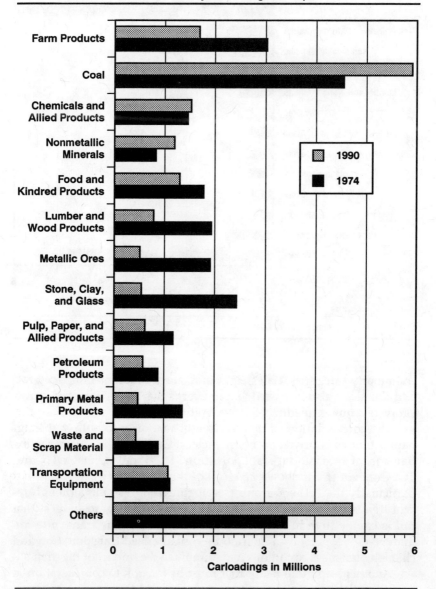

Source: Davis and Strang (1993) p. 6-28.

Intermodal containerized traffic has made it easier for rail and water-borne commerce to compete with trucks for freight. However, inter-modal traffic has been hampered in some regions of the country (such as the Atlantic northeastern corridor) by a lack of intermodal facilities and by the inability of some rail tunnels to accommodate double-stack container trains. In many areas, waterways and rail lines are not lo-cated close enough for customers to take advantage of rail and water-borne freight rates. This is partly due to the fact that railroads have cut costs by closing down low-volume lines and concentrating their busi-ness on high-volume, long-haul corridors. It is difficult for alternative transportation modes to compete with the trucking industry for the short-haul freight movements that are an important component of most rail or barge freight movements. However, the growth of inter-modal shipments may allow railroads to capitalize on their efficient long-haul rates while trucks perform short-haul operations at the ori-gin and destination. The trucking industry is already the biggest con-sumer of rail services.

Although important energy efficiencies may be achieved through multimodal and alternative freight movements, there are also many structural and geographical barriers to intermodal competition. The ability of truck freight to be moved by other modes is constrained by the location and type of customer facility. Increasingly, industry has moved away from rail lines and into office parks that are built to be serviced by trucks. Thus, business decisions about location and exist-ing investments in facilities often predetermine a company's choice of transportation services.

Perhaps the biggest limitation of alternative freight movement is that in many transportation markets, the focus of competition is not cost, but service. The trucking industry has gained a reputation for speed of delivery and reliability of service that railroads have been hard pressed to duplicate. Surveys show that freight rates are not the most important factor in freight transportation choice. Service factors, such as reliability, transit time, and claims processing, are often more important (McGinnis 1990).

However, not all businesses require precise delivery schedules or the fastest delivery times. Studies of rail/truck competition have high-lighted that significant competition occurs for cargo weights from 20,000 to 80,000 pounds. Lighter and heavier cargos outside of this range tend to be serviced by truck and rail, respectively, when service conditions permit. Even given high demands for service, rail still re-mains competitive in many segments of the freight market.

Several recent developments in the transportation industry also affect the competitiveness of alternative transportation modes, partic-

69

ularly rail. The explosion of intermodal service has facilitated more efficient multimodal competition. The integration of rail and truck services has been sped by changes in recent regulations that have permitted railroads to purchase trucking companies. Such integration allows for better logistical planning and coordination, thereby increasing service and speeding delivery times and making multimodal rail movements more competitive. Larger, multimodal transportation companies can offer one-stop shopping for transportation services and provide for longer hauls. Both of these features make multimodal cheaper and more attractive. Obviously, the limit of multimodal transportation is that a customer must ship rail-sized freight movement to start with.

Another important development in the transportation industry that may affect the feasibility of alternative-mode freight movement is the implementation of just-in-time (JIT) inventory procedures by manufacturers. JIT systems are made up of several separate purchasing, transportation, and inventory practices. Important operational characteristics include lower inventories, efficient materials handling, buyer control of transportation, fewer suppliers and carriers, and the use of long-term contracts with suppliers and carriers.

JIT inventory methods attempt to eliminate all raw material and work-in-progress inventories, relying on frequent and timely deliveries of materials to prevent stock-outs and the shutdown of production lines. Bypassing the factory receiving area, goods are delivered right on the floor of the factory where the materials are required. Coordinated inbound and outbound shipments allow one vehicle to perform both functions and reduce empty backhauls (Bookbinder and Higginson 1990).

Several features of JIT inventory procedures work against rail freight movements. JIT's demands for certainty of delivery time are more difficult for rail to meet, and since the cost of late delivery may include the shutdown of a manufacturing line, premium prices for truck hauls can be justified. Multiple delivery points and more frequent deliveries reduce the size of individual freight movements and thus the feasibility of rail movement. However, even with these drawbacks, rail movements can still capture some JIT freight.

Deregulation has given the railroads the ability to better negotiate contracts with shippers and purchasers for JIT transportation service. Further, JIT planning practices, such as tight order and delivery schedules, may make it easier for railroads to coordinate empty-car movements using distribution requirements planning (DRP). In addition, advances in communications and information technology are allowing railroads to track shipments and prevent late delivery. If containers get behind schedule, they can be pulled off the track and delivered by truck.

JIT inventory methods probably will not spread to most businesses because they can only be utilized efficiently by certain types of manufacturing operations; thus the majority of manufacturers will probably not demand JIT-quality transportation services. Nevertheless, although studies have shown that rail cannot compete effectively in COFC JIT freight movements because of the expense of container-loading equipment and the potential schedule delays associated with it, TOFC JIT movements have been implemented profitably in several locations throughout the United States (Bookbinder and Higginson 1990), illustrating that rail can compete in markets with some of the highest service demands. With advances in communications and information technology, it may be possible for the industry as a whole to begin competing more effectively in service.

Improving Energy Efficiency in the Trucking Industry

Although rail and other modes of transportation are competitive with truck freight movements in many sectors of the transportation industry, significant portions of freight must be moved by trucks because no other viable alternatives exist. Due to service requirements or deficiencies in alternative-mode infrastructure, a certain percentage of the freight market is effectively dedicated to the trucking industry.

For this segment of the transportation industry, increased energy efficiency can be achieved only by reducing the energy intensity of truck freight movements. A recent Energy and Environmental Analysis, Inc. study (EEA 1991) detailed a variety of technologies and policies through which future fuel efficiencies could be achieved. Essentially, fuel efficiencies can be achieved in two areas. Given a level of demand, energy conservation in transporting freight by truck can be accomplished by reducing energy input through operational and technological improvements and/or by increasing the number of freight ton-miles traveled per unit of energy consumed (i.e., increasing fuel productivity.)

For most vehicle types, one way to improve fuel productivity is to increase the payload capacity of the vehicle. Legal cargo capacity is determined by the difference between a vehicle's empty weight and its maximum gross vehicle weight (GVW). However, to minimize damage to pavement and bridges, each state has a system of truck size and weight limits. Truck weight limits set an upper bound to a vehicle's maximum operating weight, whereas truck size limits constrain

71

GVW by restricting a vehicle's volumetric carrying capacity. Liberalizing weight and size limits to allow trucks to operate at higher GVWs would directly influence fuel productivity by increasing payload capacity. Fuel efficiency per mile would decline, but fuel efficiency per ton-mile would increase because aerodynamic forces do not closely scale with increases in weight (EEA 1991). Further, heavier trucks can take advantage of larger, more fuel-efficient engines.

Expanding the size and weight of trucks has significant long-term costs, however. Whether it will increase highway fatalities is a subject of great dispute among researchers. It will certainly incur increased wear and tear on roads and bridges, which were designed for certain vehicle weight specifications. Critics in the railroad industry note that increasing size and weight limits will allow the trucking industry to reap the benefits of raised productivity while not paying for the infrastructure costs incurred. This, critics claim, comes on top of the already lavish subsidy that trucking has benefited from by using public roads without fully paying its way through fees and taxes. The railroads have long felt that such federal subsidies to the trucking industry have made rail less competitive and have shifted freight movements onto trucks.

Proponents of longer combination vehicles (LCVs) tout their ability to decrease congestion, cut freight costs, and increase fuel productivity. The Transportation Research Board has estimated the potential economic benefit of LCVs to be several billion dollars (Schulz 1990b). However, the railroad industry claims that such studies do not properly account for potential disruption in the rail industry, increased pollution, and more frequent highway congestion caused by greater movement of freight over roads.

A slightly less controversial way to increase the fuel productivity of trucks is to reduce empty backhauls. When vehicles backhaul empty, they are operating at zero ton-miles per gallon. This brings down their average fuel efficiency dramatically.

Empty backhauls are both a logistical and a political problem. Politically, backhauls are regulated for some intrastate movements, although no federal backhaul regulation has existed since 1980. Any carrier with Interstate Commerce Commission authority is free to backhaul as long as it is not carrying food in one direction and hazardous materials in the other. A federal effort to improve fuel productivity through reduced empty backhauls might include a federal mandate relaxing state backhaul regulations.

Empty backhauls are also a logistical problem, dependent on the ability of a given trucking company to efficiently schedule the operation of its trucks. New information and communications technology has been especially effective in reducing empty backhauls. Some large, advanced truckload carriers, such as J. B. Hunt, even use satellites to keep track of their vehicle fleets and schedule efficient delivery and pickup routes. For the most part, small trucking companies and owner-operators do not have access to this type of sophisticated technology to reduce empty backhauls. Some have suggested that government sponsorship of information clearing houses could make such technology available to small trucking operations.

JIT inventory procedures, which attempt to schedule pickups and deliveries together, also hold some potential for improving fuel efficiency through reduced empty backhauls. However, JIT procedures will probably affect only a fraction of the trucking market.

The benefits of reduced empty backhauls can be quite substantial. By some calculations, fuel productivity can be increased 30 to 60 percent. The lack of perfect information and time restrictions of drivers limit the extent to which this kind of productivity improvement can be achieved, but even taking into account these limitations, the potential energy savings are significant.

Energy conservation in trucks can also be obtained through operational and technological improvements in the design of the truck. Current diesel-powered trucks are already very fuel-efficient relative to their weight. A fully loaded diesel truck can get 7 to 8 miles per gallon (mpg) on the highway, a fuel economy of approximately 280 to 320 ton-miles per gallon. A car weighing 5,000 pounds or less fully loaded can attain a fuel economy of 26 to 30 mpg, or only about 60 to 75 ton-miles per gallon (EEA 1991). However, even given the state of current technology, fuel economy can still be further improved.

Technological improvements in engine design can enhance fuel economy in several ways. More advanced engineering can raise engine thermodynamic efficiency, reduce friction loss, decrease pumping loss, or increase turbocharger efficiency. The kind and scope of engineering improvements differ by vehicle type, but their net effect is to reduce break-specific fuel consumption. In estimating engine break-specific energy loss by engine type to the year 2002, the Engine Manufacturers Association has forecast that there will be no improvement for light-duty trucks, a 3.6 percent improvement for the medium-duty class, and a 4.8 percent improvement for the heavy-duty-class trucks (EEA 1991). The potential for achieving energy efficiencies with larger vehicles is one of the reasons put forward for adopting LCVs.

A host of other engineering technologies, such as speed control and more sophisticated fuel injection systems, can also be employed to improve fuel economy and reduce vehicle emissions. Fuel economy can also be improved by reducing a vehicle's related characteristics, such as drag, rolling resistance, and weight of accessory loads. Weight reductions are also being obtained by substituting plastic and aluminum components for steel and by using modern, lower-weight brake mean effective pressure (BMEP) engines.

More advanced aerodynamic truck designs will also bring new fuel efficiencies. New aerodynamic cab models pioneered by Kenworth came on the market in the late 1980s and continue to penetrate truck vehicle fleets. Navistar has also been a leader in truck aerodynamics and has identified achievable drag improvements in cab tractor design that could reduce drag by 25 percent. Some drag improvements may reduce payload capacity or make changing tractors more difficult, however, and thus not all of this new technology will be adopted. Nevertheless, significant gains in productivity can be achieved.

Decreasing rolling resistance will also yield significant fuel efficiencies. By reducing the number of tires and designing new and lower-profile radials, manufacturers can cut rolling resistance by about 10 percent. In Europe, four tires on two axles have been replaced with two "supertires." Although some reductions in rolling resistance may be achieved through their use, the penetration of supertires into the U.S. market is expected to occur only on a small scale.

Alternative Fuels

The trucking industry has made significant progress in improving the amount of freight moved per unit of energy as well as the efficiency of engine technology and has invested significant resources in environmental and energy-efficient technologies for diesel fuels. As a result, truckers have always been opposed to a federally mandated alternative-fuel policy since any nondiesel alternative-fuel policy would require a substantial additional investment in engineering and research. Significant lobbying by the trucking industry prior to the Clean Air Act Amendments of 1990 averted methanol alternative-fuel requirements for light-duty vehicle fleets and defined reformulated, low-sulphur diesel as an alternative fuel, and the industry currently plans to satisfy CAAA standards by using cleaner diesel and cleaner-burning engines.

Although the majority of the trucking industry has attempted to avoid nondiesel alternative-fuel solutions, there has been some progress in switching fleets to alternative fuels. United Parcel Service operates an experimental program in which city fleets are run on compressed natural gas (CNG) (Schulz 1990a), and some utilities have offered monetary subsidies for conversion to natural gas (Bohn 1990). Some regions of the country have begun converting to alternative fuels faster than others—for example, tougher California emissions standards have advanced the use of alternative-fuel vehicles on the West Coast.

Automakers have given alternative fuels some momentum by investing money in alternative-fuel truck research. General Motors (GM) and Chevrolet both have spent research money on alternative-fuel truck programs, building a variety of prototype truck designs, and bus companies such as the Flexible Bus Company in Ohio and Tecogen of Massachusetts have begun producing alternative-fuel buses for use by schools and mass transit administrations.

The penetration of alternative-fuel vehicles into the market has been slow, however. Expensive compressor equipment required for refueling makes use of CNG economical only for vehicles that operate on the same daily schedule and refuel at a central location. Other alternative fuels face the same kinds of barriers to market entry. Because infrastructure already exists for diesel refueling, diesel enjoys a significant competitive advantage, but in most areas this is not the case for any alternative fuels. Although alternative fuels can contribute substantially to truck efficiency and environmental soundness, market forces will nevertheless limit the extent of change within industry.

Conclusion

Overall, obtaining a more sustainable transportation system is going to involve the coordination of a variety of programs. Improving the environmental soundness, energy efficiency, and energy security of the current transportation system will require policymakers to juggle a series of initiatives, some of which may mitigate the impact of others. For example, allowing longer combination vehicles may increase the fuel productivity of the trucking industry, but it may also draw freight away from alternative modes of transportation; engineering design to meet environmental standards may not necessarily increase fuel productivity; and enhancements in the fuel economy of traditionally fueled vehicles may make them a more attractive option, thus decreasing energy security. In the final analysis, any successful policy for a more sustainable transportation system must balance energy security, energy efficiency, and environmental soundness as sometimes competing yet ultimately interconnected goals.

References

Army Corps of Engineers. 1988. *Waterborne Commerce of the United States.* Fort Belvoir, Va.: Water Resources Support Center.

Bohn, Joseph. 1990. "Utilities Push Natural Gas for Trucks with Varied Incentives." *Automotive News*, October 8, p. 16.

Bookbinder, J., and J. Higginson. 1990. "Implications of Just-in-Time Production on Rail Freight Systems. *Transportation Journal*, Spring, pp. 29–35.

Davis, S., and S. Strang. 1993. *Transportation Energy Data Book*. 13th ed. Oak Ridge, Tenn.: Oak Ridge National Laboratory.

Energy and Environmental Analysis, Inc. (EEA). 1991. "Analysis of Heavy Duty Truck Fuel Efficiency to 2001." Arlington, Va.: September.

Guensler, Randall, and Daniel Sperling. 1991. "Uncertainty in the Emission Inventory for Heavy-Duty Diesel-Powered Trucks." Institute of Transportation Studies, University of California at Davis.

McGinnis, Michael. 1990. "The Relative Importance of Cost and Service in Freight Transportation Choice: Before and After Deregulation." *Transportation Journal*, Fall, pp. 12–19.

Schulz, John. 1990a. "Diesel Will Remain the Primary Truck Fuel Despite Tightening of Pollution Standards." *Traffic World*, November 19, pp. 10–11.

―――. 1990b. "Truckers Hail, Railroads Assail TRB Study on Weight Fairness." *Traffic World*, July 16, pp. 13–14.

Chapter Five

Hypercars:
The Next Industrial Revolution

AMORY B. LOVINS

Conventional cars, like other technologies, have entered their era of greatest refinement just as they may become obsolete. Imagine that a seventh of U.S. GNP were derived from the Big Three typewriter manufacturers, who have gradually progressed from manual to electric to typeball models and are now making delicate refinements for the forthcoming Selectric 17. The typewriters are excellent and even profitable, selling 15 million every year. The only trouble is that the competition is developing wireless subnotebook computers. That is where the global auto industry is today—painstakingly refining designs that may soon be swept away by the integration of powerful technologies already in or entering the market. Advanced materials, software, motors, microelectronics, power electronics, electric storage devices, and computer-aided design and manufacturing will bring a revolution in both vehicles and auto manufacturing.

In September 1993, U.S. automakers and the Clinton administration announced the historic Partnership for a New Generation of Vehi-

---

Between the 1993 Asilomar conference and the publication of this book, the author has renamed the supercar concept. He now calls it the *hypercar* to avoid confusion with other usages of supercar, such as street-licensed racecars that get a couple of hundred miles per hour, not per gallon.

cles (PNGV) to develop within a decade a prototype car having tripled fuel economy. Yet this seemingly ambitious goal can be far surpassed. Well before 2003, competition, not government mandates, can bring to market cars efficient enough to carry a family coast-to-coast on one tank of fuel, more safely and comfortably than present vehicles, and more cleanly than electric cars plus the powerplants needed to recharge them. This revolution in automaking will require leaping forward to a completely new car design: the ultralight hybrid-electric hypercar (Lovins et al. 1993).

Ultralight Design

Decades of effort to improve engines and powertrains have only reduced the portion of a car's fuel energy that is lost before it gets to the wheels to about 80 to 85 percent (see Figure 5-1). About 95 percent of the resulting wheelpower hauls the car itself, so less than 1 percent of the fuel energy actually ends up hauling the driver. This inefficiency has a simple main cause: cars are made of steel, and steel is

---

Figure 5-1

Two Ways to Drive 12 Km in the City

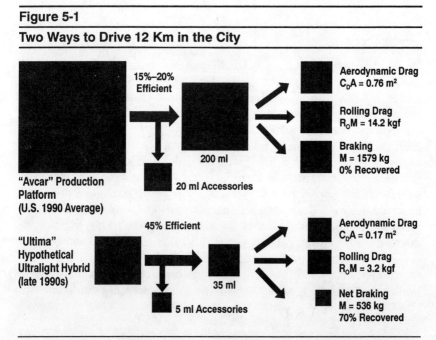

"Avcar" Production Platform (U.S. 1990 Average)

15%–20% Efficient

200 ml

20 ml Accessories

Aerodynamic Drag $C_DA = 0.76$ m^2

Rolling Drag $R_0M = 14.2$ kgf

Braking M = 1579 kg 0% Recovered

"Ultima" Hypothetical Ultralight Hybrid (late 1990s)

45% Efficient

35 ml

5 ml Accessories

Aerodynamic Drag $C_DA = 0.17$ m^2

Rolling Drag $R_0M = 3.2$ kgf

Net Braking M = 536 kg 70% Recovered

In highway driving, efficiency *falls* because there is far more irrecoverable loss to air drag (which rises as v^3) and less recoverable loss to braking.

---

heavy, so powerful engines are required to accelerate them. The oversizing cuts the engine's efficiency in half.

The incremental approach to improvement saves so little fuel because it focuses disproportionately on fine points of engine and transmission design while comparatively neglecting the basic strategy of making the car very light and aerodynamically very slippery. But doing just that—designing cars more like airplanes and less like tanks—can capture a magical synergy between minimized tractive loads and hybrid-electric propulsion.

The ultralight strategy rests on the basic physics of cars: in urban driving on a level road, drivewheel energy—typically only 15 to 20 percent of the fuel input energy—is devoted about one-third to heating the brakes when the car stops, one-third to heating the air the car pushes aside, and one-third to heating the tires and road (MacCready 1993, p. 153). On the highway, air resistance, whose force is proportional to the square of speed, accounts for approximately 60 to 70 percent of tractive energy needs.

Because about five to seven units of fuel are needed to deliver one unit of energy to the wheels, saving energy at the wheels offers immense leverage for efficiency. The keys to a superefficient car are to

- cut weight (hence the force required for acceleration) by three- to fourfold by using advanced materials, chiefly synthetic composites, while improving safety through greater strength and sophisticated design.

- cut aerodynamic drag by two-and-a-half- to sixfold through sleeker streamlining and more efficient packaging.

- cut tire and road losses by three- to fivefold through the combination of better tires and lighter weight.

Once these unrecoverable energy losses are largely eliminated, the only other place the wheelpower can go is into braking. In principle, and with careful design, regenerative braking could recover and reuse as much as 70 percent of the available kinetic energy in an urban driving cycle (U.S. DOE 1992), an efficiency that has, in fact, been demonstrated.

A hypercar would have a hybrid-electric drivetrain, making its electricity onboard from any convenient fuel rather than plugging into electric utility power. Electricity would be generated as needed by a small engine or gas turbine—for example, a 30 percent efficient Otto cycle (probably an Orbital-derivative two-stroke) or a 50 percent efficient semiadiabatic diesel engine. Other powerplants—fuel cell, thermophotovoltaic, or external-combustion—would also be suitable. The wheels would be driven by up to four switched-reluctance motors (a British technology that is inherently smaller, lighter, cheaper, stronger, quieter, and more efficient, rugged, fault-tolerant, and controllable than induction or permanent-magnet motors, though those would also suffice) and could be either hub mounted or inboard. A few kilowatt-hours' worth of batteries (and/or ultracapacitors or, soon, a carbon-fiber "superflywheel") could temporarily store the braking energy recovered from the wheel-motors for use in hill climbing and acceleration. With its power so boosted, the engine would need to handle only the average load, not the peak load, so it could shrink to about one-tenth the normal size. It would run very near its optimal point, doubling its efficiency, and turn off whenever it was not needed. Later, the internal combustion engine could be replaced by a fuel cell (ideally, a modular monolithic solid-oxide fuel cell, self-reforming and reversible, thereby also eliminating the buffer storage). Such a hybrid-electric propulsion system would weigh only about one-fourth as much as the drivetrain of a battery-electric family car, which must haul a half ton of batteries just to provide minimal range.

Both automakers and private designers have already built experimental cars that are ultralight or hybrid-electric, but generally not both. Yet combining these approaches yields extraordinary, and until now little-appreciated, synergies. Adding hybrid-electric drive to an ordinary production car increases its efficiency by about one-third to one-half (Barske 1991; Delsey 1992; Streicher 1992). Making an ordinary car ultralight, but not hybrid, as has been done with the concept cars of the mid-1980s, approximately doubles its efficiency (Bleviss 1988). But doing both together, if artfully integrated, can boost a car's efficiency by about *tenfold* (Lovins et al. 1993).

This revolution in efficiency has two main causes. First, the ultralight loses very little energy irrecoverably (to air and road friction), and the hybrid-electric drive recovers most of the rest (the braking energy). Second, saved weight compounds. When you make a heavy car one pound lighter, you really make it about a pound and a half lighter because it needs lighter structure and suspension, a smaller engine, less fuel, etc., to haul that weight around. But in an ultralight, saving a pound may save more like five pounds. Indirect weight savings snowball faster in ultralights than in heavy cars, faster in hybrids than in nonhybrids, and fastest of all in hybrid-electric ultralights (Lovins et al. 1993). All of the ingredients needed to capture these synergies are already demonstrated and need only be combined.

As far back as 1921, automakers demonstrated cars more aerodynamically slippery than today's production cars, with most of the drag

Table 5-1

Reducing Drag Coefficient, C_D

1970	Norm	~0.5–0.6
1992	U.S. average	0.33
	Best sedan	0.29
	Best productionized 2-seat	0.18
1992	Best worldwide production platform	0.255
1921	Rumpler 7-seat Tropfenwagen (midengine prototype)	0.28
1985	Ford Probe V concept car	0.137 (<F-15's C_D!)
1987	Renault Vesta II 4-seat concept car	0.186
1991	GM Ultralite 4-seat concept car	0.192
1990s	Likely practical limit with passive boundary-layer control	~0.08–0.20

Reducing Frontal Area, A (m^2)

1992	Average U.S. 4/5-seat production platform	~2.3
	2-seat Honda DX	1.8
1987	Renault Vesta II 4-seat concept car	1.64
1991	GM 4-seat Ultralite concept car	1.71

Today's typical 0.33×2.3 m^2 $C_DA = 0.76$ m^2; GM's Ultralite, 0.33 m^2; the best parameters separately shown for four-seaters, $0.137 \times 1.64 = 0.22$ m^2 (30% of today's); and edge-of-envelope, $~0.08 \times 1.5$ $m^2 = 0.12$ m^2 (16% of today's). We assume $C_DA = 0.27$ near-term, 0.17 later, ~0.13 edge-of envelope.

reduction coming from such simple means as making the car's underside as smooth as the top. Today's best experimental cars are twice as slippery still (see Table 5-1). At the same time, ultrastrong new materials make the car's shell lighter. A lighter car needs a smaller engine, and walls of ultrastrong materials can be thinner; both changes can make the car bigger inside but smaller outside. That smaller frontal area combines with a sleeker profile to cut through the air with about one-third the resistance of today's cars. Advanced aerodynamic techniques may be able to redouble this saving.

Modern radial tires, too, waste only half as much energy as 1970s bias-ply models, and the best 1990 radials about halve the remaining loss (Goodyear 1990). Rolling resistance drops further in proportion to weight; the result, allowing for a realistic range of payloads (which may weigh nearly as much as the vehicle itself), is 65 to 80 percent lower losses to rolling resistance (Lovins et al. 1993).

Table 5-2
Reducing the Mass, M, of Four-Seat Cars

Mass compounds by ~1.5x in heavy cars, ~5x in ultralights.

Typical 1990 U.S. production platforms had curb mass ~1,443 kg.
However, mainly light-metal concept cars built in ~1983–1987 included:

Manufacturer	Capacity	Model	Curb Mass
VW	5-seat	Auto 2000	779 kg
Volvo	4-seat	LCP 2000	707 kg
Toyota	5-seat	AXV Diesel	649 kg
Renault	4-seat	Vesta II	475 kg
Peugeot	4-seat	ECO 2000	449 kg

The unoptimized 1991 four-seat GM Ultralite weighs 635 kg; its C_DAM (a rough indicator of tractive loads) is 19% that of production cars. Thus <700 kg curb mass was practical long ago, <600 kg is practical now, and ~400 kg is practical ultimately. We assume 580 kg near-term, 400 kg later. (The USEPA test mass is 136 kg more.)

Reducing Tire Rolling Resistance, r_0

Modern radials' $r_0 \sim 0.007–0.010$; best mass-produced, ~0.0062; best made by 1990 with good handling (by Goodyear), 0.0048; 1993 state-of-the-art, even less. We assume 0.006–0.007, including parasitic mechanical losses.

Source: Bleviss (1988); Rocky Mountain Institute research.

In today's cars, accessories—power steering, heating, air conditioning, ventilation, lights, and entertainment systems—use about a tenth of engine power. But a hypercar would use about the same amount of energy for *all* purposes by saving most of the wheelpower *and* most of the accessory loads. Ultralights can handle nimbly without power steering, and their special wheel-motors even provide all-wheel antilock braking and antiskid traction. New kinds of head- and taillights shine brighter on a third the energy, and can save even more weight by distributing a single pea-sized lamp's light throughout the car by fiber optics. Air conditioning would need perhaps a tenth the energy used by today's car air conditioners, which are big enough for an Atlanta house. Special paints, vented double-skinned roofs, visually clear but heat-reflecting windows, solar-powered vent fans, etc., can first exclude unwanted heat; then innovative cooling systems can handle the rest, run not directly by the engine but by its waste heat.

Perhaps the most striking and important savings would come in weight (see Table 5-2). In the mid-1980s, many automakers demonstrated concept cars carrying four to five passengers but weighing as little as 1,000 pounds, versus today's average of about 3,200 pounds (Bleviss 1988). Conventionally powered, these concept cars were two to four times as efficient as today's average new car, but they did it the hard way, using mainly light metals such as aluminum and magnesium. Today, the same goal can be accomplished better with composites made by embedding glass, carbon, polyaramid, and other ultrastrong fibers in special moldable plastics.

Ultralights can be at least as safe as today's heavy steel cars, even when both kinds collide head-on at high speeds. Composites are so strong and bouncy that they can absorb far more energy per pound than metal (Kindervater 1991; Grosse 1992; Käser 1992). Materials and design are much more important for safety than mere mass, and occupant protection systems can be lightweight. For example, just a few pounds of hollow, crushable carbon-fiber-and-plastic cones can absorb the entire crash energy of a 1,200-pound car hitting a wall at 25 mph (Kindervater, personal communications, 1992–1993). Millions have watched on television as Indy 500 racecars crash into walls at 230+ mph: parts of the car buckle or break away in a controlled, energy-absorbing fashion, but despite per-pound crash energies five times those of 100 combined mph head-on collisions, the car's structure and driver's protective devices prevent serious injury. Those are carbon-fiber cars.

In 1991, 50 General Motors experts built the Ultralite, an encouraging example of ultralight composite construction (Figure 5-2). This sleek, sporty, four-seat, four-airbag concept car packs the interior space of a Chevrolet Corsica into the exterior size of a Mazda Miata (Keebler 1991; Gromer 1992; Sherman 1992). With only a 111-horsepower engine, smaller than that of a Honda Civic, its light weight (1,400 pounds) and low air drag ($C_DA = 0.76$ m^2) give the Ultralite a 135 mph top speed and 7.8-second 0 to 60 mph acceleration, comparable to that of a BMW 750iL with a huge V-12 engine. However, the Ultralite is over four times as fuel-efficient as the BMW, averaging 62 mpg—twice today's norm. At 50 mph, it cruises at 100 mpg on only 4.3 horsepower, a mere fifth of the power normally needed.

If equipped with hybrid drive, this first-cut 1991 prototype, built in only 100 days, would be *four to six times* as efficient as today's cars, easily beating the target for 2003 set by the PNGV. We have simulated 300 to 400 mpg four-seaters with "state-of-the-shelf" technology and ones getting over 600 mpg with the best ideas now in the lab. In April 1994, an experimental two-seat lightweight hybrid built by Professor Michael Seal's team at Western Washington University achieved the equivalent of 202 mpg in Los Angeles traffic; its next version will have more comfort and safety features but will weigh even less. Table 5-3

83

Figure 5-2

General Motors "Ultralite" Concept Car, 1991.

Photo courtesy of GM.

compares the vehicle parameters and modeled fuel economy of four illustrative performance classes of hypothetical advanced ultralight hybrid hypercars with the parameters of existing production cars and those of the nonhybrid GM Ultralite concept car.

Ultralight hybrids also favor ultraclean fuels. A small tank could store enough compressed natural gas or hydrogen for long range, and the high cost of hydrogen would become less important if only a tenth as much of it were needed. Liquid fuels sustainably derived from farm and forestry wastes would become ample to run an ultra-efficient transportation system without the need of special crops or fossil fuels.

Even with conventional fuel, the tailpipe of a hypercar would emit less pollution than the powerplants needed to recharge a battery-electric car. Hypercars would therefore be cleaner, even in the Los Angeles airshed, than so-called zero-emission vehicles (ZEVs) (actually elsewhere-emission). Ultralight hybrids should therefore qualify as "virtual ZEVs," and probably will.

In May 1994, the California Air Resources Board (CARB) reaf-

Table 5-3

Key Parameters and USEPA Composite Fuel Efficiencies of Selected Four-Seat Existing and Hypothetical Cars

C_DA,m^2	M, kg	r_0	E_{acc}	C_DAM	engine η	driveln η	regen η	1/100 km	mi/gal
Production cars: typical U.S. 1990									
0.76	1,443	0.009	≈1.0	1,095	~0.30	~0.60	0	8.00	2.49
Demonstrated concept car: GM Ultralite 1991 (1.5-183-kW 2-stroke engine)									
0.33	635	0.007	<1.0	208	unpubl	unpubl	0	3.79	62
Hypothetical synthetic-polymer-dominated ultralight hybrids:									
"Conservativa" worst-case illustration (uncontroversial parameters)									
0.40	700	0.008	0.80	280	0.35	0.75	0.60	2.44	97
"Gaia" near-term design ("optimized Ultralite," standard gasoline engine)									
0.27	580	0.007	0.50	154	0.30	0.90	0.70	1.61	146
"Ultima" advanced design ("state-of-the-shelf"—very light, good diesel)									
0.17	400	0.006	0.30	68	0.50	0.90	0.70	0.63	376
"Imagina" edge-of-envelope (aero++, fuel cell or best diesel, C-flywheel)									
0.13	400	0.005	0.25	52	0.56	0.96	0.88	0.38	614

Engine efficiency is peak (BSFC$_{min}$) — 280 g/kW$_{mech}$h is 1η/$_{max}$ = 0.30; driveline efficiency is engine-output-shaft-to-wheels; regenerative braking efficiency is wheel-to-wheel, including storage in/out η and square of η.

Source: Modeled after Rohde and Schilke (1980); data from Rocky Mountain Institute.

firmed its controversial 1990 requirement—which some Northeastern states now also wish to adopt—that 2 percent of car sales in 1998, rising to 10 percent in 2003, be ZEVs. Previously, *zero-emission vehicle* was deemed to mean battery-powered or fuel-cell electric cars exclusively, but mindful of hypercars' promise, CARB is now considering broadening the ZEV definition to include anything cleaner. This alternative compliance path could be a big boost both for hypercar entrepreneurs and for clean air: each car will be cleaner, and far more hypercars than battery cars are likely to be bought. By providing the advantages of electric propulsion without the disadvantages of batteries (including reduced performance at low temperatures), hypercars vault over battery cars' niche-market limitations.

Beyond the Iron Age

Moldable synthetic materials have fundamental advantages over the metals that now dominate automaking. The modern steel car satisfies often conflicting demands with remarkable skill: steel is ubiquitous and familiar, and its fabrication is exquisitely evolved. Yet superior synthetic alternatives could quickly displace old materials, as has happened before in the auto industry. U.S. car bodies switched from 85 percent wood-framed in 1920 to over 70 percent steel only six years later, making possible the modern assembly line (Abernathy 1978). Today, synthetics dominate boatbuilding and are rapidly taking over aerospace. Logically, cars are next.

Driving this transition are the huge capital costs for design, tooling, manufacturing, and finishing steel cars. For a new model, a thousand engineers spend a year designing and a year making more than a billion dollars' worth of car-sized steel dies whose cost can take decades to recover. This inflexible, costly tooling in turn demands huge production runs, maroons company-busting investments if products flop, and magnifies financial risks by making product cycles far longer than markets can be forecast. That this gargantuan process works is an astonishing accomplishment, but one that is technically baroque and economically perilous.

Moldable composites are not "black steel" and must be designed in utterly novel shapes, yet their fibers can be aligned to match stress and interwoven to distribute it, just as a cabinetmaker works with woodgrain. Two or three times fewer pounds of carbon fiber can achieve the same strength as steel (Gromer 1992); for many uses, other fibers, such as glass and polyaramid, are as good as or better than and two to six times cheaper than carbon was in 1992 (although carbon's cost disadvantage is rapidly evaporating). The biggest advantages of composites, however, emerge in manufacturing.

Only 15 percent of the cost of a typical steel car part is for the steel itself; the other 85 percent is to pound, weld, and smooth the steel (Seiss 1991). Composites and other molded synthetics emerge from the mold already in virtually the required "net shape" and final finish. Large, complex units can be molded in one piece, cutting the parts count by about a hundredfold and the assembly labor and space by tenfold (Amendola 1990). The lightweight, easy-to-handle parts fit precisely together without rework. Painting—the costliest, hardest, and most polluting step in automaking—can be eliminated by lay-in-the-mold color. If not recycled, composites last virtually forever: they don't dent, rust, or chip. They also permit advantageous car designs, including frameless monocoque bodies (like an egg, the body is the structure) whose extreme stiffness improves handling and safety.

Composites are formed to the desired "net shape" not by multiple strikes with tool-steel stamping dies, but in single molding dies made of coated epoxy. Epoxy dies wear out much faster than tool-steel dies, but they are cheap enough that it doesn't matter. Total tooling cost is about two to ten times less per copy than with steel because there are far fewer parts, only one die set is needed per part rather than three to seven for successive hits, and epoxy is far cheaper to buy and fabricate than tool steel. Stereolithography, a three-dimensional process that molds a designer's computer images directly into complex solid objects, can dramatically shrink retooling time, even roughing the epoxy dies *overnight*. Indeed, the shorter life of epoxy tools is a fundamental strategic *advantage* because it permits the rapid model changes that continuous improvement, product differentiation, and market nimbleness demand.

Together, these advantages cancel or reverse the apparent cost disadvantage of composites. Carbon fiber currently costs up to a hundred times as much *per pound* as sheet steel (though better processes and higher production volumes are shrinking this gap to as little as tenfold), yet the mass-produced cost of a composite car is probably comparable to or less than that of a steel car both at low production volumes (like Porsche's) and at high ones (like Ford's). What matters is not cost per pound, but cost per car (Amendola 1990), and what composites cost extra in materials, they make up in cheaper manufacturing.

Cultural Change and Competitive Strategy

Hypercars are not just another kind of car: they will probably be made and sold in completely new ways. Hypercars imply wrenching changes that may come far more quickly than our ability to manage them. If ignored or treated as a threat rather than grasped as an opportunity, these changes are potentially catastrophic for millions of individuals and tens of thousands of companies. Currently, automaking and associated businesses employ one-seventh of U.S. workers (Runkle 1992), approaching two-fifths in some European countries. They represent one-tenth of America's consumer spending and use nearly 70 percent of the nation's lead; about 60 percent of its rubber, carpeting, and malleable iron; 40 percent of its machine tools; 12 percent of its steel; and about 20 percent of its aluminum, zinc, glass, and semiconductors (id.). David Morris, cofounder of the Institute for Local Self-Reliance, observes: "The production of automobiles is the world's number one industry. The number two industry supplies their fuel. Six of America's ten largest industrial corporations are either oil or auto companies. . . . A recent British estimate concludes that half of the world's earnings may be auto or truck related."

With hypercars, the distribution process for automobiles could change as profoundly as the manufacturing process. On average, today's cars are marked up about 50 percent from production cost (which includes automakers' profit, plant cost, and warrantied repairs), but cheap tooling might make the optimal production scale of hypercars as small as a regional soft-drink bottling plant. Cars could be ordered directly from the local factory, made to order, and delivered to the customer's door in a day or two. (Toyota now takes only a few days longer with steel cars.) Such just-in-time manufacturing would eliminate inventory and selling costs and avoid the rebates needed to move premade stock that is mismatched to current demand. Markups would largely vanish, so hypercars could be profitably deliverable at or below today's prices even if they cost considerably more to make, which they probably wouldn't. Being radically simplified and ultrareliable, they could be maintained by onsite visits (as Ford does in Britain today), aided by plug-into-the-phone remote diagnostics. If all this makes sense today for a $1,500 mail-order personal computer, why not for a $15,000 car?

America leads, for now, both in startup-business dynamism and in all the required technical capabilities. After all, hypercars are much more like computers with wheels than they are like cars with chips: they are more a software than a hardware problem, and competition will favor the innovative, not the big. Comparative advantage lies not with the most efficient steel-stampers, but with the fastest-learning systems integrators (like Hewlett-Packard or Compaq) and with strategic-element makers (like Microsoft and Intel) more than with Chrysler or Matsushita. Barriers to market entry should be far lower for hypercars than for steel cars. As with microcomputers, the winners might be some smart, hungry, unknown aerospace engineers tinkering in a garage right now.

All this is alien to the consciousness of most (though not all) automakers today. Theirs is not a composite-molding/electronics/software culture but a die-making/steel-stamping/mechanical culture. Automakers have tens of billions of dollars and untold psychological investments sunk in stamping steel. They treat those historic investments as unamortized assets, substituting accounting for economic principles and continuing to throw good money after bad. They design cars as abstract art, then figure out the least unsatisfactory way to make them, rather than seeking the best ways to manufacture with strategically advantageous materials and then designing cars to exploit those manufacturing methods. Their institutional form, style, and speed of learning have become as ponderous as those steel-based production technologies. Most of them appear to want to write off their obsolete capabilities later when they won't have a company, rather than now when they do.

The wreckage of the mainframe computer industry should have taught us that one has to replace one's own products with better new products before someone else does. (As 3M reportedly puts it, "We'd rather eat our *own* lunch, thank you.") Until 1993, few automakers appreciated the starkness of that threat. Their strategy seemed to be to milk old tools and skills for decades, watch costs creep up and market share down, postpone any basic innovation until after all concerned had retired, and hope none of their competitors was faster. That's the you-bet-your-company strategy, because it only takes one competitor to put you out of business, and you may not even know who that competitor is until too late. The PNGV will stimulate instead a winning, risk-managed strategy: leapfrogging to ultralight hybrids.

Encouragingly, some automakers now show signs of understanding these principles. In recent months, the intellectual mold-breaking of the PNGV initiative has sparked new thinking in Detroit. The automakers' more imaginative engineers are discovering that the next gains in car efficiency should be easier than the last ones because they will come not from sweating off fat ounce by ounce, but from escaping an evolutionary trap. Although good ultralight hybrids need elegantly simple engineering, which is difficult, it is actually easier to boost efficiency tenfold with hypercars than threefold with today's cars.

Little of this ferment is visible from the outside because automakers have learned reticence the hard way. A long and unhappy history of being mandated to do (or exceed) whatever they admit they can do has left them understandably bashful about revealing capabilities, especially to Congress. In addition, any firms that harbor leapfrog ambitions will hardly be eager to telegraph them to competitors. There is a natural desire to extract any available business and political concessions and to hold back from extending to traditional adversaries (such as media, politicians, and environmentalists) any trust that could prove costly if abused or not reciprocated. For all these reasons, public pronouncements from Detroit are more likely to understate than trumpet progress. The Big Three are also progressing unevenly, both internally and comparatively: their opacity conceals a rapidly changing mixture of exciting advances and inertia. Some managers appreciate, but many do not yet, that hypercars fit the compelling strategic logic of changing how they do business, especially by radically reducing cycle times, capital costs, and financial risks. It is difficult but vital for harried managers to focus on these goals through the distracting fog of fixing flaws in their short-term operations.

The Cost of Inaction

The potential public benefits of hypercars are enormous—in oil displacement, energy security, international stability, avoided military costs, balance of trade, climate protection, clean air, health and safety, noise reduction, and quality of urban life. Promptly and skillfully exploited, hypercars could also propel an industrial renewal. They are good news for such industries—many now demilitarizing—as electronics, systems integration, aerospace, software, petrochemicals, and even textiles (which offer automated fiber-weaving techniques). However, if ignored, the opportunity could be botched, retarded, or ceded to others, with disastrous effects on U.S. jobs and competitiveness. There is abundant talent in American labor, management, government, and independent centers to guide the transition, but it is not yet seriously mobilized. The costs of that complacency are high.

Cars and light trucks, their efficiency stagnant since 1982, use 37 percent of the nation's oil, upwards of 43 percent of which is imported at a cost of around $50 billion a year (MacKenzie et al. 1992). Persian Gulf imports were cut by over 90 percent during 1977–1985, chiefly by federal standards that largely or wholly caused the efficiency of new cars to double during 1973–1986 (OTA 1991). Had we kept on saving oil as quickly after 1985 as we did for the previous nine years, then since 1985 we would not have needed a single drop of oil from the Persian Gulf. But we did not, and oil imports are now reapproaching historic highs—the direct result of twelve years of national oil policy consisting mainly of weakened efficiency standards, lavish subsidies, and the Seventh Fleet.

The national stakes therefore remain large. Even though the PNGV is starting to re-create Detroit's sense of adventure, hypercars still face formidable obstacles, both culturally within the auto industry and institutionally in the marketplace. Achieving a rapid transition with high confidence warrants public attention to improving foresight and smoothing inevitable turbulence. It may even warrant giving automakers strong incentives to pursue the leapfrog strategy boldly and encouraging customers to overcome their well-known lack of interest in buying fuel-thrifty cars in a nation that insists on gasoline cheaper than bottled water.

Market Conditioning and Public Policy

The usual prescription of economists and the Big Three automakers for greater fuel economy is stiffer gasoline taxes. After painful debate, Congress raised the gasoline tax by 4.3 cents per gallon, restoring it to well *below* its inflation-corrected historic level and returning inflation-corrected gasoline prices to about their 1972 pre-Arab-oil-embargo level. In Western Europe and Japan, taxes that raise motor fuel prices to twice or four times U.S. prices have long been in place, but new German and Japanese cars are probably less efficient than American ones, especially if statistics are corrected to similar performance, size, and features (Schipper et al. 1992). Costlier fuel is a feeble incentive to buy an efficient car because the fuel-price signal is diluted (7:1 in the United States today) by the other costs of owning and running a car, is weakened by high consumer discount rates and brief expected ownership, and is often vitiated by company car ownership and other distortions that shield many drivers from normal costs (Dolan et al. 1993).

This market failure could be corrected by strengthening government efficiency standards. However, standards, though effective and a valuable backstop, are not easy to administer, can be evaded and gamed (Ford and GM violated them for years but avoided penalties through various loopholes), and are technologically static: there is no incentive to do better. Happily, there is a market-oriented alternative: the feebate.

Under feebates, upon buying a new car, the customer pays a fee or gets a rebate; which and how much depends on how efficient the car is. Year by year, the fees pay for the rebates. (Note: feebates are not a new tax. In 1989, the California legislature agreed, approving the DRIVE+ feebate bill by a 7:1 margin, although outgoing governor George Deukmejian later vetoed it.) Better still, the rebate for an efficient new car can be based on its *difference* in efficiency compared with the old car being scrapped. Such a system would rapidly get efficient, clean cars on the road and inefficient, dirty cars off the road (one-fifth of the car fleet produces perhaps three-fifths of its air pollution). The many variants of such accelerated-scrappage incentives would encourage competition, reward Detroit for bringing efficient cars to market, and open a market niche into which to sell them. Feebates may even break the political logjam that has long trapped the United States in a sterile debate over stricter fuel-efficiency standards versus higher gasoline taxes.

Perhaps people will buy hypercars, just as they switched from vinyl records to compact discs, simply because they are a superior product—cars that by comparison make today's most sophisticated steel cars seem a bit clunky and antiquarian. If such a switch occurred, gasoline prices would become uninteresting. The world oil price would permanently crash as hypercars (and their light- and heavy-vehicle analogues) saved as much oil as OPEC now extracts. Feebates would still be helpful in emboldening and rewarding Detroit for quick adaptation, but perhaps not essential. The ultralight hybrid would sweep the market. What then?

Beyond Efficient Technology: Least-Cost Transportation

Even without hypercars, we already have too much driving by too many people in too many cars. Congestion is smothering mobility, and mobility is corroding community. We need too much travel and have too few noncar ways to do it. Driving still more miles in more cars, even if they are vastly improved, merely condemns us to running out of roads and patience rather than air and oil. Avoiding the constraint *du jour* requires far more than extremely efficient vehicles because many of the social costs of driving have less to do with fuel use than with congestion, lost time, accidents, roadway damage, land use, and other side effects of driving itself (Johnson 1992). External costs for automobiles may approach a trillion dollars a year in the United States—perhaps a seventh of the GNP—costs borne by everyone but not reflected in direct costs to drivers (Ketcham and Komanoff 1992; MacKenzie et al. 1992).

In this economic fairyland, it is hardly surprising that doubled U.S. new-car efficiency has been offset by more cars and driving, which also dilute the benefits of cleaner and safer cars. Global car registrations are growing more than twice as fast as population: 50 million cars in 1954, 350 million in 1989, and 500 million projected for the year 2000. A mere 15 percent of the world's people own 76 percent of its motor vehicles, and the other 85 percent want theirs.

Road accidents each year cost about $90 billion by killing over 40,000 Americans—about as many as killed by diabetes or breast cancer—and injuring 5 million more, not to mention extensive pollution-induced illness and social problems (MacKenzie et al. 1992). If automobility were a disease, then vast national resources would be mobilized to cure it. In fact, the cure has already been broadly defined but is complex and gradual. Sustainable transportation requires designing communities around people, not cars—rethinking land use so that we needn't travel so much to get the access we want. This in turn requires an end-use/least-cost policy framework to foster fair competition between all modes of access. We can even find ways to displace the need for physical mobility by arranging to be *already* where we want to be, thereby avoiding the transportation problem rather than having to solve it.

Creative public policy instruments can introduce market mechanisms to a transportation system long crippled by lopsided subsidies and top-down central planning—amounting to compulsory socialism for car-based infrastructure and private markets for alternatives. Most developing countries are starting to follow this bad example, but needed innovations are starting to emerge: ways to make parking and driving bear their true costs, improve competing modes, foster and monetize fair competition between all modes of access, and substitute sensible land use for physical mobility.

Whether for freight or for personal mobility, demand for traffic, as for energy or water or weapons, is not fate but choice. Cost-minimizing ways are now emerging to choose whether to invest more in cars, other modes of transport, substitutes for transport (such as videoconferencing), satellite offices, or better land use. The Intermodal Surface Transportation Efficiency Act (ISTEA) of 1991 mandates least-cost choices and lets federal transport dollars flow to the best buys, not only to highways. But in about 30 states, the opportunity for federal funding of these alternatives does not arise because the federal funds must usually match state funds that are legally restricted to road-building. It may take decades of bruising fights with highway lobbies to bring intermodalism to every state.

Quicker and more attractive than such state-by-state reforms would be new ideas that could sweep the country because they solved so many other problems too. Electric and water utilities are already starting to make markets in "negawatts" and "negagallons," making saved resources into fungible commodities subject to competitive bidding, arbitrage, futures, options, secondary markets, etc. If it is cheaper to save the resource than to supply it, entrepreneurs are thereby rewarded for doing the cheapest thing first. Why not similarly make markets in "negamiles" and "negatrips" in order to discover what it is worth to pay people to stay off the roads so we needn't build and mend them so much and suffer their delays and smog? If anyone could make money from a socially cheaper way to get access than driving cars, wouldn't we all drive much less?

New policies, whether imaginative or mundane, often diffuse more sluggishly than new technologies. Americans are reinventing the car faster than they can rethink it, and we will probably have highly efficient cars before we have figured out when not to drive them. The recent history of computers, telecommunications, and other technological fusions suggests that the switch to hypercars could come far faster than basic shifts in where people live, work, shop, and recreate or in how people choose among means of mobility. Hypercars can buy time to address these issues but cannot resolve them.

The speed and size of all these changes could be deeply disruptive as well as beneficial, but perhaps we can choose whether to make them help us or hurt us. If so, we had better start thinking about how best to make these changes, with the least pain and the most benefit, before others do them first or do them to us. If the technical and market logic sketched here is anywhere near right, we are all about to embark on one of the greatest adventures in industrial history.

Editor's Note

This chapter includes material abridged and adapted from Amory B. and L. Hunter Lovins, "Reinventing the Wheels," *The Atlantic Monthly*, January 1995, and from other publications of Rocky Mountain Institute. Amory and Hunter Lovins have subsequently written a detailed 32-page semitechnical primer on hypercars, to be published in spring 1995 under a "Supercars" listing in the *Wiley Encyclopedia of Energy Technology and the Environment* (New York: John Wiley & Sons).

References

Abernathy, W.S. 1978. *The Productivity Dilemma: Roadblock to Innovation in the Automobile Industry*. Baltimore: Johns Hopkins University Press.

Amendola, G. 1990. "The Diffusion of Synthetic Materials in the Automobile Industry: Toward a Major Breakthrough?" *Research Policy* 19 (6): 485–500.

Barske, H. 1991. "Rationelle Verwendung von Kraftstoff: Autos mit 3 Liter Benzinverbrauch, eine Utopie?" [Economical use of fuel: Automobiles with 3-liter (per 100 km) gasoline consumption, a utopia?]. In *Proceedings of the 6th Annual Conference, Environment and Renewable Energy II—Objectives 1991 to 2000*, edited by B. Löffler, pp. 13.1–14. Basel.

Bleviss, D.L. 1988. *The New Oil Crisis and Fuel Economy Technologies: Preparing the Light Transportation Industry for the 1990s*. Westport, Conn.: Quorum Books.

Delsey, J. 1992. "Environmental Comparison of Electric, Hybrid and Advanced Heat Engine Vehicles." In *Proceedings of the Urban Electric Vehicle Conference* (OECD/NUTEK/IEA, Stockholm, May 25). Paris: International Energy Agency.

Dolan, K., B.E. and B.G. Andersson, H. Nishimake, L. Schipper, R. Steiner, and W. Tax. 1993. "Fiscal Policies Affecting Automobiles in Western Europe, Japan, and the United States." LBL draft report originally prepared as an appendix to Schipper et al. 1992.

Goodyear. 1990. News release #19295-490 from Corporate Headquarters, Akron, Ohio. April.

Gromer, C. 1992. "Ultracar." *Popular Science*, April, pp. 33–35, 125.

Grosse, B. 1992. "2-28-92 Consulier GTP Barrier Impact Test." Nonproprietary excerpts provided by Consulier Automotive, Riviera Beach, Fla.

Johnson, E.W. 1992. "Taming the Car and Its User: Should We Do Both?" *Bulletin of the American Academy of Arts and Sciences* 46 (2): 13–29.

Käser, R. 1992. "Safety Potential of Urban Electric Vehicles in Collisions." In *Proceedings of the Urban Electric Vehicle Conference* (OECD/NUTEK/IEA, Stockholm, May 25). Paris: International Energy Agency.

Keebler, J. 1991. "GM Builds 100-Mpg 'Ultralite' Car." *Automotive News*, December 31, pp. 1, 31.

Ketcham, B., and C. Komanoff. 1992. *Win-Win Transportation, A No-Losers Approach to Financing Transport in New York City and the Region*. New York: Transportation Alternatives.

Kindervater, C. 1991. "Composite Structural Crash Resistance." Paper presented at the Institute for Structures and Design, Deutsche Forschungsanstalt für Luft- und Raumfahrt [German Research Establishment for Air and Space Travel] Crash User Seminar, June 3–5, Stuttgart.

Lovins, Amory B., John W. Barnett, and L. Hunter Lovins. 1993. "Supercars: The Coming Light-Vehicle Revolution." Paper presented at the Summer Study of the European Council for an Energy-Efficient Economy, Rungstedgård, Denmark, June 1–5.

MacCready, P.B. 1993. "Vehicle Efficiency and the Electric Option." In *Transportation and Global Climate Change*, edited by David L. Greene and Danilo J. Santini. Washington, D.C.: American Council for an Energy-Efficient Economy, pp. 147–158.

MacKenzie, J.J., R.C. Dower, and D.D.T. Che. 1992. *The Going Rate: What It Really Costs to Drive*. Washington, D.C.: World Resources Institute.

Office of Technology Assessment (OTA). 1991. *Improving Automobile Fuel Economy: New Standards, New Approaches*. OTA-E-504. Washington, D.C.: U.S. Congress.

Rohde, S.M., and N.A. Schilke. 1980/1981. "The Fuel Economy Potential of Heat Engine/Flywheel Hybrid Automobiles." Supplement to *Proceedings of the 1980 Flywheel Technology Symposium*. DOE/ASME/LLL, CONF-801022-Supp (Scottsdale, Arizona, October 1980); also published as SAE Special Publication P-91 (War-rendale, Pa.: Society of Automotive Engineers, 1981). See also N.A. Schilke, A.O. DeHart, L.O. Hewko, C.C. Matthews, D.J. Poz-niak, and S.M. Rohde, "The Design of an Engine-Flywheel Hybrid Drive System for a Passenger Car," SAE Paper 841306 (1984).

Ross, M. 1989. "Energy and Transportation in the United States." *Annual Review of Energy* 14: 131–171.

Runkle, D. 1992. Address to National Laboratories Conference, Warren, Michigan, January 22.

Schipper, L., R. Steiner, M.J. Figueroa, and K. Dolan. 1992. *Fuel Prices, Automobile Fuel Economy, and Fuel Use for Land Travel: Preliminary Findings from an International Comparison.* Report LBL-32699. Lawrence Berkeley Laboratory.

Seiss, R. 1991. Presentation to the Committee on Fuel Economy of Automobiles and Light Trucks, Energy Engineering Board, U.S. National Research Council, Irvine, Calif., July 8.

Sherman, D. 1992. "Using Carbon Fibers to Conserve Hydrocarbons: GM Ultralite." *Motor Trend*, February, pp. 74–76.

Streicher, W. 1992. "Energy Demand, Emissions and Waste Management of EVs, Hybrids and Small Conventional Cars." In *Proceedings of the Urban Electric Vehicle Conference* (OECD/NUTEK/IEA, Stockholm, May 25). Paris: International Energy Agency.

U.S. Department of Energy (U.S. DOE). 1992. *Notes of the Hybrid Planning Workshop* (Dearborn, Mich., September 22–23). Washington, D.C.: U.S. Department of Energy.

Chapter Six

Alternative Fuels and Greenhouse Gas Emission Policy

LAURIE MICHAELIS

The International Energy Agency (1993) has recently carried out a study of the potential of alternative fuels to reduce greenhouse gas emissions from the use of cars. Drawing on an analysis of the life-cycle energy use and greenhouse gas emissions associated with cars operating on different fuels and in different regions, this study looks in detail at economic and policy issues.

The use of alternative fuels and electricity from renewables has the *technical potential* to reduce the life-cycle greenhouse gas emissions from car use by 80 percent, but these energy sources are more expensive than gasoline. The *economic potential* for greenhouse gas emission reduction is smaller. Alternative-fuel cars using diesel, liquified petroleum gas (LPG), and compressed natural gas (CNG) can have life-cycle greenhouse gas emissions 10 to 30 percent lower than those from gasoline cars, and they may be cheaper to use than gasoline cars for some drivers. The *market potential* is smaller still, as alternative-fuel and electric cars are less convenient to use than gasoline cars and they are unlikely to be taken up by all the drivers for whom they are cheaper than gasoline cars.

Alternative-fuel use is generally encouraged in order to reduce oil dependency and local air pollution. The reduction of greenhouse gas emissions is an additional argument for their use. Although they could be promoted as part of a greenhouse gas abatement strategy, their uptake would not be affected much by the energy and carbon taxes recently discussed in the European Community and the United States.

Transport policy approaches that take account of the wider range of negative environmental and social effects of car use may have more effect on greenhouse gas emissions than programs focused entirely on alternative fuels. Measures that internalize the social costs of congestion, accidents, air pollution, and oil dependency can all contribute to reducing greenhouse gas emissions.

Energy Use by the Transport Sector

In the 30-year period between 1960 and 1990, the share of oil in Organisation for Economic Cooperation and Development (OECD) countries' transport energy use rose from 92 to 99 percent, increasing from 319 million tonnes of oil equivalent (Mtoe) to 888 Mtoe (IEA 1991, 1992).[1] Oil use in other OECD sectors expanded until the early 1970s, then declined following the 1973/1974 and 1979/1980 price rises, so that transport is now the main oil-using sector. The OECD transport sector, including international shipping, now uses marginally more energy than industry and more than any of the other final users of energy.

Nearly all of the growth in transport energy is taken up by road transport, which is now responsible for over three-quarters of OECD transport energy use and carbon dioxide (CO_2) emissions. Air transport and international shipping make up most of the rest. Between 1970 and 1990, car use throughout OECD countries increased by amounts ranging from 40 percent in the United States to 100 percent in Japan. Although fuel consumption per car-kilometer fell by around 25 percent in the United States in the same period, it has changed very little in most other countries. In addition, vehicle occupancy dropped by 5 to 20 percent, resulting in higher energy use per passenger-kilometer in most countries.

Transport activity is important both for the creation and for the consumption of wealth: industrial and commercial efficiency depends on the mobility of personnel and goods, and the car is perhaps the single most important consumer good. At the same time, transport, especially road use, causes environmental and social damage and costs. Thus, as OECD societies continue to mature, policymakers are shifting

---

[1] Following IEA convention, 1 Mtoe = 41,868 TJ (lower heating value).

their attention from the need for infrastructure to the problems of congestion, accidents, air pollution, and oil import dependence.

As a result of the continuing increases in travel and freight traffic, combined with slow improvements in fuel economy, transport energy use in OECD Europe is expected to expand until 2010. In the latest results from a business-as-usual scenario using the International Energy Agency's world energy model (IEA 1994), transport energy use grows at 1.9 percent per annum to 2000 and then at 1.4 percent per annum to 2010. In this scenario, by 2010, transport CO_2 emissions are 35 percent higher than in 1991, and transport has increased its share of total emissions from about 27 to 29 percent.

Life-Cycle Greenhouse Gas Emissions from Cars

Using a model developed by Mark DeLuchi (1991) at the Institution of Transportation Studies, University of California at Davis, the IEA has calculated life-cycle greenhouse gas emissions for alternative-energy cars. DeLuchi's model calculates emissions of CO_2, carbon monoxide (CO), methane (CH_4), volatile organic compounds (VOCs), nitrous oxide (N_2O), nitrogen oxides (NO_x), and chlorofluorocarbons (CFCs). The model accounts for emissions in vehicle manufacture, in all stages of fuel supply, and in vehicle operation and includes second-order effects from the supply of fuels and electricity used in the life cycle. It also calculates the radiative forcing[2] caused by life-cycle greenhouse gas emissions in CO_2-equivalent terms, using the global warming potential concept.

DeLuchi's model was supplied to the IEA configured for fuel mixes in electricity generation and refineries in the United States and was adapted to reflect IEA projections for the year 2005 of average energy inputs to electricity generation and refining in North America and OECD Europe, as obtained with the World Energy Outlook model. This refined model was used to calculate life-cycle emissions for a Volkswagen Golf (hypothetical model year 2005, but actually 1991), operating on a variety of energy carriers. Figure 6-1 illustrates a set of results of these calculations.

As shown in Figure 6-1, it is technically possible to reduce greenhouse gas emissions by about 80 percent by using alternative fuels. If cars are manufactured using renewable energy sources, a reduction of

---

[2] "Radiative forcing" is the effect of the raised concentration of greenhouse gases on the net vertical radiation flow at ground level.

Figure 6-1

**Life-Cycle Greenhouse Gas Emissions
(Hypothetical Model Year 2005)**

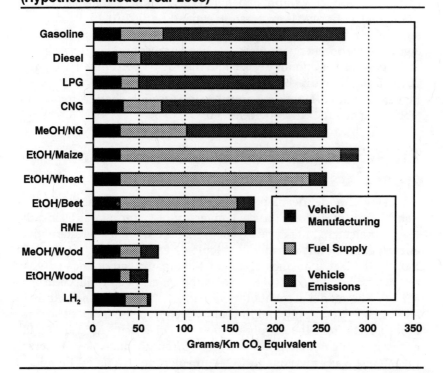

90 percent or more is possible. However, this technical potential is unlikely to be achieved in the short term, nor would it be cost-effective to attempt to achieve it as a means of reducing greenhouse gas emissions. A better indication of emission reductions that might be obtained in practice is given by the economic potential.

Economic Potential for Emission Abatement

For at least the next 20 years, most of the fuels for which life-cycle emissions are shown in Figure 6-1 are likely to be more expensive to produce than gasoline. Exceptions are diesel, LPG, and CNG. Levelized costs of driving were calculated in the study for gasoline, diesel, and CNG, taking account of variations in such factors as vehicle cost, weight, annual distance traveled, lifetime, and fuel economy. Assumptions regarding the engine life for diesel cars are particularly important for determining their levelized cost for high-mileage users.

The IEA study calculated the driving costs in two IEA member countries: the United States and France. The car and energy markets in these countries differ in several important respects: French cars are typically about one-third lighter than American cars, and their fuel consumption is about 35 percent lower. Car prices are similar in the two countries, but in France, fuel taxes are much higher. A key factor affecting the cost of diesel cars is the stringency of emission standards in the two countries: in France, the European Community standards in force and those anticipated for 1996 explicitly allow for the use of the diesel cars currently available. In the United States, standards to be enforced from the mid-1990s will exclude the use of these cars, so more advanced technology will be required if diesel is to be used.

In this study, a higher cost was assumed for diesel cars in the United States, reflecting the use of advanced fuel injection or exhaust control systems. This premise resulted in a high cost of switching from gasoline (Figure 6-2) for the average driver, although not for very high-mileage drivers with a discount rate below 5 percent (see Figure 6-3). The advantage at high mileage arises because diesel car engines are more durable than gasoline engines. The study calculations assume that diesel and gasoline cars are both limited to a ten-year maximum life by body wear and corrosion and that they are limited by engine wear to a maximum distance of 200,000 kilometers (km) for the gasoline car and 250,000 km for the diesel car. Only the very small proportion of drivers expecting to exceed about 25,000 km per year, using the same car over about ten years, would find diesel cars cheaper than gasoline cars. Thus, the economic potential for diesel cars in the United States (that is, the share of the market justified by their life-cycle cost relative to gasoline) is very small.

CNG cars are likely to have lower levelized costs than gasoline cars for the average American driver, but their reduced driving range on a full tank and the limited refueling network is likely to confine them to niche markets for some time. CNG cars could be built with the same driving range as gasoline cars, but only at the expense of storage and/or passenger space, and at a higher cost.

Under the conditions tested, diesel cars are likely to be cheaper on a levelized cost basis than gasoline cars for a high proportion of French drivers because of the low excise duty on diesel relative to gasoline. When taxes are excluded from the analysis (see Figure 6-4), the switch from gasoline to diesel reduces costs only for high-mileage drivers or when a diesel car model is offered at about the same price

Figure 6-2

Cost of Switching from Gasoline in the United States (Taxes Excluded)

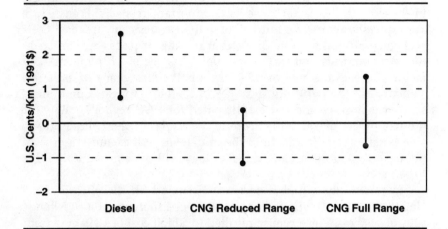

Figure 6-3

Cost of Switching from Gasoline to Diesel in the United States (Taxes Excluded)

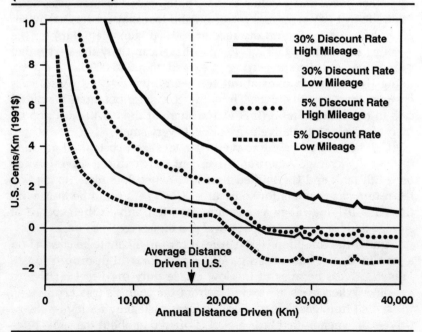

as the gasoline model. It is difficult to identify exactly which diesel model competes with which gasoline model as they have different handling characteristics. Nevertheless, diesel cars are currently available in Europe at prices similar to those of the gasoline models with which they appear to compete. The economic potential for diesel cars in France is quite high, and much of this potential is already taken up.

In France, CNG cars with reduced driving range are likely to have levelized costs about the same as those for gasoline. However, using a CNG car with full driving range is likely to be more expensive than using a gasoline car on a levelized basis.

The economic potential for CNG cars in both France and the United States is large if we consider financial costs alone. However, CNG cars are not perfect substitutes for gasoline cars because of their reduced range, their long filling time, and at present, the lack of CNG filling stations. If the problem of reduced range is addressed through increased fuel storage capacity, the cost of CNG cars is likely to rise so that they are more expensive than gasoline cars while the other disadvantages remain. As a result of these disadvantages, the market potential for CNG cars is probably quite small. They are unlikely to achieve significant market share except where their use is mandated or in niche markets, such as commercial and government fleets.

The IEA study concludes that alternative fuels are unlikely to result in the reduction of aggregate transport greenhouse gas emissions by more than 5 percent without additional intervention in the market.

Figure 6-4

Cost of Switching from Gasoline in France (Taxes Excluded)

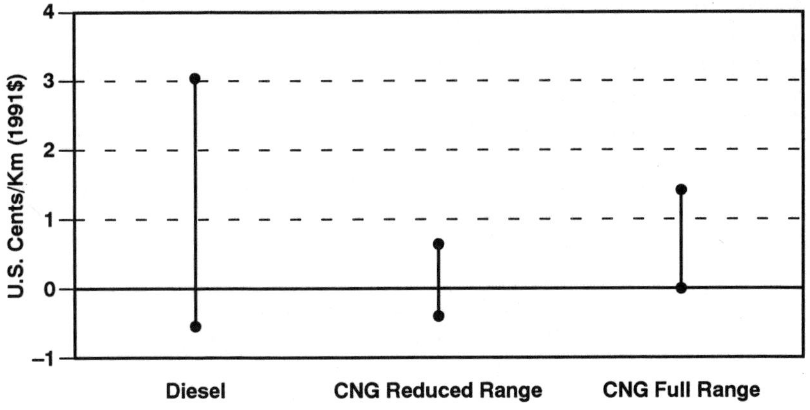

Cost of Greenhouse Gas Emission Abatement

In order to consider the attractiveness of alternative fuels as means of reducing greenhouse emissions, the IEA has calculated the costs of fuel switching per tonne of CO_2-equivalent emission reductions. The results, illustrated in Figures 6-5 and 6-6, indicate that, in both the United States and France, CNG cars with reduced range give emission abatement costs below $200 per tonne of CO_2 equivalent. In both countries, the cost of abatement could be negative. However, it should be remembered that CNG cars have life-cycle greenhouse gas emissions only around 10 percent lower than those of gasoline cars.

Switching to diesel offers roughly 20 percent emission reduction relative to gasoline, but as Figure 6-5 shows, in the United States the switch from gasoline to diesel costs more than $200 per tonne of CO_2 equivalent, making this an unattractive option relative to other alternative fuels. Methanol (MeOH) from wood gives roughly 80 percent emission reduction at less than $200 per tonne of CO_2 equivalent.

The costs for ethanol (EtOH) from maize and methanol from

Figure 6-5

Cost of Reducing Greenhouse Gas Emissions by Switching from Gasoline in the United States (Taxes Excluded)

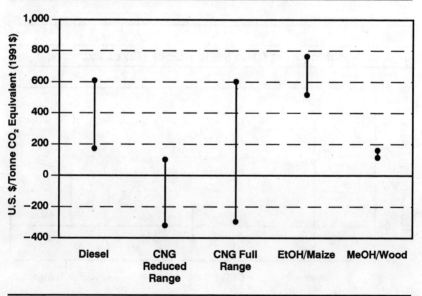

Figure 6-6

Cost of Reducing Greenhouse Gas Emissions by Switching from Gasoline in France (Taxes Excluded)

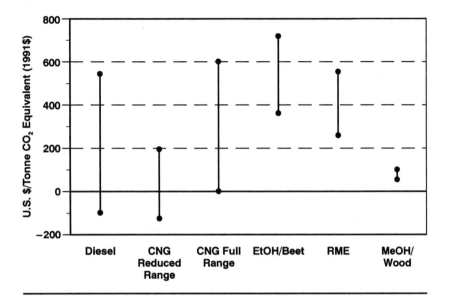

wood are calculated as production costs minus agricultural subsidies. They are intended to give some indication of the cost of using biofuels to achieve energy and environmental objectives with agricultural intervention taken as a fait accompli. For this calculation, existing U.S. agricultural subsidies[3] have been included on a flat per-hectare basis for both maize and wood, although this is not the way they are currently applied.

In France, diesel cars are currently cheaper than gasoline cars on a levelized basis for the average driver. Diesel cars could potentially make up about half of the car fleet and more than half of the aggregate car mileage, thereby offering a 10 percent reduction in greenhouse

---

[3] The subsidy figure used is the "producer subsidy equivalent" (PSE) calculated by the OECD (1992). PSEs include direct government subsidies and the effects of price supports (i.e., excess cash flows from consumers to producers due to the difference between domestic market prices and border prices). They are used here as an ad hoc indication of the value of maintaining land in production. An alternative might be to apply the PSEs on a flat per-worker basis, reflecting the value of keeping people in rural employment.

forcing caused by car use. Nevertheless, maintaining the diesel share of the market could require a significant continuing tax differential between gasoline and diesel, with unwanted macroeconomic effects. The effect of this tax differential on aggregate mileage is unclear. A high gasoline tax would push mileage by gasoline car owners down, whereas a low diesel tax would push mileage by diesel car owners up relative to a fuel-neutral taxation approach. The overall effect depends on the level of gasoline tax that would be adopted if there were no differential. Assuming the differential to be chosen so that government revenues are constant, it is likely that aggregate mileage would be slightly reduced.

Policy Measures to Promote Alternative Fuels

Governments use a variety of policy measures to promote the use of alternative-fuel vehicles and other technical changes. Perhaps the most important of these measures are

- fuel taxes and subsidies
- new-car taxes and rebates
- mandated alternative-fuel-vehicle sale and purchase
- subsidized fueling networks
- research, development, and demonstration funding

Fuel Taxes and Subsidies

Many European governments have made use of their traditionally high gasoline taxes to encourage the use of alternative fuels through tax exemptions or lower rates of duty. It is generally easier to promote fuels that are very similar to conventional fuels and that do not require significant changes in vehicle technology than it is to promote fuels that require consumers to buy a new and unfamiliar vehicle type. This is illustrated in Figure 6-7, which compares the market penetration of diesel in France with that of unleaded gasoline in the United Kingdom. A lower price for unleaded gasoline in the United Kingdom led consumers to switch rapidly to the new fuel, an experience shared by many European countries. For diesel in France, however, the lower fuel price was a necessary but not sufficient condition for consumers to switch from gasoline. The process is delayed by the need for manufacturers to design, produce, and improve diesel cars to the point at which they are seen by consumers to be good substitutes for gasoline cars. By 1990, diesel cars had achieved market acceptance and constituted 32 percent of new-car sales in France, but it will take some years before the car fleet as a whole is over 30 percent diesel.

Figure 6-7

Fuel Pricing and Market Share

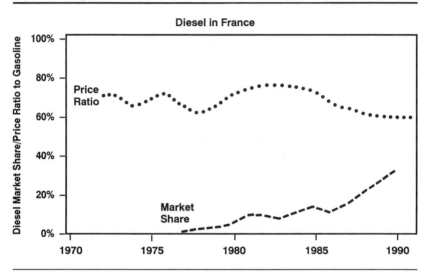

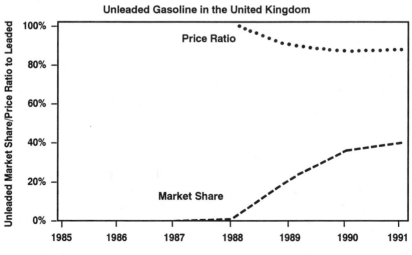

Diesel car drivers in France pay 3.3 U.S. cents per km less in fuel tax than gasoline car drivers, and their CO_2-equivalent greenhouse gas emissions are 64 grams per km lower than those of gasoline car drivers.

New-Car Taxes and Rebates

The possibility of a car tax related to fuel economy has long been discussed in all of the OECD regions. Car purchase tax waivers and subsidies have also been used to encourage consumers to buy alternative-fuel vehicles or convert their gasoline cars to operate on alternative fuels. Fiscal measures related to car purchase may be more effective than fuel taxes, since consumers generally behave as if they use very high discount rates, which means that very large fuel price signals are needed to have an effect on car purchase decisions. Even commercial fleet purchasers will frequently write off their new-car purchases over a period of four years—effectively using a 25 to 30 percent discount rate. If the government operates with a 5 percent discount rate, car purchasers will appear to place too much emphasis on the car price and too little on fuel and other operating costs. Where taxes are being used as an instrument to change consumer behavior rather than to raise revenue, it will be much more effective to tax cars than to tax fuels. Some natural gas utilities have found it effective to offer reduced price or free conversions of gasoline cars to operate on CNG while recouping the conversion costs through a margin on CNG sales.

Mandated Alternative-Fuel-Vehicle Sale and Purchase

Both sales and purchases of alternative-fuel vehicles have been mandated in the United States, and such mandates have been an effective policy measure for stimulating research and development worldwide. They follow the common approach to reducing air pollution from cars, in which governments have generally used regulatory rather than fiscal measures.

Nevertheless, regulators may run into difficulties if they aim to achieve substantial market penetration of alternative fuels through regulation. Experience with the introduction of unleaded gasoline indicates that, when the new fuel is more expensive than the traditional fuel, drivers are likely to go out of their way to avoid using it. Although purchase mandates are effective in initiating a new technology to the market, new fuels will only be successful when they are cheaper to use than conventional fuels or when tax differentials are used to make them cheaper.

Subsidized Fueling Networks

The lack of infrastructure for distributing alternative fuels is a key barrier to their introduction. In many OECD countries, natural gas utilities have taken the initiative in establishing CNG filling stations. OECD governments have found it harder to justify direct support for investment in alternative-fuel networks although when a government is firmly committed to a particular fuel, this is an important element of a policy package to promote it.

Research, Development, and Demonstration Funding

Research, development, and demonstration may be justified even when direct intervention in the market is not justified. This axiom applies especially when there is uncertainty about future energy supplies and environmental issues. Many oil market analysts consider it unlikely that oil prices will rise significantly over the next 20 to 30 years, which reduces the motivation to develop alternative energy sources for transport. Even so, supply disruptions could occur, and IEA governments have a shared commitment to address the risk. Similarly, the risks associated with greenhouse gas emissions are uncertain, and many governments wish to protect themselves against the possibility of severe effects while avoiding large expenditures that may later prove to have been unnecessary. In this context, most governments have some research and development activities related to alternative fuels, and many are involved in demonstration programs.

The Role of Alternative Fuels in Policy

This chapter has so far focused on the role of alternative fuels in policy to reduce greenhouse gas emissions. In fact, alternative fuels may have important influences or roles in other areas of interest to policymakers. Perhaps one of the most important of these areas is in the development of domestic industry and energy services. Alternative fuels may also be a means of reducing the external costs of transport, especially those due to air pollution.

Relevance of Alternative Fuels for Macroeconomic Objectives

Figure 6-8 shows the breakdown of the cost of switching from gasoline cars to diesel or CNG cars for the average driver in the

Figure 6-8

Breakdown of Costs of Switching from Gasoline in the United States (Fuel Taxes Included)

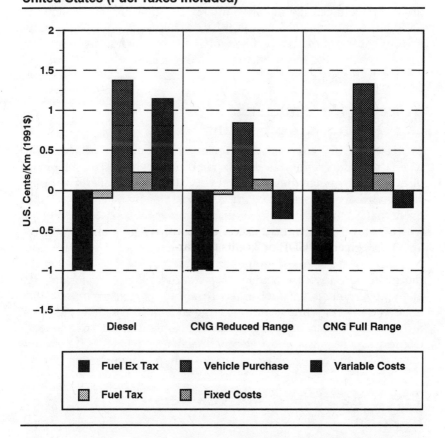

United States. As this graph shows, the main cost in each case is for the vehicle although for the diesel car, nonfuel variable costs (maintenance and repairs) are also significantly increased. The main saving is in fuel costs. This transfer of consumer expenditure from petroleum fuels (imported at the margin) to manufactured goods and skilled labor may help to serve macroeconomic objectives.

Internalizing the Externalities of Car Use

Concern about the wider range of social impacts of car use, including congestion and accidents, is rising, and there is a long history of government action to deal with these problems. Such action may also have an effect on energy use and greenhouse gas emissions. Although little confidence can be placed in the precise figures of externality valuations given in the literature, they may give some indication of the depth of concern about different issues.

In studies of the externalities of car use, congestion generally emerges as one of the highest costs. Newbery (1990) estimates the marginal external cost due to congestion for a driver in a congested city street at 36 pence (about 60 U.S. cents) per km, about double the driver's direct costs of driving. He estimates the United Kingdom average marginal external cost due to congestion at 3.4 pence per km (about 6 U.S. cents). The more recent World Resources Institute (WRI) estimate of $100 billion in congestion costs for the United States (MacKenzie et al. 1992) amounts to about 2.5 cents per car-km,[4] which is less than 10 percent of direct driving costs. Quinet (1989) has put total travel time costs in the OECD at 6.8 percent of gross domestic product (GDP), which for the United States would amount to around 7 cents per car-km, with the excess travel time due to congestion only around 2 percent of GDP, or 2 cents per car-km.

The external cost of accidents is generally assessed to be lower than that due to congestion although such estimates are heavily dependent on the relative costs assumed for loss of life and wasted time. WRI put external accident costs (not paid by the driver) in the United States at $55 billion (MacKenzie et al. 1992). For cars, the cost works out to roughly 1 cent per km. Quinet (1989) has estimated accident costs at 2 percent of GDP, which would be 1 to 2 cents per km for cars. The cost of accidents is heavily dependent on the value attached to human life, and national estimates for the external cost of transport accidents range from 1.1 to 3 percent of GDP, or 0.5 to 3 cents per car-km (Quinet 1994). Estimates also vary according to whether costs associated with avoiding accidents have been included. The costs of seatbelts, helmets, and other safety devices are assumed by some analysts not to be externalities because they are bought by the road users themselves. However, many road users, including pedestrians, choose to take expensive precautions to guard against other people's behavior. When these costs are included as accident externalities, the overall cost is in the upper end of the 0.5 to 3 cents-per-car-km range.

---

[4] This is derived from $100 billion spread over 1.5 trillion car-miles and 0.6 trillion truck-miles, with the approximation that one truck causes the same amount of congestion as two cars. Note that this is the average cost, whereas Newbery calculates the marginal cost, which is more appropriate for determining a level for congestion pricing.

The external costs of air pollution from transport are estimated to be lower than those of accidents, with Quinet (1989) putting them at 0.4 percent of OECD GDP. This figure includes pollution from all types of vehicle, but it would be in the region of 0.1 to 0.3 cents per km for cars. Other national estimates of air pollution costs range from 0.03 to 1.05 percent of GDP. Internalizing these costs would have some effect on the attractiveness of switching to alternative fuels when the alternatives cause significantly less local pollution than gasoline.

External costs associated with greenhouse gas emissions cannot currently be evaluated, and those who have attempted to do so come out with wide ranges. WRI uses an avoidance cost approach to arrive at a figure of $27 billion for the external cost associated with transport CO_2 emissions in the United States (MacKenzie et al. 1992). This evaluation amounts to about 0.6 cents per km. Estimates based on damage costs of global warming are currently very crude. Pearce et al. (1992) give hypothetical costs in the region of $10 to $30 per tonne of carbon emitted, associated with gross world product (GWP) losses in 2050 of 1 percent to 3 percent. This estimate translates to 0.2 to 0.8 cents per km for a gasoline car.

Analysts do not agree as to whether an externality can be attached to security of supply problems in consuming oil. The choice to buy a gasoline-powered car can affect oil security by raising oil demand. At current levels of oil demand, such an increase could give the suppliers a stronger position in the market although at higher demand levels and prices, the oil market may be more stable as it becomes economic to recover oil from more diverse sources. The presence of an external cost associated with the risk of supply interruptions or price rises is questionable—the risk is faced by the user of the gasoline. However, some analysts deem that motorists do not take adequate account of the risks to others associated with their choice to consume gasoline. These risks might include the loss of essential services (such as food distribution) if fuel for freight transport were to become unavailable, and the loss of life and property if military intervention were undertaken to protect oil supplies. Estimates of the externality associated with oil security range from zero to around 0.6 cents per car-km (MacKenzie et al. 1992; Hogan 1993).

Government policies to internalize the costs associated with local air pollution, greenhouse gas emissions, and oil security would have some effect on the attractiveness of alternative fuels. The total of these externalities appears from the above discussion to be somewhere in the range of 0.25 to 2.5 cents per car-km. However, it should be noted that this is the average external cost, whereas an economically efficient tax should be chosen to reflect the marginal cost. If a vehicle tax were applied to new gasoline car purchases to reflect, say, 1 cent per km in hypothetical external costs that could be avoided by using alternative fuels, new-car prices would rise by an average of $1,000 or more. Such a price increase would affect the demand for cars, and the use of a sliding tax scale to reflect a car's fuel consumption would encourage purchasers to buy more efficient or smaller cars.

Most externalities are higher per km driven for urban driving than for rural or highway driving: congestion is mainly an urban problem; exhaust emissions are more likely to affect people in cities than in country lanes; accidents to nondrivers are most frequent in urban and residential areas; and fuel consumption and greenhouse gas emissions tend to be higher in urban areas. External costs associated with urban driving could be half or more of the direct costs paid by the driver. Many IEA member countries are exploring measures to internalize costs for urban drivers in particular, giving considerable attention to fees or taxes for road use and parking. Such fees operate mainly through reducing urban car use and to some extent through encouraging drivers to reschedule trips. One study in the Netherlands (NOVEM 1992) found that combined measures of this type could reduce greenhouse gas emissions from cars in the Randstad region by around 17 percent in 2010.

Conclusions

Alternative-fuel options can be divided into four main groups:

- Fuels that offer little or no life-cycle greenhouse gas emission abatement but that may be attractive from the perspective of other areas of government policy. Synthetic liquid fuels using fossil fuel inputs, including some biomass-derived fuels, fall into this group, as do CNG used in existing vehicles and electric vehicles using power from some existing generation mixes.

- Alternatives available now or expected to become available by 2005, including diesel, LPG, CNG in optimized engines, and electric vehicles using power from existing generation mixes. These options can reduce life-cycle greenhouse gas emissions by 10 to 25 percent.

- Synthetic fuels from wood or other low-input biomass feedstocks. Production processes are not yet technically demonstrated, but the fuels could offer 60 to 80 percent life-cycle greenhouse gas emission reduction.

- Fuels derived from completely renewable sources, including hydrogen produced by electrolysis of water using electricity generated by renewable sources, synthetic fuels from zero-input biomass feed-stocks, and electric vehicles powered by electricity from renewable sources. All would depend on large-scale replacement of the existing fossil-based energy system. Such fuels could result in a greater than 80 percent life-cycle greenhouse gas emission abatement.

Governments can encourage the use of alternative fuels through taxes and subsidies on fuels and cars, through mandates to use the fuels, and through investment in infrastructure. Where the technologies would help to protect against long-term risks, government spending may be necessary to ensure that research, development, and demonstration occur.

The externalities that have been identified with car use probably do not justify the level of fiscal intervention that appears to be necessary to introduce alternative fuels requiring substantially different car technology. Other strategies to reduce greenhouse gas emissions may have greater potential at lower cost. There are potential synergies between policies aimed at reducing congestion, improving road safety, promoting security of energy supply, and reducing greenhouse gas emissions. Alternative-fuel programs address only the last two concerns. We are now beginning to see a tendency to take a comprehensive view of transport policy: well-integrated policy packages may be more effective in reducing greenhouse gas emissions than technology-focused measures aimed at promoting alternative fuels.

References

DeLuchi, Mark. 1991. *Emissions of Greenhouse Gases from the Use of Transportation Fuels and Electricity.* ANL/ESD/TM-22. Vol. 1. Argonne, Ill.: Argonne National Laboratory Center for Transportation Research.

Hogan, W.W. 1993. "Energy Externalities, Energy Taxes, and Economic Efficiency." Paper presented at the meeting of the International Association for Energy Economics, Bali, July 29.

International Energy Agency (IEA). 1991. *Energy Balances of OECD Countries, 1960–1979.* Paris: OECD.

———. 1992. *Energy Balances of OECD Countries, 1989–1990.* Paris: OECD.

———. 1993. *Cars and Climate Change.* Paris: OECD.

———. 1994. *World Energy Outlook.* 1994 edition. Paris: OECD.

MacKenzie, J.J., R.C. Dower, and D.D.T. Chen. 1992. *The Going Rate: What It Really Costs to Drive.* Washington, D.C.: World Resources Institute. June.

Newbery, D.M. 1990. "Pricing and Congestion: Economic Principles Relevant to Pricing Roads." *Oxford Review of Economic Policy* 6 (2): 22–38.

NOVEM. 1992. "Transport Policy, Traffic Management, Energy and Environment." Consultants' report to the IEA.

Organisation for Economic Cooperation and Development (OECD). 1992. *Agricultural Policies, Markets and Trade: Monitoring and Outlook, 1992.* Paris.

Pearce, D., C. Bann, and S. Georiou. 1992. *The Social Cost of Fuel Cycles.* Report to the UK Department of Trade and Industry. London: HMSO.

Quinet, E. 1989. "Evaluation du coût social des transports" [Evaluation of the social costs of transport]. In *Proceedings of the 5th World Conference on Transportation Research.* Yokohama.

———. 1994. *The Social Costs of Transport: Evaluation and Links with Internalisation Policies in Internalising the Social Costs of Transport.* European Conference of Ministers of Transport. Paris: OECD.

Chapter Seven

Emission Reductions of Alternative-Fuel Vehicles: Implications for Vehicle and Fuel Price Subsidies

MICHAEL QUANLU WANG

To help tackle urban air pollution problems, various laws and regulations introducing alternative-fuel vehicles (AFVs) have been proposed or adopted in the United States. However, despite the legislative and regulatory activities promoting AFVs, few studies have been carried out to compare dollars-per-ton emission control cost-effectiveness among various AFV types. A recent study conducted by Wang et al. (1993) showed that AFV cost-effectiveness can vary significantly with different values for such parameters as AFV costs, AFV emission reductions, and baseline gasoline vehicle (GV) emissions. That study established ranges of AFV cost-effectiveness according to two AFV cost cases (a high-cost case and a low-cost case) and two AFV emission reduction cases (a low AFV emission reduction case and a high AFV emission reduction case). However, the effect of individual cost and emission parameters on AFV cost-effectiveness was not explicitly tested.

Using a set of base-case values assumed from the model in the above study, this chapter estimates the effect of various cost and emission parameters on AFV cost-effectiveness in order to show the differences in cost-effectiveness among various AFV types. In addition, a sensitivity analysis tests the importance of major emission and cost parameters in determining AFV cost-effectiveness. In this analysis, AFV cost-effectiveness is calculated for various cases representing variations in values for major emission and cost parameters in order to show the plausible range of cost-effectiveness for various AFV types.

To put AFVs into the economic cost/benefit perspective, the per-vehicle monetary value of emission reductions for various AFV types is estimated from AFV life-cycle emission reductions and assumed dollar values per ton of emissions. AFV fuel or vehicle price subsidies are then designed to be equal to the calculated dollar values of AFV emission reductions. Fuel or vehicle subsidies designed in this way are intended to reflect society's willingness to pay to use AFVs for the sake of their emission reductions and will hopefully encourage their use.

Ten AFV types are addressed: GVs fueled with reformulated gasoline (RFG) (for presentation purposes, GVs fueled with RFG are named as an AFV type here); M85 flexible-fuel vehicles (FFVs); M100 FFVs; dedicated methanol vehicles (both M85 and M100); E85 FFVs; dual-fuel liquefied petroleum gas vehicles (LPGVs); dual-fuel compressed natural gas vehicles (CNGVs); dedicated CNGVs; and electric vehicles (EVs). GVs fueled with conventional gasoline serve as the baseline comparison vehicle. 1995 model-year compact passenger car projections are used to calculate vehicle emissions and costs; this implies that baseline GVs will meet the federal Tier I emission standards.

Input Parameters for AFV Cost-Effectiveness Calculation

Emission control cost-effectiveness of a particular AFV type is calculated from the life-cycle incremental cost of the AFV type divided by its life-cycle emission reductions. It is thus essential to estimate AFV life-cycle incremental costs and emission reductions.

AFV Life-Cycle Incremental Costs

The calculation of AFV life-cycle incremental costs here takes into account initial vehicle purchase prices, expenditure on fuels, vehicle maintenance costs, the cost of inspection and maintenance (I/M) programs, and vehicle lifetime. Given the value difference of cost items occurring in different years, the present value (PV) of life-cycle costs is calculated by discounting future costs to present costs. The life-cycle incremental cost for a particular AFV type is the difference in the PV of life-cycle costs between the AFV type and baseline GVs. The PV of vehicle life-cycle costs is calculated with the following equation. (*Note:* throughout this chapter, cost items are presented as the costs to consumers in 1990 constant dollars.)

$$PV_{cost} = IP + \sum_{i=1}^{n} [(FC_i + MC_i + Misc_i)/(1 + r)^i]$$

where:

PV_{cost}	= present value of vehicle life-cycle costs
IP	= initial price of a new vehicle
n	= vehicle lifetime (years)
i	= vehicle age
FC_i	= annual fuel cost
MC_i	= annual vehicle maintenance cost
$Misc_i$	= annual miscellaneous cost (such as the I/M cost)
r	= real-term discount rate (assumed 6 percent here)

Values adopted for the input parameters in the above equation are presented in Tables 7-1 through 7-4.

The EPA has recently adopted an enhanced I/M program that requires vehicles to be tested as they are driven on chassis dynamometers (U.S. EPA 1992). A biennial enhanced program with a cost per test of $40 is assumed here for all internal combustion engine vehicle types (but not for EVs, because EVs themselves do not produce emissions).

Note that CNGVs are assumed to last 13 years and EVs 15 years, whereas baseline GVs last for 12 years. To calculate life-cycle incremental costs for CNGVs and EVs, a second GV is assumed after the 12 years. The annualized cost of the second GV is considered together with the total cost of the first GV in calculating incremental costs of CNGVs and EVs.

AFV Life-Cycle Emission Reductions

Vehicle exhaust and evaporative emissions of seven air pollutants are considered in estimating AFV emission reductions: three criteria pollutants (nonmethane organic gases [NMOG], carbon monoxide [CO], and nitrogen oxides [NO_x]) and four air toxic pollutants (benzene, 1,3-butadiene, formaldehyde, and acetaldehyde).

To be consistent with the PV of AFV life-cycle incremental costs, the PV of AFV life-cycle emission reductions is calculated by discounting annual AFV emission reductions. Annual emission reductions by a particular AFV type are estimated with annual emissions of baseline GVs and emission reduction rates by AFV type.

Annual Emissions of Baseline GVs

Annual emissions of baseline GVs are calculated with annual grams-per-mile emission rates and annual vehicle-miles traveled

119

Table 7-1

Lifetime, Incremental Prices, and Fuel Economy Changes of Alternative-Fuel Vehicle Types (1990$)

Vehicle Type	Lifetime (years)	Incremental Price ($)	Mpg Increase (energy equivalent)
GV	12	N/A[a]	0%[b]
Methanol and ethanol FFVs	12	300	5%
Dedicated MV	12	100	15%
Dual-fuel LPGV	12	1,000	0%
Dual-fuel CNGV	13	1,500	0%[c]
Dedicated CNGV	13	1,000	5%[c]
EV	15	Various[d]	N/A[e]

Source: Most values here are based on Wang et al. (1993), pp. 95–97, 111.

[a] Not applicable. A retail price of $15,000 is assumed for GVs fueled with both conventional gasoline and RFG. RFG can be used in GVs without vehicle modification or design changes, though such modification or design changes for using RFG can certainly increase RFG emission benefits reduction.

[b] An in-use fuel economy of 27 miles per gallon (mpg) is assumed for 1995 model-year compact gasoline cars. EPA shows a lab-tested fuel economy of 29.5 mpg for 1993 model-year compact cars under the 55/45 combined cycle (Murrell et al. 1993). In-use fuel economy is roughly 10% less than lab-tested fuel economy for the combined cycle. Therefore, in-use fuel economy for 1993 model-year compact gasoline cars is about 26.6 mpg. It is assumed here that in-use fuel economy for the 1995 model year (the model year considered in this chapter) is 0.4 mpg higher than that for 1993 model year and that the fuel economy of GVs fueled with RFG will be the same as that of GVs fueled with conventional gasoline on an energy-equivalent basis.

[c] It is assumed here that the lean-burn strategy will not be used in CNGVs because of its problem with NOx emission control.

[d] Incremental EV prices vary significantly with battery technology. EV batteries need to be replaced intermittently during the EV lifetime. Because of this, EV costs are calculated differently. Assumptions regarding EV battery performance and cost are presented in Table 7-4.

[e] Not applicable. EV per-mile electricity consumption is presented in Table 7-4.

(VMT). Grams-per-mile emission rates are estimated with Mobile5A for exhaust emissions of NMOG, CO, and NO_x and for evaporative emissions of NMOG. In using Mobile5A, an enhanced I/M program, federal Tier I emission standards, and the Stage II technology to control refueling emissions in gasoline service stations are assumed.

GV air toxic emissions are calculated with Mobile5A-estimated NMOG emissions and a weighted distribution of each of the four air toxic pollutants in GV NMOG emissions (see Wang et al. [1993]).

Emission Reduction Rates by AFV Type

AFV emission reductions are affected by type of emission control technologies installed on vehicles, designed tradeoffs between vehicle emissions and vehicle performance, and tradeoffs in emissions among

Table 7-2

Annual Vehicle-Miles of Travel and Maintenance Costs of a Compact Gasoline Car (1990$)

Age (years)	Annual VMT	Maintenance Cost[a] ($)
1	12,900	132
2	12,600	289
3	12,300	368
4	11,900	415
5	11,500	447
6	11,000	468
7	10,600	477
8	10,100	488
9	9,600	488
10	9,100	489
11	8,700	86
12 and up	8,200	478

Source: FHWA (1992), p. 112.

[a] Including scheduled and unscheduled costs and cost of engine oil changes. It is assumed here that vehicles with internal combustion engines (GVs, MVs, LPGVs, CNGVs, and ethanol vehicles) will have identical annual maintenance costs. Because of reliable electric motors and on-board electric systems, it is assumed here that EV annual maintenance costs will be 60% of the costs presented in the table.

different pollutants, all of which are influenced by desired AFV target emissions for meeting certain emission rates. A set of base-case AFV emission reduction rates based on data presented in Wang et al. (1993) is assumed here (see Table 7-5).

NMOG emission reduction rates for the ten AFV types considered here are adjusted, with their ozone reactivity adjustment factors developed from the maximum incremental reactivity (MIR) of individual hydrocarbon (HC) species. Ozone reactivity adjustment factors can also be developed from the maximum ozone reactivity (MOR) of individual HC species, but the MIR scale reflects atmospheric conditions in which small changes in HC concentrations have large effects on ozone formation, whereas the MOR scale reflects conditions in which ozone formation is primarily controlled by atmospheric NO_x concentration.

Emission reduction rates by AFV type for some pollutants (see Table 7-5) are subject to great uncertainty. For example, EVs can increase or decrease NO_x emissions, depending upon the types of powerplants used for generating electricity for EVs. Methanol vehicles (MVs) and CNGVs can increase or decrease NO_x emissions, depend-

Table 7-3

Prices and Energy Contents of Motor Fuels (1990$)

Fuel	Price[a] ($/gal, or as noted)	Btu/gal[b] (based on low heating value)
Conventional gasoline	1.30	115,000
RFG[c]	1.46	114,000
Pure methanol	0.92	56,800
Ethanol	1.50[d]	76,000
LPG	0.95	84,000[e]
CNG	9.5[f]	N/A
Electricity	6.5[g]	N/A

[a] A federal road excise tax of $0.18 and a state road excise tax of $0.14 per gallon of gasoline equivalent are applied to each fuel. For detailed assumptions, see Wang et al. (1993), p. 113.
[b] Except for compressed natural gas and electricity, energy contents of fuels are needed to convert gasoline-equivalent fuel economy to fuel economy of a particular fuel.
[c] California's phase 2 gasoline is assumed here.
[d] A blender's income tax credit equivalent to $0.60 per gallon of ethanol is excluded here. Although the credit is currently in effect, it is not clear whether it would stay if ethanol vehicles were mass introduced. In addition, to level the playing field for various AFV types, the credit should be taken out, at least for a social evaluation of AFV cost-effectiveness.
[e] At a pressure of about 200 psi.
[f] Price is in $/$10^6$ Btu.
[g] Price is in cents per kilowatt-hour (kWh).

ing on the emission control strategies employed. Thus, the presented emission reduction rates should be interpreted with caution.

Primary formaldehyde emissions from motor vehicles are included in estimating AFV formaldehyde emission impacts here. Secondary formaldehyde emissions can be formed in the atmosphere from motor vehicle tailpipe emissions; however, these secondary emissions are not included here.

Calculation of a Composite Tonnage of AFV Emission Reductions

With the above procedure and data, the PV of life-cycle AFV emission reductions is calculated for each of the seven pollutants. The cost-effectiveness of a particular AFV type can be calculated for each pollutant by allocating the incremental cost of the AFV type among the seven pollutants. Alternatively, a composite tonnage of emission reductions can be calculated from the emission reductions of the seven pollutants, and the cost-effectiveness of controlling the composite tonnage can be calculated for the AFV type. Because of the difficulty (sometimes impossibility) of allocating the incremental cost among the seven pollutants, the latter method is used here.

The composite tonnage of emission reductions is calculated as the weighted average of emission reductions for each of the seven pollu-

---

Table 7-4

Costs and Performance of Electric Vehicle–Related Components (1990$)

EV price without battery (as % of GV price)	80
EV electricity consumption (kWh/mi)	0.4
Price per battery ($)	9,375
Battery life-cycle VMT	63,750
Home recharging system cost ($/yr)	32

Source: For detailed information, see Wang et al. (1993), p. 114.

Table 7-5

Alternative-Fuel-Vehicle Emission Reduction Rates (as Percentage of Gasoline Vehicle Emissions)

AFV Type	NMOG[b]	CO	NO$_x$	Exhaust Emissions 1,3-Butadiene	Benzene	Formaldehyde	Acetaldehyde	Evaporative Emissions[a] NMOG[b]	Benzene
RFG[c]	−20	−20	0	−25	−25	20	0	−15	−25
M85 FFVs	−55	−10	−10	−80	−85	280	−75	−60	185
M100 FFVs	−60	−10	−10	−80	−85	245	−75	−75	−100
M85 dedicated vehicle	−65	−15	−10	−85	−90	195	−80	−85	10
M100 dedicated vehicle	−70	−20	−10	−85	−90	160	−80	−85	−100
E85 FFVs	−30	−10	−10	−80	−90	40	825	−40	185
Dual-fuel LPGVs	−70	−30	0	−95	−95	15	−50	−100	−100
Dual-fuel CNGVs	−90	−30	0	−95	−99	70	−65	−100	−100
Dedicated CNGVs	−90	−40	−10	−95	−99	40	−70	−100	−100
EVs	−95	−95	−60	−100	−100	−95	−100	−100	−100

[a] 1,3-Butadiene, formaldehyde, and acetaldehyde are absent in evaporative emissions. Therefore, evaporative emission reduction rates are not applicable to these three air pollutants.
[b] These are NMOG emissions adjusted by the ozone reactivity adjustment factor for each fuel. NMOG emission reductions for MVs and ethanol vehicles are solely due to their lower reactivity adjustment factors. NMOG emission reductions for EVs are solely due to mass NMOG emission reductions. NMOG emission reductions for LPGVs and CNGVs are due to both mass NMOG emission r eductions and lower reactivity adjustment factors.
[c] These are emission reductions of California's phase 2 reformulated gasoline, which were estimated by the California Air Resources Board (CARB 1991, p. 55).

---

tants, using the following weighting factors developed by Wang et al. (1993): 1 for NMOG, 0.49 for CO, 1.40 for NO_x, 10 for benzene, 9.37 for 1,3-butadiene, 1.31 for formaldehyde, and 0.31 for acetaldehyde. The weighting factors for NMOG, CO, and NO_x were developed from the estimated emission values of the three pollutants in southern California. The weighting factors for the four air toxics were generated from their estimated cancer risk factors and their residence time in the atmosphere.

AFV Emission Control Cost-Effectiveness

Finally, AFV cost-effectiveness is calculated with the above-estimated AFV life-cycle incremental costs and emission reductions. The calculated AFV cost-effectiveness for each of the ten AFV types is presented in Figure 7-1.

As the figure shows, CNGVs are the most cost-effective AFV type in controlling emissions. In fact, the control cost of dual-fuel CNGVs is negligible, whereas the control cost of dedicated CNGVs is negative, meaning that use of dedicated CNGVs actually results in net cost savings. Dual-fuel LPGVs, RFG, and dedicated methanol vehicles (both M85 and M100) are the next most cost-effective vehicle types. Control costs of these AFV types are between $2,500 and $4,000 per ton of emissions reduced. Methanol FFVs and EVs are less cost-effective, with control costs ranging from $7,500 to $10,000. E85 FFVs are the least cost-effective vehicle type, with a control cost above $15,000.

Note that this ranking of the ten AFV types is according to their per-ton emission control costs, which indicate the cost to reduce one ton of emissions. The cost-effectiveness does not show what quantity of emissions an AFV type can reduce at the given cost. The per-vehicle monetary value of emission reductions, which explicitly indicates the total amount of emissions each AFV type can reduce, is calculated below for each AFV type.

Caution must be taken in comparing the AFV cost-effectiveness calculated here with that calculated in other studies. Whereas the cost-effectiveness here is for a composite tonnage of emission reductions for seven pollutants, the cost-effectiveness in other studies may be for a specific pollutant (e.g., NMOG or NO_x).

Sensitivity Analysis of AFV Emission Control Cost-Effectiveness

The AFV cost-effectiveness presented in Figure 7-1 is based on the assumed values for cost and emission parameters affecting AFV cost-effectiveness. Changes in parameter values certainly cause

Figure 7-1

Alternative-Fuel-Vehicle Emission Control Cost-Effectiveness (Composite Tonnage, 1990$)

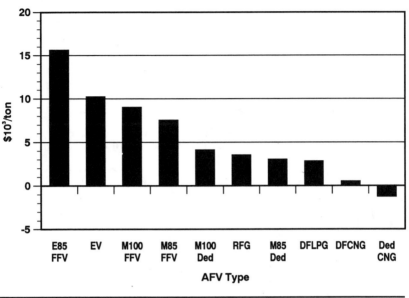

changes in AFV cost-effectiveness, and therefore a sensitivity analysis is conducted here to assess the importance of major cost and emission parameters in determining the magnitude and plausible ranges of AFV cost-effectiveness.

Cases for the Sensitivity Analysis

AFV incremental prices, fuel prices, and emission reductions are important factors in determining AFV cost-effectiveness, but these three parameters are subject to great uncertainties. Therefore, in the sensitivity analysis, three cases are established to represent these three parameters, and in each case, a low value and a high value are assumed for each parameter. Tables 7-6 and 7-7 show the low and high values for the AFV incremental-price and fuel-price cases, respectively. For the AFV emission reduction case, a set of low AFV emission reduction rates is calculated by assuming that AFV emissions are increased by 20 percent over the AFV emissions under the base-case AFV emission reduction rates assumed in Table 7-5; a set of high AFV emission reduction rates is calculated by assuming AFV emissions are decreased by 20 percent (for EVs, an emission reduction rate of 100 percent is assumed for all pollutants, reflecting the fact that EVs generate zero tailpipe emissions).

Two additional cases are established to represent baseline GV emissions and air toxic emissions. One case, based on conclusions drawn in a National Research Council study (NRC 1991), assumes that actual on-road GV emissions are four times as great as the emissions estimated with Mobile5A for exhaust emissions of NMOG, CO, and air toxic pollutants. The other case excludes emissions of the four air toxic pollutants in calculating AFV cost-effectiveness, which is in-

Table 7-6

Sensitivity Analysis Case: Alternative-Fuel-Vehicle Incremental Prices (1990$)

AFV Type	Low Value	High Value
Methanol and ethanol FFVs	100	500
Dedicated MV	0	200
Dual-fuel LPGV	800	1,200
Dual-fuel CNGV	1,300	1,700
Dedicated CNGV	800	1,200
EV	USABC LG[a]	Lead-acid[b]

[a] EV prices are essentially determined by battery costs. The long-term battery goal established by the U.S. Advanced Battery Consortium (USABC) is adopted here for the low EV price case. Wang et al. (1993, p. 114) estimated a per-battery cost of $8,750 and a battery lifetime VMT of 170,000 for the USABC long-term goal (therefore no battery replacement is needed during EV lifetime). The long-term goal has a high per-battery cost, but also high performance and long lifetime; therefore vehicle life-cycle battery total cost is low.
[b] A lead-acid battery is adopted here for the high EV price case. A per-battery cost of $4,500 and a lifetime VMT of 27,000 are assumed for lead-acid battery. The lead-acid battery has a low per-battery cost, but also low performance and short lifetime; consequently, the EV life-cycle battery cost is high.

Table 7-7

Sensitivity Analysis Case: Fuel Prices ($/Gal or as Noted, 1990$)

Fuel	Low Price	High Price
RFG	1.36	1.56
Methanol	0.82	1.02
Ethanol	1.20	1.80
LPG	0.75	1.20
CNG ($/$10^6$ Btu)	8.0	11.0
Electricity (cents/kWh)	4.5	8.5

Figure 7-2

Alternative-Fuel-Vehicle Emission Control Cost-Effectiveness for Eight Cases (1990$)

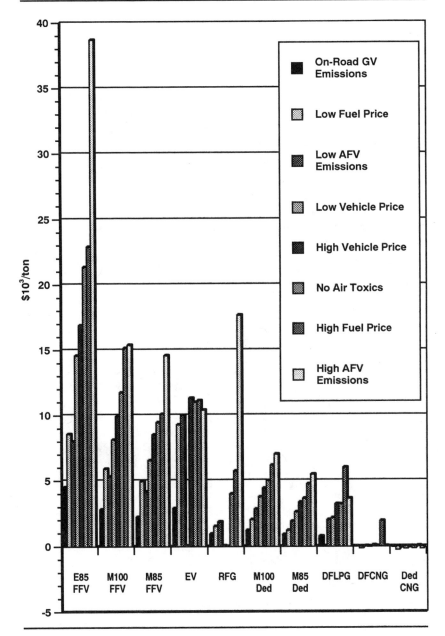

tended to demonstrate the importance of air toxic pollutants in determining the magnitude of AFV cost-effectiveness.

Sensitivity Analysis Results

The dramatic impacts of changes in values for major cost and emission parameters on AFV cost-effectiveness for each of the cases are shown in Figure 7-2 (see chapter Appendix 7-1 for the numerical results of AFV cost-effectiveness). Except for CNGVs, whose cost-effectiveness shows little variation among the assumed cases, AFV cost-effectiveness varies widely for each AFV type. For ethanol and methanol FFVs, RFG, and dedicated methanol vehicles, the lowest control cost occurs for the on-road GV emission case, whereas the highest control cost occurs for the low emission reduction cases. Cost-effectiveness varies from $4,500 to $38,700 for ethanol FFVs; from $2,500 to $15,000 for methanol FFVs (both M85 and M100); from $1,000 to $17,600 for RFG; and from $1,000 to $7,000 for dedicated methanol vehicles (both M85 and M100). Baseline GV emissions, AFV emission reductions, and fuel prices are the three important factors determining the cost-effectiveness of these AFV types.

Cost-effectiveness of EVs is generally around $10,000, except for two cases: the U. S. Advanced Battery Consortium (USABC) long-term battery-goal case and the on-road GV-emission case. For the USABC long-term-goal case, EVs have virtually zero control cost. For the on-road GV-emission case, EV control cost is about $3,000.

The control cost of dual-fuel LPGVs ranges from virtually zero for the low fuel price case to $6,000 for the high fuel price case, meaning that LPG price is the predominant factor determining LPGV control cost.

The ranking of the ten AFV types according to their cost-effectiveness remains essentially unchanged for each of the cases. That is, CNGVs are the most cost-effective vehicle type; methanol and ethanol FFVs are the least cost-effective vehicle types; and RFG, EVs, dedicated methanol vehicles, and dual-fuel LPG vehicles fall in between. However, there are two exceptions: (1) RFG for the low AFV emission reduction case can become as expensive as methanol FFVs, and (2) EVs with the USABC long-term battery goal can become as cost-effective as CNGVs.

Per-Vehicle Monetary Value of AFV Emission Reductions

A given amount of emissions is reduced by a given AFV type during its lifetime. In economics, the amount of emission reductions can be converted into dollar values. Per-vehicle monetary values of AFV emission reductions are calculated from dollars-per-ton emission values and tons of emissions reduced over the AFV's lifetime.

Dollars-per-Ton Emission Values

The dollar value of emissions can be calculated by means of two general methods: a damage estimate method and a control cost estimate method. The damage estimate method estimates dollar values of the damages created by emissions and requires estimation of the physical impacts of emissions, such as health and welfare impacts, and the valuation of the estimated impacts. The method requires emission estimates, simulation of emission transport, estimated exposure of receptor populations, and establishment of dose/response relationships for those populations.

In the control cost estimate method, emission control costs of some given control measures are estimated and then treated as the monetary opportunity benefits of the emissions reduced by other control measures.

Table 7-8 summarizes imputed values of eliminating one ton of emissions for three criteria pollutants—volatile organic compounds (VOCs), CO, and NO_x—as presented in several studies. As can be seen from the table, the emission values based on the damage estimate method are consistently lower than those based on the control cost estimate method. However, because of great uncertainties involved in the damage estimate method, this result by no means indicates that current emission standards lead to excess control of emissions.

Table 7-8 suggests that emission values estimated for California are much higher than those for other regions. To reflect this difference, two sets of values are used here: one set for California and another for other U.S. regions (see Table 7-9). In determining emission values for each set, those values estimated by the control cost estimate method have been given primary consideration.

The four air toxic pollutants are classified as carcinogens, and their most damaging effect is resultant cancer incidence. Wang et al. (1993) assumed damage factors (developed by considering cancer risk factors and residence time in the atmosphere) for the four toxic pollutants relative to NMOG as follows: 10 for benzene, 9.37 for 1,3-butadiene, 1.31 for formaldehyde, and 0.31 for acetaldehyde. These factors, together with the NMOG emission values in Table 7-9, have been used to determine emission values for each air toxic pollutant.

129

Table 7-8
Summary of Imputed Emission Values ($/Ton, 1990 $)

Study	Imputed Value	Estimating Method	Target Region
		VOC	
Bernow and Marron (1990)	5,570	Control cost	Ozone nonattainment areas
	30,450	Control cost	Southern California
CEC (1993)	7,280	Damage estimate	South Coast Air Basin
	19,920	Control cost	South Coast Air Basin
Chernick and Caverhill (1991)	3,700	Control cost	California
	340	Control cost	Out of California
	5,570	Control cost	Massachusetts
Wiel (1991)	1,240	Control cost	Nevada
So. Calif. Gas (1991)	3,640	Control cost	South Coast Air Basin
So. Calif. Edison (1991)	2,760	Damage estimate	South Coast Air Basin
	19,450	Control cost	South Coast Air Basin
		CO	
Bernow and Marron (1990)	860	Control cost	Urban areas
CEC (1993)	3	Damage estimate	South Coast Air Basin
	9,800	Control cost	South Coast Air Basin
Chernick and Caverhill (1991)	900	Control cost	Massachusetts
Wiel (1991)	970	Control cost	Nevada
So. Calif. Gas (1991)	200	Control cost	California
		NO_x	
Bernow and Marron (1990)	6,830	Control cost	Northeast United States
	275,100	Control cost	Southern California
CEC (1993)	15,270	Damage estimate	South Coast Air Basin
	27,830	Control cost	South Coast Air Basin
Chernick and Caverhill (1991)	13,190	Control cost	California
	3,070	Control cost	Out of California
	6,830	Control cost	Massachusetts
	1,870	Damage estimate	New York
	1,720	Damage estimate	Unspecified
Wiel (1991)	7,140	Control cost	Nevada
So. Calif. Gas (1991)	12,790	Control cost	South Coast Air Basin
So. Calif. Edison (1991)	4,780	Damage estimate	South Coast Air Basin
	27,160	Control cost	South Coast Air Basin

Note: The cited studies presented emission values in constant or current dollars of various years. The emission values have been converted into 1990 constant dollars via the consumer price index. Emission values estimated by the California Energy Commission (CEC) were presented in $/ton/year. It was determined, by checking the original data sources from which CEC derived its estimates and CEC's adjustments to value estimates, that CEC's estimates were actually in $/ton.

Table 7-9

Emission Damage Values for California and Elsewhere (\$/Ton, 1990\$)

	Emission Value	
Pollutant	California	Other U.S. Regions
NMOG	20,000	5,000
CO	5,000	950
NO_x	26,000	7,000

Present Value of AFV Life-Cycle Emission Reductions

The present value of life-cycle emission reductions by AFV type is calculated by discounting annual emission reductions by the AFV type over its lifetime. Annual AFV emission reductions are, in turn, calculated from annual baseline GV emissions and from AFV emission reduction rates. The method and assumptions for calculating AFV emission reductions have been presented above.

The sensitivity analysis shows that baseline GV emissions are important in determining AFV cost-effectiveness. In addition, it is believed that actual on-road NMOG and CO exhaust emissions from GVs are two to four times higher than the emissions estimated with models developed by the EPA or the California Air Resources Board (NRC 1991). Because of the uncertainty and the importance of baseline GV emissions, two sets of these emissions are assumed here: the first uses the GV emissions estimated with Mobile5A; the second employs the Mobile5A-estimated GV emissions multiplied by a factor of four for the exhaust emissions of NMOG, CO, and air toxics.

Per-Vehicle Dollar Value of AFV Emission Reductions

The per-vehicle dollar value of emission reductions by AFV type is calculated by multiplying total emission reductions by dollars-per-ton emission values per AFV type. As seen in Table 7-10, four sets of AFV emission reduction values have been calculated from the two sets of imputed emission values (California and non-California values) and the two sets of baseline GV emissions (Mobile5A-estimated and on-road adjusted GV emissions).

131

Table 7-10

Present Value of Per-Vehicle Dollar Value of Alternative-Fuel-Vehicle Emission Reductions ($/Ton, 1990$)

GV Emissions	Non-California Values		California Values	
	Mobile5A Estimated	On-Road Adjusted	Mobile5A Estimated	On-Road Adjusted
RFG	460	1,700	2,170	8,110
M85 FFV	800	2,590	3,340	10,970
M100 FFV	920	2,770	3,800	11,720
M85 dedicated	1,030	3,200	4,330	13,750
M100 dedicated	1,140	3,570	4,850	15,550
E85 FFV	660	2,200	2,790	9,440
Dual-fuel LPGV	1,260	4,160	5,540	18,600
Dual-fuel CNGV	1,360	4,570	5,900	20,240
Dedicated CNGV	1,550	5,170	6,840	23,260
EV	2,740	8,740	12,430	41,200

Per-vehicle AFV emission reductions can be worth thousands to tens of thousands of dollars, depending on vehicle types and assumptions about per-ton emission values and baseline GV emissions. Among the ten AFV types, EVs have the highest emission reduction values; CNGVs and LPGVs have the next-highest values; dedicated methanol vehicles are next; methanol FFVs have low values; and RFG and E85 FFVs have the lowest values. The magnitude of the emission reduction values reflects the magnitude of per-vehicle emission reductions. That is, EVs have the largest amount of total emission reductions, whereas RFG and E85 FFVs have the smallest amount of total emission reductions.

Per-vehicle emission reduction values are very different with per-ton emission values and baseline GV emissions. Between the lowest value (combination of the non-California emission values and Mobile5A-estimated GV emissions) and the highest value (the combination of the California emission values and on-road adjusted GV emissions), the per-vehicle emission reduction value for a given AFV type can be changed by more than a factor of 12.

The per-vehicle emission reduction values in Table 7-10 are attributable to emission reductions for each of the seven pollutants, and the contribution of each air pollutant to emission reduction values varies among the ten AFV types. (Note that emissions of some air toxic pollutants may be increased by certain AFV types, thus contributing to decreases in per-vehicle emission reduction values. See Table 7-5 for the air toxic increases by certain AFV types.) The order of the pollutants, in terms of the significance of their contributions, is CO, NMOG, benzene, and 1,3-butadiene for RFG; NMOG, benzene, CO, and NO_x for methanol and ethanol vehicles; NMOG, CO, benzene, and 1,3-butadiene for LPGVs and CNGVs; and CO, NMOG, benzene, and NO_x for EVs.

Magnitude of Vehicle or Fuel Subsidies Based on AFV Emission Reduction Values

Life-cycle costs for most AFV types are higher than those for baseline GVs. The higher life-cycle costs for RFG, methanol, and ethanol vehicles are predominantly caused by increases in per-mile fuel costs, whereas the higher life-cycle costs for LPGVs, CNGVs, and EVs are caused by increases in vehicle initial prices. To encourage use of AFVs for curbing air pollution problems, price subsidies equal to dollar values of AFV emission reductions need to be provided to AFV users.

Two types of AFV subsidies can be designed: vehicle price subsidies and fuel price subsidies. It is commonly assumed that vehicle initial prices affect the purchasing choice of vehicle types and that fuel prices affect vehicle usage. Initial vehicle price subsidies would therefore encourage the purchase of LPGVs, CNGVs, and EVs (battery subsidies could be designed for EVs to reduce battery-replacement costs). Per-vehicle price subsidies could be set equal to the dollar value of the vehicle's emission reductions.

Per-mile fuel costs for methanol and ethanol vehicles and for RFG are higher than those for GVs fueled with conventional gasoline. In addition, high methanol and ethanol costs relative to gasoline on a per-mile basis may encourage FFV users to switch from methanol and ethanol to gasoline, resulting in no emission reduction benefits from FFVs. Life-cycle fuel price subsidies on methanol and ethanol, set at a level equal to per-vehicle emission reduction values, could prevent such a fuel switch.

Table 7-11 presents the estimated fuel price subsidies for RFG, methanol, and ethanol vehicles and vehicle price subsidies for LPGVs, CNGVs, and EVs. As the table shows, the amount of fuel or vehicle subsidies based on AFV emission reduction values is substantial. In fact, with California emission values and on-road adjusted GV emissions, fuel subsidies or vehicle subsidies are far greater than fuel prices, or even vehicle prices themselves. To actually provide these amounts of subsidies may be unrealistic. How-

Table 7-11

Vehicle and Fuel Price Subsidies for Alternative-Fuel Vehicles (1990$)

$/Ton Value	Non-California Value		California Value	
GV Emissions	MB5 Estimated	On-Road Adjusted	MB5 Estimated	On-Road Adjusted
Fuel Price Subsidy (Cents/Gal)				
RFG	13	47	59	222
Methanol (based on M85 FFV)	16	50	65	213
Methanol (based on M100 FFV)	13	40	54	168
Methanol (based on M85 dedicated)	22	68	92	393
Methanol (based on M100 dedicated)	18	56	76	243
Ethanol (based on E85 FFV)	16	54	68	229
Vehicle Price Subsidy ($/Vehicle)				
Dual-fuel LPGV	1,260	4,160	5,540	18,600
Dual-fuel CNGV	1,360	4,570	5,900	20,240
Dedicated CNGV	1,550	5,170	6,840	23,260
EV	2,740	8,740	12,430	41,200

ever, because these subsidies were calculated relative to conventional GVs, conventional gasoline vehicles could be taxed at their emission damage values, and use of AFVs would have relative advantages even without subsidies.

Table 7-11 shows four different methanol price subsidies for a given case, depending on the type of methanol vehicle (i.e., M85 FFVs, M100 FFVs, M85 dedicated, and M100 dedicated). In reality, it would be impossible to differentiate methanol price subsidies based on methanol vehicle types. For practical purposes, the average of the four methanol price subsidies may need to be adopted.

Providing the amounts of fuel or vehicle price subsidies estimated above for AFVs would reduce life-cycle AFV costs substantially. Table 7-12 presents the AFV life-cycle cost changes with inclusion of vehicle or fuel price subsidies. As the table shows, after the subsidies, use of most AFV types in fact leads to net cost savings for the case with California emission values or the case with non-California emission values but on-road GV emissions. Net cost savings vary among the ten AFV types. The greatest cost savings, over $30,000 per vehicle, occur for EVs for the case with California emission values and on-road adjusted GV emissions. The results imply that, by taking into account AFV

Table 7-12

**Changes in Alternative-Fuel-Vehicle Life-Cycle Costs
with Inclusion of Vehicle or Fuel Subsidies
(Relative to Gasoline Vehicle Life-Cycle Costs) (1990$)**

$/Ton Value	Non-California Value		California Value	
GV Emissions	Mobile 5A Estimated	On-Road Adjusted	Mobile 5A Estimated	On-Road Adjusted
RFG	170	−1,070	−1,540	−7,480
M85 FFV	710	−1,080	−1,830	−9,460
M100 FFV	1,110	−750	−1,780	−9,700
M85 dedicated	−240	−2,410	−3,540	−12,960
M100 dedicated	120	−2,310	−3,590	−14,290
E85 FFV	2,060	520	−70	−6,720
Dual-fuel LPGV	−260	−3,160	−4,540	−17,600
Dual-fuel CNGV	−1,260	−4,470	−5,800	−19,240
Dedicated CNGV	−2,150	−5,770	−6,940	−23,860
EV	6,910	910	−2,770	−31,550

emission reduction values, use of AFVs in California (where the worst air pollution problems occur) will probably make economic sense. In other U.S. regions, if one believes that actual on-road GV emissions are much higher than estimated, use of all AFV types except E85 FFVs will make economic sense.

The calculations for AFV subsidies here take into account AFV emission reduction benefits only. AFVs may have other social benefits as well, such as reductions in CO_2 emissions and increases in energy security achieved by diversifying energy sources for the transportation sector (use of RFG, however, may not achieve energy security benefits). Providing the subsidies reflecting these benefits would certainly make AFVs even more attractive.

Conclusions

The estimated emission control cost-effectiveness of ten AFV types shows that CNGVs are the most cost-effective AFV type in regulating air-pollutant emissions; E85 FFVs are the least cost-effective AFV type; methanol vehicles, LPGVs, and EVs fall in between. A sensitivity analysis of various cases representing changes in values for major cost and emission parameters suggests that the cost-effectiveness of CNGVs changes very little; they are always the most cost-effective vehicle type. Cost-effectiveness of other vehicle types can change dramatically with changes in values for major cost and emission parameters. However, the ranking of the ten AFV types according to their cost-effectiveness remains essentially unchanged, except that under certain circumstances (i.e., high fuel costs, low emission reductions), ethanol and methanol FFVs and RFG could become very expensive.

Per-vehicle dollar values of emission reductions are estimated to be significant. Fuel or vehicle price subsidies that are equal to emission reduction values can change AFV life-cycle costs dramatically. In fact, providing the fuel and vehicle price subsidies estimated here for AFVs would change most AFV types from net cost increases to net cost decreases.

Acknowledgments

This work was sponsored primarily by the U.S. Department of Energy, Deputy Under Secretary for Policy, Planning, and Analysis, Office of Environmental Analysis, under contract W-31-109-ENG-38. Early work was sponsored by the California Institute for Energy Efficiency, when the author worked in the Institute of Transportation Studies, University of California at Davis. The author thanks Mark DeLuchi of the Institute of Transportation Studies, University of California at Davis; David Greene of Oak Ridge National Laboratory; Jeff

---

Appendix 7-1

Alternative-Fuel-Vehicle Emission Control Cost-Effectiveness for Various Cases ($/Ton, 1990$)

AFV Type	Base Case	Case 1: AFV Prices Low	High	Case 2: Fuel Prices Low	High	Case 3: AFV Emission Reductions Low	High	Case 4: On-Road GV Emissions	Case 5: No Air Toxics
RFG	3,620	N/A	N/A	1,510	5,730	17,660	1,850	940	3,990
M85 FFV	7,520	6,530	8,520	4,950	10,090	14,580	4,170	2,220	9,450
M100 FFV	9,030	8,130	9,920	5,900	12,150	15,380	5,310	2,820	11,730
M85 dedicated	2,940	2,600	3,350	1,210	4,740	5,470	1,890	890	3,640
M100 dedicated	4,090	3,760	4,410	2,020	6,160	7,010	2,820	1,210	5,000
E85 FFV	15,730	14,570	16,890	8,570	22,890	38,670	8,010	4,510	21,340
DF LPGV	2,680	2,150	3,220	30	6,000	3,640	2,010	760	3,210
DF CNGV	250	−270	760	−1,420	1,910	320	190	70	290
Dedicated CNGV	−1,270	−1,700	−850	−2,580	40	−1,590	−1,040	−360	−1,470
EV	10,200	50	11,306	9,270	11,120	10,410	10,000	2,890	11,000

Alson of the U.S. Environmental Protection Agency; and Dan Santini of Argonne National Laboratory for their helpful comments and suggestions. The author is solely responsible for the content of this chapter.

References

Bernow, S.S., and D.B. Marron. 1990. *Valuation of Environmental Externalities for Energy Planning and Operations. May 1990 Update.* Boston: Tellus Institute. May.

California Air Resources Board (CARB). 1991. *Proposed Regulations for California Phase 2 Reformulated Gasoline.* Technical support document. Sacramento. October 4.

California Energy Commission (CEC). 1993. *Electricity Report.* P104-92-001. Sacramento. January.

Chernick, P., and E. Caverhill. 1991. "Methods of Valuing Environmental Externalities." *Electricity Journal,* March, pp. 46–59.

Federal Highway Administration (FHWA). 1992. *Cost of Owning and Operating Automobiles, Vans, and Light Trucks, 1991.* Report prepared by Jack Faucett Associates, Bethesda, Md. Washington, D.C.: Federal Highway Administration, Office of Highway Information Management, U.S. Department of Transportation. April.

Murrell, J.D., K.H. Hellman, and R.M. Heavenrich. 1993. *Light-Duty Automotive Technology and Fuel Economy Trends Through 1993.* EPA/AA/TDG/93-01. Ann Arbor, Mich.: U.S. Environmental Protection Agency, Office of Air and Radiation, Office of Mobile Sources, Emission Control Technology Division, Control Technology and Applications Branch. May.

National Research Council (NRC). 1991. *Rethinking the Ozone Problem in Urban and Regional Air Pollution.* Washington, D.C.: National Academy Press.

Southern California Edison Company. 1991. "Testimony of Southern California Edison Company in Response to the Commission's Order Instituting Investigation and Order Instituting Rulemaking to Develop Utility Involvement in the Market for Low-Emission Vehicles, Exhibit A." Rosemead, Calif. October 23.

Southern California Gas Company. 1991. "Testimony Before California Public Utility Commission in the Matter of the Application of Southern California Gas Company for Authority to Revise Its Rates and Recover Costs for Implementation of Its Natural Gas Vehicle Market Development Program." Los Angeles. June 14.

U.S. Environmental Protection Agency (U.S. EPA). 1992. "Inspection/Maintenance Program Requirements. Final Rule." *Federal Register* 57: 52950–53014.

137

Wang, Q., D. Sperling, and J. Olmstead. 1993. *Emission Control Cost-Effectiveness of Alternative-Fuel Vehicles.* Technical paper 931841. Warrendale, Penn.: Society of Automotive Engineers.

Wiel, S. 1991. "The New Environmental Accounting: A Status Report." *Electricity Journal*, November, pp. 46–55.

Chapter Eight

A Social Cost Analysis of Alternative Fuels for Light Vehicles

MARK FULMER AND STEPHEN BERNOW

In this chapter, we present a social cost analysis of alternative fuels for light-duty vehicles—gasoline, natural gas, methanol, and electricity—taking into account projected improvements in vehicle efficiencies and changes in vehicle emissions requirements. More accurately, this analysis might be considered a *partial* social cost analysis because other impacts that may not be fully internalized—such as energy security, congestion, water pollution, accidents, safety, and noise—have not been included. Also, technologies such as solar- and hydrogen-fueled cars, which are not expected to be market-ready within the decade, have not been considered.

We applied a societal perspective in five respects, as follows: First, we applied monetary environmental externality costs to air pollutant emissions. Second, we included all costs of the different vehicles, without regard to whether the cost would be incurred by the fuel provider, vehicle owner, or other. Third, we ignored taxes, subsidies, and other transfer payments.[1] Fourth, we used a societal discount rate of 3 percent real. Finally, we took the full fuel cycle into account by

---

[1] Because fuel taxes are used to pay for the necessary road infrastructure, they should ideally be included in a social cost analysis. They were not included here because of state-to-state variations, particularly with respect to alternative fuels.

estimating the "upstream" emissions from fuel extraction, production, and delivery.

We applied two sets of monetized environmental externality costs (cost per ton of pollutant emitted) to the direct vehicle emissions: one set adopted by the California Public Utility Commission, based on southern California air quality regulations, and a second set adopted by the Massachusetts Department of Public Utilities for electric utility resource planning (Bernow and Marron 1990; California PUC 1991). These reflect conditions in two different settings: a severely polluted, densely populated urban area (the South Coast Air Quality Management District [SCAQMD] in southern California) and a less polluted urban area. Both sets of values are based principally on the "regulators' revealed preference" method, in which the marginal costs of pollution control at the point of emissions embodied in existing environmental policy and regulation are used for the externality values in utility sector planning. The lower (Massachusetts) values were applied to the upstream emissions throughout the analysis.[2]

Ideally, integrated energy/environmental planning for transportation would address the complex tradeoffs between mode choice and related land use, frequency and distance of trips, environmental impacts in media other than air, and other economic factors. However, because the integrated planning paradigm is relatively new and most alternatively fueled vehicles are in their infancy, we took a limited approach, examining the costs and benefits of alternative vehicle fuels relative to those of major competing fuels in light-duty vehicles and holding other factors constant.

Assumptions

Two basic scenarios were evaluated, referred to as "near-term" and "longer-term." For natural gas and methanol vehicles (NGVs and MVs), the longer-term scenario assumes a *well-developed* market: factory-built dedicated vehicles and high sales at the public refueling stations. For electric vehicles (EVs), the longer-term scenario assumes a long battery life and the low end of the incremental cost estimates. The near-term scenario for natural gas– and methanol–fueled vehicles assumes the present, *minimally developed* market: retrofitting existing cars and low load factors at the public refueling stations. The near-

---

[2] It can be argued that because large amounts of petroleum refinery capacity are located in highly populated and polluted areas (e.g., New Jersey, southern California, and Houston, Texas), the congested urban values might be more appropriate.

term EV scenario assumes near-term forecasts of battery life and incremental vehicle costs. The basic vehicle model and operating characteristics (miles driven, driving conditions) were assumed constant across the different fuels.

Vehicle Cost and Performance

Table 8-1 presents the vehicle costs of the alternatively fueled vehicles. As the table shows, NGVs are anticipated to be about 17 percent more costly than gasoline vehicles in the near term and about 7 percent more costly in the longer term. The bulk of this additional cost is for the high-pressure compressed natural gas cylinder necessary to store the on-board fuel. MVs are expected to be only marginally more expensive than gasoline vehicles in the near term and equivalent in the longer term. EVs are assumed to be 70 percent more expensive than gasoline vehicles in the near term and 15 percent more expensive in the longer term, with the majority of the additional costs being due to the batteries. All costs in the longer-term scenario account for the additional costs necessarily incurred by the internal combustion engine vehicles (ICVs) in order to meet more stringent emissions requirements (CARB 1990).

The standard gasoline vehicle, MV, and near-term NGV are assumed to have a vehicle life of about 125,000 miles, or 12 years at our assumed annual vehicle-miles traveled. EVs are assumed to have a somewhat extended life—150,000 miles (15 years). This is due to a simpler powertrain and the fact that electric motors have much longer lives than internal combustion engines. The one-year life extension for NGVs in the longer term is due to the anticipated advantage of reduced engine wear with gaseous fuels.[3]

This reduction in NGV engine wear also accounts for the reduced maintenance cost estimated for NGVs in the longer-term scenario. The reduced EV maintenance costs are due to the relative simplicity of the EV drivetrain relative to vehicles with internal combustion engines (e.g., DeLuchi 1992). The reduced insurance cost for EVs is due to the fact that insurance costs are levelized over more years, and that insurance costs in the latter years are not only discounted more but also are lower because of reduced insurance coverage of the older vehicle (DeLuchi 1992). Note that this analysis does not take into account

---

[3] Much of the engine wear in a liquid-fueled engine comes during the cold start, when the fuel condenses and then combusts on the cylinder walls.

Table 8-1

Vehicle Costs of Gasoline and Alternatively Fueled Vehicles, Near-Term and Longer-Term Scenarios (1992$)

	Gasoline (a)	Natural Gas (b)	Methanol (c)	Electricity (d)
Vehicle costs [1]				
Near term	$14,000	$16,500	$14,400	$24,000
Longer term	$14,370	$15,400	$14,370	$16,170
Vehicle life, years [2]				
Near term	12	12	12	15
Longer term	12	13	12	15
Levelized annual maintenance cost [3]				
Near term	$436	$436	$436	$291
Longer term	$436	$353	$436	$291
Levelized annual insurance cost [4]				
Near term	$468	$484	$468	$443
Longer term	$468	$471	$468	$443
Fuel costs ($/GJ)				
High fuel [5]	$8.09	$4.25	$14.00	$13.89
High distribution [6]	$1.14	$4.02	$3.51	$7.01
High total	$9.23	$8.27	$17.51	$20.90
Low fuel [5]	$6.28	$3.75	$9.00	$8.33
Low distribution [6]	$1.14	$2.14	$2.13	$7.01
Low total	$7.42	$5.89	$11.13	$15.34
Vehicle efficiency				
Near term (l/100 km) [7]	7.8			
Relative to gasoline [8]		1.00	1.00	3.4
Longer term (l/100 km) [7]	4.7			
Relative to gasoline [8]		1.1	1.15	2.9

(1) (a) Longer-term gasoline vehicle incremental costs from CARB (1990) (emissions control improvement) and Union of Concerned Scientists (1991) (efficiency improvement).
    (b) Incremental NGV costs based on DeLuchi et al. (1988), CARB (1990), U.S. DOE (1990), and U.S. EPA (1990).
    (c) Incremental methanol costs based on estimates from DeLuchi et al. (1988), CARB (1990), Krupnick et al. (1990), OTA (1990), and U.S. DOE (1990).
    (d) Incremental electric vehicle costs based on estimates from CARB (1990) and U.S. DOE (1990).
(2) (a) Based on a 192,000–km vehicle life.
    (b) Natural gas vehicle life assumed to be the same in near term, and 1 year (8.3 percent longer in the longer term). The longer life of NGVs is due to reduced engine wear during cold starts. DeLuchi et al. (1988) estimate NGV to have 23 percent longer life than gasoline equivalent.
    (c) Assumes same life as gasoline vehicle
    (d) Based on DeLuchi (1992), which estimates EV having 33 percent longer life than standard gasoline vehicles (mileage basis).
(3) (a) From FHWA (1990) and DeLuchi (1992). Levelized over life of vehicle.

(b) In longer term, assumes maintenance at 80 percent of that of gasoline vehicle (DeLuchi et al. 1988).
(c) Assumes the same as gasoline vehicles.
(d) From DeLuchi (1992).
(4) (a) From DeLuchi (1992.) Assumes collision damage insurance is carried for first 5 years.
    (b) Calculated using methodology in DeLuchi (1992). Assumes that the vehicle carries collision damage insurance for first 6 years.
    (c) Assumes the same as gasoline vehicles.
    (d) From DeLuchi (1992). Assumes that the vehicle carries collision damage insurance for first 6.5 years.
(5) (a) From EIA (1993), Tables D3 and E3. Levelized from 1995 to 2010.
    (b) From EIA (1993), Tables E3 and F3, delivered industrial price. Levelized from 1995 to 2010.
    (c) Based on estimates from DeLuchi et al. (1988), Krupnick et al. (1990), U.S. DOE (1990) and U.S. EPA (1990).
    (d) Assumes range of fuel and operating cost for existing coal-steam or natural gas combined-cycle powerplants.
(6) (a) From U.S. EPA (1989).
    (b) From DeLuchi et al. (1988).
    (c) From U.S. EPA (1990).
    (d) Assumes $500 for home recharger, levelized over life of vehicle.
(7) (a) Based on Union of Concerned Scientists (1991), Table C7.
    (b) Based on DeLuchi et al. (1988).
    (c) Based on DeLuchi et al. (1988).
    (d) Based on Union of Concerned Scientists (1991), Table C15. UCS (1991) assumes that EVs will increase in efficiency, however not as quickly as gasoline and other IC engine vehicles.

other possible differences, such as in collision or liability insurance rates, between EVs and gasoline vehicles.

The base gasoline vehicle efficiencies in the two scenarios are based on data from the Union of Concerned Scientists (1991).[4] In the near term, no efficiency advantages are assumed for MVs or NGVs, but in the longer term, we assume some increased efficiencies due to the implementation of engines optimized around the higher octanes of the alternative fuels.

The particularly high efficiency of electric vehicles illustrates two interesting points related to motor efficiency and vehicle design. First, electric motors are much more efficient than any kind of heat engine, the efficiency of the latter being ultimately limited by thermodynamics. Thus EVs are inherently more efficient per unit of energy *directly* consumed by the vehicle. However, when the efficiency of the power-plant supplying electricity to the vehicle is taken into account, the primary fuel use per mile traveled by an EV is comparable to that of combustion engine-driven vehicles. Second, because of the very low energy and power density of the batteries, many efficiency improvements—such as very low drag design, very light materials, and low-

[4] It should be noted that the Union of Concerned Scientists (1991) assumes a large increase in fuel economy for the longer-term scenario—up to 50 miles per gallon. This aggressive value should not be seen as a prediction, but rather as a "high-end" assumption in the analysis. The impacts on the results of differing efficiency assumptions are addressed in the sensitivity analysis section of our results.

friction tires—will likely be standard on EVs.[5] In contrast, NGVs are not likely to have these added efficiency measures. In fact, most North American NGVs are large, less efficient, American-built automobiles or light trucks.

Fuel Costs

The electricity and gas costs used here reflect North American utility *marginal costs*, including transmission and distribution. Marginal costs more accurately reflect the true resource cost than do rates or tariffs, and their use eliminates the assumption of political or strategic pricing of the fuels.[6] For gasoline and methanol, we assume that the market prices reflect producers' marginal costs of gathering, transporting, and refining the fuels. The costs of gasoline and natural gas powerplant fuel were taken from the U.S. Department of Energy's long-range energy outlook (EIA 1993). Methanol prices were based on various estimates for the production and distribution cost of methanol (DeLuchi et al. 1988; CARB 1990; Krupnick et al. 1990; OTA 1990; U.S. DOE 1990).

Because of the differences among the states and ever-evolving energy policy, all sales taxes, fuel taxes, and government grants are excluded from our analysis.

Vehicle Emissions

The vehicle emissions factors presented in Tables 8-2 and 8-3 are used throughout the analysis. In the near-term scenario, we assume gasoline vehicle emissions meet the requirements of the 1990 federal Clean Air Act Amendments (CAAA). In the long-term scenario, we assume gasoline vehicle emissions meet the requirements of the California ultra-low-emissions vehicle (ULEV) standards. Tailpipe emissions from alternatively fueled vehicles in either scenario are assumed to be the lower of either the appropriate standard or published estimates of vehicle emissions characteristics.

It is likely that EVs would be recharged during off-peak hours when low-operating-cost "baseload" units would be on the operating margin of the utility system. The mix of such units and their emissions factors would differ from one utility system to another, particularly in

---

[5] Most of the vehicle efficiency enhancements assumed on EVs could be applied to the other vehicles as well. However, in general, these enhancements are seen as justifiable only on EVs because of their particularly poor energy storage capabilities.

[6] Ideally, electricity and gas tariffs would send the appropriate market signals reflecting the marginal resource costs.

Table 8-2

Pollutant Emissions Factors for Gasoline, Methanol, and Natural Gas Vehicles (Grams Pollutant per Mile)

	Near Term [a]			Longer Term [b]		
	Gasoline	Natural Gas	Methanol	Gasoline	Natural Gas	Methanol
CO_2	307	230	477	184	125	477
NO_x	0.4000	0.4000	0.4000	0.2000	0.2000	0.2000
VOC	0.1250	0.0625	0.0838	0.0400	0.0100	0.0268
CO	3.4000	1.4000	3.4000	1.7000	0.2000	1.7000
TSP	0.0032	0.0000	0.0000	0.0032	0.0000	0.0000
SO_x	0.0470	0.0000	0.0000	0.0470	0.0000	0.0000

Note: Species other than those shown will be emitted: however, data are less complete for these species, and their contribution to net externality costs are assumed to be small relative to those shown above and are therefore omitted. MV and NGV particulate and SO_x emissions are assumed to be negligible relative to those of gasoline vehicles. See text for further discussion and references on emissions characteristics.

[a] Near term assumes gasoline vehicles meet the emissions promulgated in the 1990 U.S. Clean Air Act Amendments (CAAA). CO_2 values based on 7.8 l/100 km gasoline efficiency. NGVs VOC emissions are assumed to be 50 percent less than gasoline standards (including reactivity adjustments). Methanol VOC emissions are assumed to be 33 percent less than gasoline standards (including reactivity adjustments). Methanol vehicles CO emissions are assumed to meet applicable standards (i.e., no emissions benefits). NGVs and methanol vehicles NO_x emissions are assumed to meet applicable standards (i.e., no emissions benefits). MV and NGV particulate and SO_x emissions are assumed to be negligible relative to that of gasoline vehicles.

[b] Longer term assumes gasoline vehicles meet California ultra-low-emissions-vehicle (ULEV)requirements. CO_2 values based on 4.7 l/100 km gasoline efficiency. NGVs and methanol vehicles NO_x emissions are assumed to meet applicable standards (i.e., no emissions benefits). Methanol vehicles CO emissions are assumed to meet applicable standards (i.e., no emissions benefits). NGVs and methanol vehicles NO_x emissions are assumed to meet applicable standards (i.e., no emissions benefits).

the near term, and could change over time as cleaner plants are brought into service. In the near-term scenario, we have assumed that EVs would be charged with power generated from a mix of existing coal plants with the characteristics of those now serving the north-central United States. In the longer-term scenario, we have assumed that EVs would be charged with power generated from a new natural gas combined-cycle powerplant with steam injection for nitrogen oxides (NO_x) reduction and an oxidizing catalyst for carbon monoxide (CO) and volatile organic compounds (VOCs) reduction. To the degree that a different mix of marginal plants is available during EV recharging times or could evolve over time, the marginal externality costs (as well as the marginal cost of electricity for recharging) would

Table 8-3

Pollutant Emissions Factors for Electric Generation and Electric Vehicles

	NO_x	SO_x	CO_2	CH_4	CO	TSP	VOC
Existing north-central U.S. coal (meeting 2000 standards) (gm/kWh)	2.3700	4.1800	937	0.0062	0.1320	0.2244	0.0220
Effective electric vehicle emissions at 0.222 kWh/km (near-term scenario) (gm/km)	0.5261	0.9280	208	0.0014	0.0293	0.0498	0.0049
New natural gas combined cycle (gm/kWh)	0.2762	0.0021	416	0.0001	0.0769	0.0454	0.0294
Effective electric vehicle emissions at 0.156 kWh/km (longer-term scenario) (gm/km)	0.0431	0.0003	65	1.56E-05	0.0120	0.0071	0.0046

Source: UCS (1991), Technical Appendices, Tables H3, I1, I2, I3.

differ from those assumed here.[7] However, the two technologies chosen represent a reasonable envelope of "clean" and "dirty" technologies that could realistically be used for EV charging.

Upstream Emissions

The air emissions due to oil, gas, and coal extraction, processing, and transportation included in the analysis are shown in Table 8-4. The primary source for upstream emissions estimates is DeLuchi 1991. These values were corroborated and supplemented with data from U.S. DOE 1983 and Frische 1990.

The "downstream" pollution associated with equipment disposal is not addressed here. However, earlier work at Tellus Institute on the pollution generated during the life cycle of various materials indicates that the majority of pollution impacts occur in production and operation rather than in disposal (Tellus 1991).

Valuing Air Emissions Externalities

To value the air emissions in a social cost analysis, we applied the externality values presented in Table 8-5 to the tailpipe emissions of

---

[7] In the United States, a number of utility systems currently have a surplus of base-load coal-generating capacity; thus existing coal could remain on the operating margin for several years.

Table 8-4

**Upstream Pollutant Emissions
(Pound per MMBTU Consumed by Vehicle)**

Pollutant	Natural Gas	Gasoline	Methanol	Coal	Electricity generated from Natural Gas
CH_4[a]	0.42	0.14	0.26	2.12	0.53
CO[a]	0.16	0.21	0.16	0.09	0.24
$NMHC$[a]	0.01	0.02	0.02	0.01	0.02
NO_x[a]	0.24	0.18	0.44	0.10	0.35
CO_2[a]	70.19	70.69	101.25	18.93	46.51
SO_x[b]	2.86E-06	0.09	2.86-E06	0.01	7.15E-06

[a] CH_4, CO, NMHC, NO_x, and CO_2: Natural gas, gasoline emissions calculated from DeLuchi (1991), Vol. 1, Tables 2, 3, 10. Electric emissions from DeLuchi (1991), Vol. 1, Tables 2, 3; Vol. 2, Table D-8.

[b] SO_x: Natural gas and coal from U.S. DOE (1983), extraction, production, and transportation. Gasoline from Frische (1990). Methanol assumed to be produced from natural gas and thus has the same SO_x emissions as gas.

Table 8–5

Environmental Externality Costs (Levelized $/Ton) (1992$)

	NO_x	VOC	CO	CO_2	CH_4	TSP	SO_x
Urban/suburban[a]	$6,793	$5,539	$909	$23	$230	$4,180	$1,568
Congested urban[b]	$28,524	$20,374	$909	$23	$220	$6,171	$21,306

[a] Urban/suburban values are those adopted in Massachusetts for use in electric resource planning (Bernow and Marron 1990).

[b] Congested urban values from California PUC (1991). Applicable to the greater Los Angeles area.

the vehicles and to the powerplant emissions for electric vehicles. In both scenarios, we considered two sets of externality values, nominally referred to as "congested urban" and "urban/suburban." The congested urban values are derived from air quality regulation in the Los Angeles area, and the urban/suburban values are those adopted in Massachusetts for electric resource planning.

Other values could be used within the same framework. For example, recent values were developed by the California Energy Commission for the SCAQMD region (CEC 1993), based on "damage costing" techniques, which attempt to estimate impacts at the ends of the various pollutant pathways and to value them using market or marketlike behavior. The externalities for which these values were estimated included primarily human health, visibility, and crop impacts.

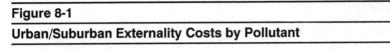

Figure 8-1

Urban/Suburban Externality Costs by Pollutant

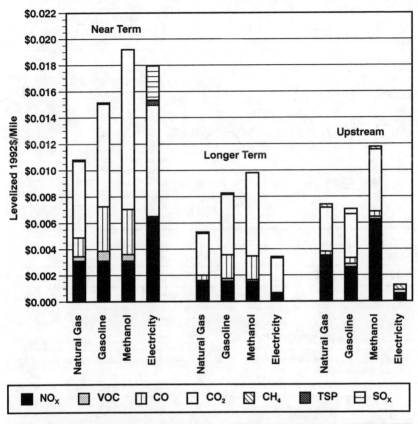

The CEC values for sulfur dioxide (SO_2), NO_x, and VOCs are between one-third and one-half of the PUC values, whereas the CEC value for TSP is about eight times the PUC value. A discussion of the "damage costing" and "regulators' revealed preference" approaches to externalities valuation can be found in Bernow and Biewald (1993).

The upstream emissions were valued at the lower urban/suburban costs throughout the analysis.[8] A more detailed analysis of externalities would distinguish between localized urban pollution and more dispersed regional pollution, and between demographic, climatological, and emissions patterns. The contributions of the individual

---

[8] See note 2, above.

pollutants to the overall externality cost are shown in Figure 8-1. For the urban/suburban values, NO_x and carbon dioxide (CO_2) emissions contribute the most to the externality costs. For the vehicles using internal combustion engines, CO emissions also contribute; for EVs, sulfur oxides (SO_x) emissions contribute substantially.[9] In the longer term, CO_2 emissions dominate the overall externality cost for all four fuels, owing to the dramatic reductions in other pollutants from more stringent regulations. The congested urban environmental externality value for EVs is relatively large because of the combination of higher SO_x emissions and the very high value placed on sulfur emissions in the Los Angeles area by regulators in California. For the upstream emissions, NO_x and CO_2 emissions account for the majority of the externality costs.

It is also important to note that the net emissions costs in the longer-term scenario are much less than in the near-term scenario because of the projected vehicle efficiency improvements, the very stringent emissions requirements, and in the case of the EVs, the relatively clean and efficient electricity generation.

Results

In both the near-term and longer-term scenarios, we calculated the life-cycle cost of owning and operating a light vehicle using gasoline or one of the alternative fuels, both with and without environmental externalities. In addition, the sensitivity of these results to input assumptions was explored, and critical parameters identified.

Baseline Results

Table 8-6 summarizes the life-cycle costs with and without environmental externalities. In the near term, with only direct costs included (e.g., not environmental externalities), gasoline vehicles have the lowest cost, followed by natural gas, methanol, and electric vehicles. In the longer-term scenario, electric vehicles have the lowest direct cost, followed by natural gas, gasoline, and methanol vehicles.

The inclusion of environmental externalities increases the cost of travel, but because the net externality values are so similar among the fuels (except electricity), they do not change the cost relationships between the different fuels. Nor are the externality costs particularly

---

[9] The large impact of SO_x emissions is due to our assumption that the electricity generated for EVs will come from coal. In regions where the marginal baseload fuel is natural gas, hydro, or nuclear, the SO_x emissions impacts will be greatly reduced.

high relative to the other costs of purchasing and operating a vehicle. In the near-term scenario, the congested urban environmental externality cost makes up less than 10 percent for the combustion engine

Table 8-6
Levelized Average Cost of Travel ($/Mile) (1992$)

COST COMPONENTS

| | | | | Externality Values | | |
| | | | | | Tailpipe/Powerplant | |
	Vehicle	Insurance and Repair	Fuel	Upstream	Congested Urban	Urban/ Suburban
Near term						
Natural gas	$0.167	$0.091	$0.031	$0.007	$0.011	$0.021
Gasoline	$0.141	$0.091	$0.036	$0.007	$0.015	$0.028
Methanol	$0.145	$0.091	$0.063	$0.012	$0.019	$0.030
Electricity	$0.202	$0.075	$0.020	$0.001	$0.018	$0.071
Longer term						
Natural gas	$0.146	$0.083	$0.017	$0.004	$0.005	$0.010
Gasoline	$0.145	$0.091	$0.022	$0.004	$0.008	$0.015
Methanol	$0.145	$0.091	$0.034	$0.006	$0.010	$0.015
Electricity	$0.138	$0.074	$0.016	$0.002	$0.003	$0.005

TOTALS

| | | With Externalities | |
| | | Tailpipe/Powerplant at | |
	Without Externalities	Congested Urban Costs	Urban/ Suburban Costs
Near term			
Natural gas	$0.289	$0.307	$0.317
Gasoline	$0.269	$0.291	$0.303
Methanol	$0.299	$0.330	$0.341
Electricity	$0.297	$0.316	$0.369
Longer term			
Natural gas	$0.245	$0.254	$0.259
Gasoline	$0.258	$0.270	$0.277
Methanol	$0.270	$0.286	$0.291
Electricity	$0.228	$0.233	$0.235

Note: Calculations based on Tables 8-1 through 8-5.

vehicles and about 25 percent for the EV. In the long-term scenario, these fractions are even less. However, it is important to note that we assume vehicles that pollute much less than typical 1992 new cars, let alone the aging fleet on the road today. If the urban/suburban externality values were applied to the tailpipe emissions of the U.S. 1988 fleet average (UCS 1991), the resulting externality cost would be almost three times greater than that of gasoline vehicles in the near-term scenario, and almost five times greater in the longer-term scenario. On the other hand, computer simulations using MOBIL5 and measurements of actual on-road emissions characteristics tend to be higher than the standards used here, indicating that our estimates of the emissions contributions to total costs for the IC engine vehicles are relatively conservative.

The assumption of the type of fuel used to generate the electricity for the EV is critical to these results. If in the near-term scenario, a new natural gas combined-cycle powerplant were assumed, then EVs would have life-cycle costs comparable to those of natural gas vehicles (but still not as low as for gasoline). On the other hand, if an existing coal-fired powerplant were assumed to be used in the longer-term scenario, then the EV's advantage would disappear. Finally, if EVs were charged using a renewable resource, the externality costs would be even lower, potentially making electricity the least-cost fuel. These scenarios highlight the important point that if air emissions externalities are included in transportation analysis, the marginal electric generating facilities serving the EVs must be identified and their emissions characteristics understood.

A second interesting variation considers the near-term scenario in which the vehicles are located in a highly polluted urban area but the marginal electric generating station is located in a more remote area. When the congested urban externality values are used for the tailpipe emissions and the urban/suburban values are used for regionally dispersed powerplant emissions, electric vehicles come close in cost to natural gas and methanol (but still not as low as gasoline) vehicles.

Sensitivity of Results to Key Parameters

Figure 8-2 illustrates the sensitivity of the results to variations in a number of important parameters. The x-axis in Figure 8-2 shows the fuel cost, including all fuel production, distribution, and infrastructure costs; the y-axis is the levelized cost per mile of travel.

For each fuel in Figure 8-2, there are two "boxes." The lower box for each fuel assumes the vehicle characteristics and costs of the longer-term scenario; the upper box for each fuel assumes the vehicle characteristics and costs of the near-term scenario. The bottom margin of each box represents the cost per mile of travel without environmental externalities. The top margin of each box is the cost per mile when the congested urban externality values are included. The area enclosed by the box represents the range of costs that could be expected for the given vehicle cost and efficiency assumptions.

The sensitivity of the results to fuel costs is seen in the slope of the bottom of each box. The steeper the slope, the less fuel-efficient the vehicle and the more sensitive the cost per mile is to fuel cost. However, none of the vehicles shown here is particularly sensitive to fuel cost; an almost 50 percent increase in fuel cost for NGVs increases the per-mile cost by only 3.5 percent. Even in the most sensitive case, methanol in the near term, a 50 percent increase in fuel costs increases the per-mile cost by only 5.4 percent.

Figure 8-2 also illustrates that the cost per mile of travel is highly sensitive to assumptions concerning vehicle cost and efficiency. The large gap between the near-term-scenario EV box and the longer-term-scenario EV box results primarily from the huge variation in assumed vehicle cost. The difference between the near-term-scenario box and the longer-term-scenario box for both methanol and natural gas results in each case from a combination of moderate differences in assumed vehicle cost between the two scenarios and the higher fuel efficiency assumed in the longer-term scenarios. The gap between the near-term and longer-term boxes for gasoline results exclusively from increased fuel efficiency in the longer-term scenario. The near-term and longer-term boxes in the methanol and the natural gas scenarios overlap slightly because the longer-term costs with environmental externalities happen to be greater than the near-term scenario costs without environmental externalities.

Limitations and Uncertainties

The large "gaps" between the near-term and longer-term sensitivity boxes in Figure 8-2 for the same fuel (which are due to differing assumptions on alternative-fuel-vehicle cost and fuel economy) make it very difficult to draw definitive conclusions regarding the relative merits of alternative vehicle fuels. Although it is true that in the longer term, EVs look to have a potential cost-per-mile advantage, if the vehicle costs do not come down as much as projected, if the vehicle life advantage assumed here does not occur, or if one of many other assumptions proves to be inaccurate, the results would change—i.e., stay in the range of the upper (near-term scenario) box.

Figure 8-2

Sensitivity of Levelized Average Cost of Travel to Fuel Cost, Externality Values, Vehicle Cost, and Efficiency

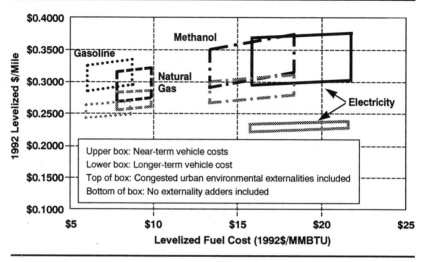

Market uncertainty, characteristics of service, and consumer behavior are very important issues treated only cursorily in this study. The ranges that the alternatively fueled vehicles can travel between refueling are generally significantly less than those of a gasoline vehicle (OTA 1990). EVs will not be able to be charged in four minutes or less, as can gasoline, methanol, and even natural gas vehicles (OTA 1990). Vehicles using different fuels will perform differently; MVs are expected to have *better* power and acceleration than gasoline vehicles, but with potential difficulties starting in cold weather. NGVs are anticipated to have slightly reduced performance relative to gasoline vehicles (because of the increased weight of the fuel cylinder), but decreased engine wear (DeLuchi et al. 1988). EVs will be much quieter and are expected to have reduced maintenance costs. How will consumers react to these differences? How should policymakers take these factors into account when contemplating alternative-fuel policies? These are important questions whose answers are beyond the scope of this study.

A related issue not explicitly dealt with in this study is the dynamics of technological change. The analyses here are, for the most part, snapshots of current technologies and present one possible projection of the future. How would a region or nation move from the present status quo to one of the longer-term scenarios described here? If technology progresses significantly differently than in our assumptions here, particularly in terms of vehicle costs, then the result could tilt in favor of or against any of the fuels. On the other hand, would different policies contribute to or retard the pace of technological change to different degrees for different technologies?

With regard to externalities, it should be noted that this analysis includes only air emissions, and not other nonpriced impacts on the environment, human health, and amenity. Also, the tailpipe emissions estimated here for the various IC engine vehicles are based on *standards*; rigorous modeling and empirical studies indicate that actual *on-road* emissions are generally higher than the standards and would result in still higher externality costs.

Finally, it should also be reiterated that this analysis is from a "societal" perspective and hence uses a low, societal discount rate. Using a higher, corporate or individual discount rate would tend to penalize vehicles with higher up-front costs, primarily EVs, and favor those with higher annual operating costs. The analysis is based on avoided fuel cost and ignores the fact that the costs would be split among various parties (fuel suppliers, federal and state governments, individual users, etc.). Full retail prices are not reflected. In particular, fuel taxes are not included; therefore, an individual user's perspective would be different.

Policy Implications

A key to setting policies on alternative fuels is understanding the goals that the policies are to meet, as fuel choice is not an end in itself. By including only direct and environmental externality costs, we have implicitly assumed that the goal of alterative fuels in light-duty vehicles is primarily improved air quality, subject to economic efficiency (i.e., which vehicle type is the least cost). Other quite reasonable goals for an alternative-fuel policy might include energy security, domestic economic development, or safety. Moreover, alternative-fuel policy is itself best placed within the broader context of integrated transportation energy and environment policy. Then, issues of urban congestion, land use, and the quality and place of *mobility* within the broader frame of access to goods, services, and other societal activities must come into play. Working toward these other goals might, in some cases, conflict with or, in others, contribute to the specific environmental goals addressed here. Nonetheless, our discussion focuses on policies that address environmental goals and how alternative vehicle fuels might fit in.

Standard Setting

Setting tailpipe and evaporative emissions standards is the most common transportation environmental policy and has resulted in the dramatic reductions in emissions seen since the early 1970s. Figure 8-1 indicates that setting standards can still be effective in reducing emissions. Emissions standards currently address only CO, NO_x, and VOCs. The externality savings of the reductions in the near-term standards (1990 Clean Air Act) to the longer-term standards (California ULEV) is still significant, let alone the difference in emissions between the typical cars on the road today and the levels assumed in the near-term scenario.

Setting tight standards also limits the effectiveness of using alternative fuels. Some of the inherent emissions benefits of using natural gas or methanol are eliminated when more stringent standards are applied to gasoline. For example, in both the near term and longer term, natural gas vehicles potentially offer significant CO reductions relative to gasoline or methanol, but in the longer term, the absolute CO savings is much less.

"Tailpipe" standards do not affect electric vehicles. Thus, although EVs can contribute to pollution reduction in congested metropolitan areas, there are regional pollution increases from their power supply sources. The emissions of EVs are set by the marginal generating mix supplying the EV and the stationary source emissions standards governing those facilities.[10] The large improvement seen from the near-term to the longer-term scenario is due solely to the different generating supply assumptions (coal in the near term, natural gas combined cycle in the longer term) and is not connected to any particular standard.

Efficiency Improvements

Improvements in vehicle efficiency, no matter the policy mechanism used to induce them, significantly decrease CO_2 and SO_x emissions, as well as all upstream emissions because of the reduction in fuel use. Although most transportation/air quality discussions—and regulations—have focused on CO and ozone precursors, *50 percent or more of the externality costs assumed here come from CO_2 alone.*[11] The exter-

---

[10] In addition to point source standards, the systemwide SO_2 limitations embodied in Title IV of the 1990 Clean Air Act Amendments also limit emissions from electric generation, particularly from baseload coal units.

[11] This result is a strong function of the CO_2 externality value used in the analysis. The externality value for CO_2 is very uncertain, and dollar-per-ton estimates have been made that are both significantly higher and lower than the one used here.

nality costs of the upstream emissions are often on the same order of magnitude as those of the direct emissions. Clearly, no matter what fuel is used, increased efficiency has a role to play in reducing pollution from transportation.

Within a given set of emissions standards and vehicle efficiency assumptions, the use of fuels other than gasoline can have significant benefits, but these benefits are generally on the same order of magnitude at best as the improvements gained from setting stricter standards and efficiency improvements. Policies encouraging alternative fuels can be effective in reducing emissions, but alternative fuels alone should not be the only vehicle-oriented policy addressing air quality issues.

The Elusive "Level Playing Field"

Given our conclusion that alternative fuels have a role to play in transportation environmental planning and policymaking, the large question becomes which fuel or fuels to support through which policy instruments. The analysis presented here and analyses elsewhere cannot point to a definitive "winner" in all contexts and conditions; differences in underlying conditions (e.g., location) and the uncertainty in many variables (e.g., vehicle mileage) could result in different fuels being least-cost. Therefore one approach, rather cavalierly put, is to "level the playing field"—let all the alternative fuels compete and "may the best fuel win." Of course, the winner may not be a single fuel, as different mixes of transportation fuel at different times and in different contexts may evolve.

A difficulty with this approach is that the least-cost solution in the long term may suffer from a poor starting position. For example, gasoline clearly has huge advantages in its existing infrastructure, and although natural gas has a nearly national transmission/distribution system in place, it does not yet have a widespread refueling system. By letting the market pick the winners, the implementation of options that in the longer term might be superior could be significantly impeded. Thus, focused policy initiatives to help maintain a level playing field *over the longer term* may be needed.

The electric vehicles in this analysis are a good example. Clearly, a huge amount of research and development is needed before EVs could be expected to make a significant dent in the light-vehicle market on economic merits alone. Policymakers at both the federal and state levels, recognizing the long-term potential of EVs, have chosen to support EV research financially, whereas the California LEV standards have gone as far as to effectively mandate a niche for EVs. Another promising vehicle type, fuel-cell vehicles, will likely need a similar publicly supported R&D effort to become marketable.

Other Policy Instruments

This discussion so far has centered on technology-oriented policy: what government can do to affect the technology in the marketplace—through emissions standards, efficiency improvements, or support of less polluting alternative fuels. However, the other side of the emissions equation is vehicle-miles traveled (VMT). A "clean" vehicle driven a lot could be, on the whole, more polluting than a less clean one driven less. Although promulgating standards and mandating fuels are somewhat easier solutions, policies to reduce VMT, particularly in regions out of Clean Air Act ozone attainment, might be more effective in reducing transportation-related emissions.

Pollution and/or fuel taxes may play a role in affecting driving behavior as well as vehicle purchase decisions and fuel choice.[12] Fees and/or restrictions on parking access in urban areas might also play a role, affecting congestion as well as urban air pollution. Incentives to reduce VMT either through trip reduction, van pooling, or mode shifting for commuters could also be effective in solving a number of problems at once. Land use decisions and infrastructure investments are important policy considerations that can interact with the other approaches. Enhanced vehicle inspections and maintenance requirements are being enacted in a number of states as an emission reduction strategy. Although analysis of these policies is beyond the scope of this paper, they should not be ignored when addressing the air pollution impacts of light-duty vehicles, no matter what the fuel.

Conclusions

In the near term, new gasoline vehicles will likely have the lowest direct costs and the lowest social cost when either set of environmental externalities is included. However, these results assume that gasoline vehicles will soon meet the relatively stringent requirements of the 1990 federal Clean Air Act Amendments, which restrict emissions to levels much lower than is typical of cars on the road today.

In the longer term, we find electricity to have the lowest direct costs and the lowest cost when either set of environmental externalities is included. However, the great uncertainty in key assumptions,

---

[12] Revenue-neutral pay-as-you-drive insurance is one such option that has been suggested.

such as externality values, vehicle costs, or electric generation source, does not allow for definitive conclusions. Any number of reasonable and plausible changes in the assumptions could tilt the balance in favor of any of the fuels examined here. As noted earlier, however, the balance might ultimately tilt toward a mix of vehicle fuels, depending on the context.

The inclusion of environmental externalities affects the relationship between EVs and the vehicles using internal combustion engines. When the power supplying an EV is generated with existing, relatively dirty coal powerplants, then the externality costs of the sulfur emissions add significantly to the cost of EVs. If new, clean-burning gas combined-cycle (or renewable) technology is applied, the reduced externality values relative to the internal combustion engine alternatives provide electric vehicles a significant savings.

References

Bernow, Stephen, and Bruce Biewald. 1993. *Environmental Sustainability as a Goal in Resource Planning and Policy.* Washington, D.C.: U.S. Congress, Office of Technology Assessment.

Bernow, Stephen, and Donald Marron. 1990. *Valuation of Environmental Externalities for Energy Planning and Operations.* May 1990 update. Boston: Tellus Institute.

California Air Resources Board (CARB). 1990. *Proposed Regulations of Low-Emissions Vehicles and Clean Fuels.* Staff report. Sacramento.

California Energy Commission (CEC). 1993. *1992 Electricity Report. Appendix F: Air Quality.* January. Sacramento.

California Public Utilities Commission (PUC). 1991. *Decision 91-06-022.* June 5. Sacramento.

DeLuchi, Mark. 1991. *Emissions of Greenhouse Gases for the Use of Transportation Fuels and Electricity.* Report ANL/ESD/TM-22. Argonne, Ill.: Argonne National Laboratory, Center for Transportation Research.

———. 1992. *Hydrogen Fuel-Cell Vehicles.* Research Report UCD-ITS-RR-92-14. Davis: University of California, Institute of Transportation Studies.

DeLuchi, Mark A., Robert A. Johnston, and Daniel Sperling. 1988. *Methanol Versus Natural Gas Vehicle: A Comparison of Resource Supply, Performance, Emissions, Fuel Storage, Safety, Costs, and Transitions.* SAE Technical Paper 881656. New York: Society of Automotive Engineers.

Energy Information Administration (EIA). 1993. *Annual Energy Out-*

look: Long Range Projections. Washington, D.C.: U.S. Department of Energy.

Federal Highway Administration (FHWA). 1991. *Cost of Owning and Operating Automobiles, Vans and Light Trucks, 1991*. Washington, D.C.: U.S. Department of Transportation, Office of Highway Information Management, Federal Highway Administration.

Frische, Ewe. 1990. *Total Emissions Model for Integrated Systems (TEMIS)*. Darmstadt, Germany: OKO Institut.

Krupnick, Alan J., Margaret Walls, and Michael A. Toman. 1990. *The Cost Effectiveness and Energy Security Benefits of Methanol Vehicles*. Discussion paper QE90-25. Washington, D.C.: Resource of the Future.

Office of Technology Assessment (OTA). 1990. *Replacing Gasoline: Alternative Fuels for Light-Duty Vehicles*. OTA-E-365. Washington, D.C.: U.S. Congress, Office of Technology Assessment.

Tellus Institute. 1991. *CSG/Tellus Institute Packaging Study: Assessing the Impacts of Production and Disposal of Packaging and Public Policy Measures to Alter Its Mix*. Boston, Mass.

Union of Concerned Scientists (UCS). 1991. *America's Energy Choices: Investing in a Strong Economy and a Clean Environment*. Technical Appendices. Cambridge, Mass.

U.S. Department of Energy (U.S. DOE). 1983. *Energy Technology Characterizations Handbook*. DOE/EP-0093. Washington, D.C.

———. 1990. *Assessment of Costs and Benefits of Flexible and Alternative Fuel Use in the U.S. Transportation Sector. Technical Report Four: Vehicle and Fuel Distribution Requirements*. DOE/PE/0095P. Washington, D.C.

U.S. Environmental Protection Agency (U.S. EPA). 1989. *Analysis of the Economic and Environmental Effects of Methanol as an Automotive Fuel*. Special report. Ann Arbor, Mich.: U.S. EPA, Office of Mobile Sources.

———. 1990. *Analysis of the Economic and Environmental Effects of Compressed Natural Gas as a Vehicle Fuel*. Vol. 1: *Passenger Cars and Light Trucks*. Special report. Ann Arbor, Mich.: U.S. EPA, Office of Mobile Sources.

Chapter Nine

A Consumer Surplus Analysis of Market-Based Demand Management Policies in Southern California

MICHAEL CAMERON

The severity of urban traffic congestion and mobile-source air pollution may be significantly reduced with market-based incentives. Policies such as congestion pricing and smog fees have become more attractive to policymakers who, faced with strict legal mandates and shrinking budgets, seek to manage travel demand rather than accommodate it through additions to infrastructure.[1] This chapter proposes a framework for analyzing the societal net benefits of market-based demand management policies and illustrates that framework by estimating the costs and benefits of a $0.05-per-mile VMT (vehicle-miles of travel) fee in Southern California.[2]

There is considerable evidence that the current price paid to travel fails to include the real and substantial costs of mobile-source air pollution and congestion. Additionally, the increasingly common government practice of using retail sales taxes and property taxes to help fi-

---

[1] The federal Clean Air Act Amendments (CAAA) of 1990 and the Intermodal Surface Transportation Efficiency Act (ISTEA) of 1991, plus a host of state laws, call for reductions in urban transportation resource consumption.

[2] The quantitative analysis in this paper is based on a recent Environmental Defense Fund report, *Efficiency and Fairness on the Road: Strategies for Unsnarling Traffic in Southern California* (Cameron 1994). Full documentation of the data and methods of analysis are contained in the appendices of that report. Copies are available from Environmental Defense Fund, 5655 College Avenue, Oakland, CA 94618.

nance public transportation infrastructure means that the current price fails also to include all public resource costs. Failure of the market price to reflect the full costs of transportation consumption means the price people currently pay to travel is artificially low, with the result that motorists are choosing to take trips whose benefits are less than their costs.

Market-based demand management policies—such as VMT fees, congestion pricing, parking pricing, and smog fees—have been proposed to increase the price paid to travel so that it reflects full costs. The corrected price will increase net benefits of the transportation system by eliminating those trips whose costs exceed their benefits. However, despite the appeal of market-based policies in some policy circles, many questions about these policies remain unanswered. Although some quantitative analysis of the effects of market-based policies on pollution and congestion has taken place, a full analysis of their costs and benefits is lacking (Bay Area Economic Forum 1990; Cameron 1991; Reason Foundation 1992). This chapter uses the consumer surplus model of economics to estimate the net societal benefits of market-based demand management policies, specifically applied to Southern California's surface transportation system.

Using the Consumer Surplus Model to Estimate Net Transportation Benefits

The position that transportation demand should be managed implicitly assumes that transportation consumption is excessive, and furthermore that the net benefits of our urban transportation systems are not as high as they could be. A method is needed to examine the effects on net benefits of policies that reduce consumption. The first step of that analysis is to establish a baseline of current net benefits. The second step is to measure the effects on net benefits of the changes in consumption brought about by demand management policies. The consumer surplus model of economics can be used for both steps.

Under the consumer surplus model, the total societal net benefits of the transportation system are equal to the sum of the net benefits to all individuals.[3] The net benefits of the transportation

---

[3] In addition to consumer surplus, the total benefits of the transportation system to society include the profits earned by suppliers of transportation services, such as vehicle manufacturers, road construction companies, and fuel companies. The value of the transportation system to suppliers is termed producer surplus. Although the current public policy focus is on the value of the transportation system to users, or consumers, a more thorough approach would consider both the consumer and producer surplus of the transportation system.

system to a single individual are equal to the net benefits of all the trips taken by that person. The net benefits of any single trip are equal to its benefits minus its costs. To calculate societal net benefits, therefore, the model requires information on the benefits and costs of each trip taken.

The benefits of a trip to a person can be measured by that person's willingness to pay for it. Presumably, people value some trips more highly than others. For example, a person typically is willing to pay more for a trip to work than for a trip to the movies. In theory, it is possible to order all of the trips a person wishes to make from the most valuable to the least. In economic theory, such an ordering is referred to as a demand schedule or curve. For any price of travel, a demand curve reveals how much travel a person will conduct and how much a person values different levels of travel.

The cost of a trip includes direct costs, such as those of purchasing and operating automobiles and building roads, and indirect costs, such as the congestion and air pollution that stem from the trip. For the transportation market to maximize net benefits, the market price paid to travel must reflect no more and no less than the total costs of travel. If, as previously suggested, the current market price fails to include the costs of congestion and pollution and therefore is artificially low, people will take trips whose value is lower than their true costs, and net benefits will be lower than they could be.

The consumer surplus framework is a useful model for understanding efficient levels of demand for transportation consumption. Rarely, however, are transportation problems or their proposed solutions analyzed with this framework, even though data exist to do so. With reasonably accurate data on consumer demand and on the full social costs of travel, the consumer surplus model can be used to estimate the net benefits of the transportation system. Similarly, with benefit and cost data for demand management policies, the consumer surplus model can be used to perform policy analysis and to estimate the effects of policies on net benefits.

Net Benefits of Southern California's Transportation System

Transportation consumption underlies Southern California's infamous air pollution and traffic congestion. There are few, if any, other metropolitan areas with more widespread agreement that transportation demand should be constrained. Frustration over the problem is reflected in four major laws that threaten the region with financial

Table 9-1

Benefits and Costs of Surface Transportation, Southern California, 1991 (Billions of Dollars)

Benefits	
Automobile travel	$78.2
Public transit	1.5
TOTAL BENEFITS	**$79.7**
Costs	
Automobile expenses	$34.1
Transit fares	0.3
Taxes	4.2
Air pollution	3.7
Congestion	7.7
TOTAL COSTS	**$50.1**
Net Benefits	$29.6

Source: Cameron (1994), p. 7.

sanctions if it does not significantly reduce the air pollution and congestion costs of its transportation system.[4]

Southern California is home to approximately 15 million people, who own and operate over 7 million vehicles (Diamant 1993). In 1991, approximately 101.5 billion miles of travel were logged on the region's 155,000 lane-miles of roads (Cameron 1994, p. 6). Table 9-1 indicates that the value to the region's residents of their 1991 transportation consumption, based on their willingness to pay for both automobile and public transit trips, was approximately $79.7 billion.[5] In exchange, residents paid approximately $34.1 billion in direct expenditures, mostly on their automobiles. They also paid $4.2 billion in transportation taxes and fees. Indirectly, residents experienced approximately $3.7 billion in transportation-related pollution costs and $7.7 billion in congestion costs. Table 9-1 indicates that the total of all costs was approximately $50.1 billion. The annual net benefit, or consumer surplus, for the region is estimated to be $29.6 billion.

---

[4] The federal Clean Air and Intermodal Surface Transportation Efficiency Acts and the California State Clean Air and Congestion Management Acts contain significant mandates for reducing transportation consumption.

[5] The demand curve and estimate of the value of mobility is for household and personal travel demand only. It does not include the value of the transportation system to the region's businesses, which in 1991 owned and operated 1.8 million commercial vehicles.

Value of Mobility

Arguably the most difficult valuation of an applied consumer surplus model is estimation of the demand function for travel. The estimated $78.2 billion of automobile benefits shown in Table 9-1 was calculated from the demand curve represented in Figure 9-1, which shows regional demand for VMT as a function of cost. In 1991, residents drove 101.5 billion miles in response to automobile ownership and operating costs of approximately $0.37 per mile.

The analytic techniques for deriving the rest of the points on the curve were developed by Greig Harvey and are elements of his TRIPS model.[6] This model is a sophisticated travel forecasting method that, among other things, estimates the effects of price changes on auto ownership, trip frequency, destination choice, and mode choice. The travel forecasting method of TRIPS is based on the individual travel behaviors of 15,000 households in Southern California. The model's database includes information from the trip diaries kept by each traveler, as well as information on demographics, auto ownership, and transportation options (time and length of trip by auto, bus, etc.) for origin-destination pairs.

To estimate the demand function in Figure 9-1, the model relies on behavioral equations defined from historically observed individual travel behaviors. The estimate of how much regional VMT would decrease in response to increases in operating costs is based on choices individuals actually made when confronted with different prices.

Because the range of real-world price changes is relatively small, the ability of the model to accurately predict changes in consumption that result from changes in price is roughly limited to increases of $0.20 per mile above the current operating cost, which is approximately $0.10 per mile driven. At an operating cost of $0.30 per mile ($0.57 per mile total cost), the TRIPS model estimates that regional travel would have been only 67 billion miles in 1991 (Figure 9-1).

Theoretically, to measure willingness to pay and the full value of current levels of mobility requires a demand function that covers all levels of travel consumption. Practically, it is not possible to model Southern California's demand function with accuracy below 67 billion miles consumed annually. To estimate the value of current levels of travel, it was necessary to make a judgment about the relative size of the remaining part of the curve (the part between 0 and 67 billion

---

[6] All references to the TRIPS methodology are taken from Greig Harvey's appendix on the methodology of TRIPS in Cameron (1994).

Figure 9-1

Annual Demand for VMT, Southern California Households, 1991

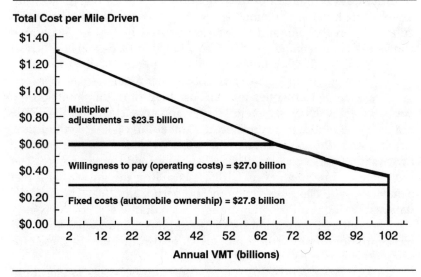

Total Cost per Mile Driven

Multiplier adjustments = $23.5 billion

Willingness to pay (operating costs) = $27.0 billion

Fixed costs (automobile ownership) = $27.8 billion

Annual VMT (billions)

Source: Cameron (1994), p. I-8.

vehicle-miles consumed per year). In this instance, the area beneath the remaining demand function was estimated to be roughly 40 percent of the estimated area.[7] The total area estimated was roughly $78.2 billion. The same model (TRIPS) and methodology were used to estimate the benefits of transit trips to be $1.5 billion (Cameron 1994, Appendix I, pp. 10–12).

The estimate of the gross value of the transportation system need not be more precise than this. The most practical use of the consumer surplus model is in estimating changes in net benefits that result from policy changes. The price and consumption levels that would be provoked by market-based demand management policies fall well within the TRIPS estimated portion of the demand function (above 67 billion miles annually), meaning the remaining part does not factor into the calculation of changes in net benefits. The best possible estimate of the value of the region's transportation system to its users in 1991, given available data, is $79.7 billion per year.

---

[7] Full documentation of the methods for estimating the market demand curve for travel is contained in Cameron (1994, Appendix I, pp. 4–9).

Direct Out-of-Pocket Expenditures

The estimate that the region's residents spent roughly $34 billion in direct out-of-pocket expenditures is taken from the 1991 travel survey of 15,000 Southern California households.[8] Spread over the 101.5 billion miles of vehicle travel, the average cost of owning and operating a vehicle in Southern California in 1991 was $0.37 per mile (Cameron 1994, p. 24).

According to the TRIPS model, the average perceived operating cost was $0.10 per mile driven (Cameron 1994, p. 24). The regional cost of vehicle ownership and operation, spread over the entire population, was over $2,400 per person.

Transportation Taxes

In 1991, taxes that generated revenue solely for expenditure on the region's surface transportation system raised $5.3 billion (Diamant 1993, Table 3-1).[9] Excluding commercial transportation taxes, the amount paid by the region's residential population equaled $4.2 billion. State and federal gasoline taxes raised roughly 36 percent; motor vehicle registration and license fees raised 29 percent; retail sales taxes generated 29 percent; and transit fare revenues represented 7 percent of total government transportation revenues. These figures exclude property taxes that contribute to local government general funds, from which public transportation expenditures are often made.

Pollution Costs

The vast majority of air pollutants in the South Coast Air Basin come from the region's vehicle fleet. Federal health-based air quality standards are unmet for four of the six criteria pollutants regulated by the federal Clean Air Act. In a 1989 study of human exposure to the region's air pollution, the annual health benefits of achieving the federal air quality standards for ozone and particulate matter were estimated to be $9.4 billion (Hall 1989, p. E-15). Given the mobile-source share of 49 percent of ozone precursors and 37 percent of particulate matter (mostly entrained road dust), the health costs of mobile-source air pollution were estimated to be $3.7 billion (South Coast Air Quality Management District 1991).

---

[8] This amount does not include transportation taxes and fees.

[9] All public finance figures and references are taken from Adam Diamant's appendix in Cameron (1994).

167

Significantly, this assessment does not include the health effects of carbon monoxide, nearly all of which is generated by the region's vehicle fleet. This valuation also fails to account for nonhealth costs of air pollution, such as damage to buildings, materials, and agriculture. Furthermore, the $9.4 billion of annual health benefits is what would be achieved by bringing current emissions down to the level needed to meet federal standards. Presumably there would be additional health gains if emissions were even lower. For these reasons, the $3.7 billion of pollution costs associated with the transportation system is a conservative number.

Congestion Costs

The estimate of $7.7 billion in annual congestion costs is based on calculations by TRIPS of the total hours of recurring delay on the region's roads and on implicitly derived values of the time people lose sitting in traffic. TRIPS' estimates of delay rely on data on interzonal peak and off-peak travel times provided by the Southern California Association of Governments (SCAG). The values of time used, which are based on people's wage rates, are the same as those used by SCAG's transportation forecasting models. For the calculations in this study, the average person's value of time is assumed to be $6.80 per hour (Cameron 1994, p. 17). The number of hours of delay in 1991 was 903 billion hours, or an average of 11 minutes per day per person (Cameron 1994, Appendix I, p. 19).[10] Significantly, this estimate does not include the costs of commercial delay, increased accidents, or extra fuel and maintenance costs. A separate study that included these costs estimated the total cost of congestion in the region to be $9.4 billion annually (SCAG 1988, Table B-5).

Net Transportation Benefits

On the basis of these valuations of benefits and costs, the net benefits of Southern California's transportation system are estimated to be $29.6 billion per year (see Table 9-1) for the 1991 level of transportation consumption. This figure does not include land costs, noise pollution costs, climate change costs (from CO_2 emissions), or the security costs of dependence on imported oil. It also does not include the value

---

[10] Higher-income individuals, whose time is assumed to be more valuable, are exposed to more delay than lower-income individuals. For this reason, the estimate of regional congestion costs is more than the average amount of personal delay multiplied by the average wage rate.

or costs of the transportation system to businesses. A more thorough analysis would include each of these.

By itself, the calculation of net benefits is useful for putting the importance of the transportation system into context. For example, the $39 billion of direct household spending on surface transportation (see Table 9-1) represents approximately 11 percent of the region's $370-billion-per-year economy.[11] More important, however, is the information the model provides on the benefits and costs of levels of travel other than those actually experienced in 1991. This information permits analysis of the net benefits of any type of transportation policy, including public investments in infrastructure, regulatory policies for changing travel behavior or technology, and market-based demand management policies.

Estimation of the Benefits of Market-Based Demand Management Policies in Southern California

Pollution and congestion costs in Southern California are estimated to be approximately 23 percent of total surface transportation costs (see Table 9-1). Since these costs increase with the amount of travel conducted, they are operating costs of the transportation system. Spread over the 101.5 billion miles of travel in 1991, regional pollution costs of $3.7 billion and congestion costs of $7.7 billion equaled $0.11 per mile driven.

Though pollution and congestion are true operating costs, they are not included in the price people pay to operate their vehicles. If they were included, the price paid to drive, which currently is $0.10 per mile, would roughly double. According to the consumer surplus model, this significant distortion in the price currently paid to travel should lead people to take trips whose value is less than their true costs and should result in lower net benefits from the transportation system than are possible. In theory, therefore, market-based demand management policies that would increase the price paid to travel should yield an increase in net benefits in Southern California. The Southern California consumer surplus model just presented can be used to test this hypothesis.

A variety of market-based demand management policies exist to choose from, including congestion pricing, parking pricing, smog fees,

---

[11] Regional economic product taken from U.S. Dept. of Commerce, Bureau of Economic Analysis (1990).

and VMT fees. Congestion pricing would assess fees at points in the road network, and at times of the day, that are prone to congestion. The level of fee would vary with the level of recurring congestion and at each place and time would be set to keep demand within the physical constraints of the road system. The principal benefit of congestion fees would be reduced congestion, though they would yield emission reduction benefits as well.

Parking pricing has been proposed to offset the common practice of employer-subsidized parking. One survey of Southern California discovered that more than 90 percent of employers provide free parking for their employees and that the effect of free parking on transportation demand is greater than the effect of giving away free gasoline would be (Willson et al. 1989, p. i). An innovative market-based policy intended to counter this price distortion, termed "parking cashout," is being implemented in California. Employers who provide subsidized employee parking are required by law to offer employees the choice of keeping their subsidized parking place or, instead, taking

---

Table 9-2

Comparison of Transportation Benefits and Costs With and Without a $0.05 VMT Fee, Southern California, 1991 (Billions of Dollars)

	Current Transportation System	$0.05-per-mile VMT Fee	Change
Benefits			
Automobile travel	$78.2	$74.3	($4.0)
Public transit	1.5	1.9	0.4
TOTAL BENEFITS	$79.7	$76.2	($3.5)
Costs			
Automobile expenses	$34.1	$30.9	($3.2)
Transit fares	0.3	0.4	0.1
Taxes	4.2	3.9	(0.3)
Air pollution	3.7	2.2	(1.5)
Congestion	7.7	5.7	(2.0)
VMT fee	–	4.5	
New revenues	–	(4.1)	0.4
TOTAL COSTS	$50.1	$43.5	($6.6)
Net Benefits	$29.6	$32.7	$3.0

Source: Cameron (1994), p. 28.

---

the cash equivalent of the subsidy. This policy is also a centerpiece of President Clinton's Climate Action Plan.

Smog fees would charge motorists for the amount of pollution they emit from their vehicles, thus increasing the cleanliness of the vehicle fleet and reducing the total amount of travel. The fees would also substantially reduce pollution costs and have mild congestion reduction benefits (Cameron 1991, p. 37).

VMT fees would charge motorists a flat fee for every mile driven, regardless of any particular mile's contribution to congestion or pollution. Although VMT fees are a less precise pricing instrument than congestion or smog fees, they would reduce both congestion and pollution. Because a vehicle's VMT would be easier to monitor than its contribution to congestion or pollution, VMT fees could be easiest to implement.

The potential of market-based demand management policies to reduce consumption and increase net benefits can be illustrated by estimating the effects of a $0.05-per-mile VMT fee on net benefits in Southern California (see Table 9-2). Regional net benefits would increase by $3.0 billion (rounded), from $29.6 to $32.7 billion per year. The fee would reduce consumption of travel, which means valued trips would be eliminated, but the cost savings of reduced pollution and congestion, and reduced spending on transportation, would yield positive net benefits. The costs and benefits of such a fee are discussed in the following sections.

Value of Mobility

Since every trip a person takes is of some value, any trip not taken as a result of a VMT fee will represent a loss, or cost. One effect of demand management policies is to reduce the gross quantity and value of travel. The TRIPS model identified those auto trips taken in 1991 that, in light of a $0.05-per-mile operating cost increase, would have been eliminated.[12] These trips equaled 11 percent of all VMT taken in 1991.

From the information in the demand curve in Figure 9-1, it is possible to estimate the value, measured by willingness to pay, of the 11 percent of travel eliminated (Cameron 1994, p. 29). Table 9-2 indicates that the $0.05-per-mile VMT fee would lead to a decrease in the gross value of travel in the region from $79.7 billion to $76.2 billion per year. The

---

[12] TRIPS modeled the VMT fee as a cost that motorists would experience frequently (i.e., billing would be monthly or more frequent). If the fee were collected infrequently, such as in the form of an annual VMT fee, the effects on demand would be smaller.

value of foregone trips would be approximately $3.5 billion. This includes an increase in transit benefits since one effect of increasing the price of auto travel would be to shift some trips onto public transit.

Private Out-of-Pocket Expenditures

Because people would travel less in response to efficiency fees, they would spend less money operating and maintaining their vehicles. Efficiency fees would also induce some people to not own a car, or induce families to own fewer cars, so ownership costs such as depreciation, insurance, and registration would also go down. Table 9-2 indicates that a $0.05-per-mile VMT fee would result in a decrease in regionwide transportation expenditures from roughly $34.1 billion to $30.9 billion per year, a savings of $3.2 billion. This estimate is also made by the TRIPS model, which has information on the costs of the trips foregone.

Pollution Costs

Reduced levels of travel and reduced stop-and-go travel would result in less air pollution. The TRIPS database contains information on the emissions of vehicles, including diurnal, startup (cold and hot), and running emissions, differentiated by age class of vehicle and by type of pollutant. These data are related to average trip speeds and trip lengths to provide estimates of mobile-source emissions and to capture the details of how emissions performance relates to travel behavior.

Using this information, TRIPS estimates that a $0.05-per-mile VMT fee would result in roughly a 9 percent reduction in mobile-source ozone precursors and an 11 percent reduction in auto-related particulate matter (Cameron 1994, p. 29).[13] From the estimated health costs of air pollution cited in the previous section, these reductions would reduce health costs from $3.7 billion to $2.2 billion per year, or by $1.5 billion.

Congestion Costs

Reductions in VMT would lead to reductions in congestion. The TRIPS model estimates the effects of changes in price on changes in trip frequency, destination choice, and mode choice. These changes are

---

[13] Most particulate matter emissions related to mobile sources comes from entrained road dust. This analysis assumes that entrained road dust will decrease in proportion to VMT.

modeled for their effects on corridor volumes and hence on delay. Since reduced delay would in turn lead to increased trip taking, TRIPS performs an iterative analysis to estimate the equilibrium level of congestion.

A $0.05-per-mile VMT fee would reduce hours of recurring delay by 29 percent, from 903 billion hours annually to 644 billion. Given the valuations of time used by SCAG's forecasting models, Table 9-2 indicates that congestion costs would be reduced by $2.0 billion from $7.7 to $5.7 billion annually.

Transportation Taxes

Reductions in overall travel would result in lower tax revenues. Less gasoline would be consumed, so less would be paid in gas taxes. Fewer automobiles would be registered and licensed. The TRIPS model estimates both changes in fuel consumption and changes in auto ownership. In response to a $0.05-per-mile VMT fee, fuel consumption would decrease from 6.3 billion gallons per year to 5.6 billion gallons. In the long run, vehicle ownership would be reduced by approximately 6 percent. These decreases in taxable resource consumption would result in a smaller tax base and in modest savings for individual travelers, as indicated in Table 9-2. The regional total of lost revenue would be approximately $300 million. These lost revenues could be replaced by revenues from the new fees.

Efficiency Fee Costs

The efficiency fee would represent a new cost to motorists. In the case of a VMT fee, motorists would pay directly in proportion to the amount they drive. Table 9-2 indicates that a $0.05-per-mile VMT fee would generate $4.5 billion of new public revenue. Although these funds would accrue in the public treasury, they would be experienced as a cost by travelers.

Expenditure of New Efficiency Fee Revenue

Unlike other policies to reduce congestion, such as road construction, or policies to reduce emissions, such as new emission technologies, market-based policies do not require significant new investments in transportation capital. Thus the revenues from the fees would be available for a wide range of public uses. Table 9-2 indicates that, after using some of the new revenues to replace lost tax revenues and to pay for increased transit capacity to meet increased demand for transit, $4.1 billion would be available for public expenditure.

Net Transportation Benefits

The net change in transportation benefits, as presented in Table 9-2, is the sum of all these changes. A $0.05-per-mile efficiency fee would increase regional net benefits of the transportation system from $29.6 billion to $32.7 billion, a gain of $3.0 billion per year. Individuals lose some valued travel and the money they pay in fees. They gain time savings, health benefits, savings from reduced spending on automobile use, and savings from public spending of the fee revenues.

From the valuations of transportation benefits and costs used in this study, it appears that market-based demand management policies that reduce consumption would increase the net benefits of Southern California's transportation system. This analysis supports the widely held assumption that the least valued trips being taken on Southern California's roads are worth less than they cost and the assumption that consumption of transportation resources in the region is excessive. With the help of the TRIPS model, this version of the consumer surplus model can be applied to analyze other market-based demand management policies and at different rates.

Strengths and Weaknesses of the Consumer Surplus Model

As a practical matter, representation of transportation benefits and costs in monetary terms is an imprecise and even contestable exercise. The value of mobility is captured by the consumer demand function, or willingness to pay for it. There are no discreet units of measure for mobility, however, so a close proxy, such as vehicle-miles of travel, must be used instead. In fact, demand for mobility is quite different from demand for miles of travel. It is difficult to estimate the value of mobility.

Measuring the value of mobility to a person based on that person's willingness to pay for it is contestable since willingness to pay is significantly influenced by the distribution of wealth in society. Although the value of mobility certainly is reflected in a person's willingness to pay for it, so too is the amount of money available to the person in the first place. Existing data show that high-income individuals are willing to pay more to travel than those with low incomes, though it is not clear that the mobility of high-income individuals is more valuable.[14] The consumer surplus model implicitly accepts the distribution of wealth in society.

---

[14] The EDF report (Cameron 1994) from which this chapter is excerpted contains a detailed analysis of the differences in willingness to pay across income groups.

The valuation of different costs is also open to debate. It is very difficult to estimate accurately in monetary terms the value of clean air, a stable climate, or energy security. Similarly, traditional methods for measuring congestion costs value lost time in terms of people's wage rates. Critics who would contest the willingness-to-pay method for valuing benefits since it is biased by income distribution might also contest this method for valuing time.

These difficulties in measuring transportation values, although they may seem to limit the usefulness of the consumer surplus model, actually render it more useful in one critical respect. In the real world, all transportation policy choices involve tradeoffs among the many transportation values. More often than not, the value of transportation benefits and costs is implicitly assigned. In fact there is no single or objectively correct valuation of the benefits of mobility or the costs of pollution, congestion, and energy security. The consumer surplus model forces analysts and policymakers to focus explicitly on the relative importance of different transportation benefits and costs, facilitates comparisons of different value systems, and illustrates how critical those values are in determining what are beneficial transportation policies.

Conclusion

The consumer surplus model provides a useful method for evaluating the net benefits of different levels of transportation consumption. It is also a powerful tool for estimating the benefits of different policy approaches. Perhaps the most useful aspect of the model is that it forces policymakers to focus on the multiple purposes of the transportation system and to be explicit about the relative importance of those purposes.

This chapter has applied the consumer surplus model to estimate the baseline net benefits of annual (1991) transportation consumption in Southern California to be $29.6 billion, based on a gross value of $79.7 billion and total costs of $50.1 billion. The model was also used to estimate the benefits of a sample market-based demand management policy in Southern California, indicating that a $0.05-per-mile VMT fee would yield a 10 percent increase in regional net transportation benefits, from $29.6 billion to $32.7 billion per year.

References

Bay Area Economic Forum. 1990. *Market-Based Solutions to the Transportation Crisis*. San Francisco: Bay Area Economic Forum. May.

Cameron, Michael. 1991. *Transportation Efficiency: Tackling Southern California's Air Pollution and Congestion*. Oakland, Calif.: Environmental Defense Fund and Regional Institute of Southern California. March.

————. 1994. *Efficiency and Fairness on the Road: Strategies for Unsnarling Traffic in Southern California*. Oakland, Calif.: Environmental Defense Fund. February.

Diamant, Adam. 1993. *Public Finance of Surface Transportation in Southern California: 1989–1991*. Oakland, Calif.: Environmental Defense Fund. December.

Hall, Jane. 1989. *Economic Assessment of the Health Benefits from Improvements in Air Quality in the South Coast Air Basin*. Fullerton, Calif.: California State University.

Reason Foundation. 1992. *Congestion Pricing for Southern California: Using Market Pricing to Reduce Congestion and Emissions*. September.

South Coast Air Quality Management District (SCAQMD). 1991. *Final 1991 Air Quality Management Plan*. Diamond Bar, Calif. July.

Southern California Association of Governments (SCAG). 1988. *Congestion in the Los Angeles Region: Costs Under Future Mobility Strategies*. Los Angeles. March.

U.S. Department of Commerce, Bureau of Economic Analysis. 1990. *Survey of Current Business, May 1988 and April 1989*. Washington, D.C.

Willson, Richard, et al. 1989. *Parking Subsidies and Commuter Mode Choice: Assessing the Evidence*. Los Angeles: Southern California Association of Governments. July.

Steering with Prices: Fuel and Vehicle Taxation as Market Incentives for Higher Fuel Economy

JOHN M. DECICCO AND DEBORAH GORDON

Just over 20 years ago, King Faisal of Saudi Arabia cut his country's oil output by 25 percent and ordered an embargo of oil supply to the United States and several other Western nations. By the time the embargo ended in March 1974, Saudi Arabia and other members of the Organization of Petroleum Exporting Countries (OPEC) had increased their profits to $10 per barrel from under $2 per barrel six months earlier (Stobaugh and Yergin 1979). The sharp turns in energy-related markets, such as those for automobiles and automobile transportation, over the past two decades are clear evidence that one can "steer with prices." However, the question still facing us is, Who's in the driver's seat? It seems that policymakers in the United States are at best in the front passenger seat, speaking in the driver's ear while listening to a chorus of back-seat drivers made up of researchers and representatives of industry, government, and nongovernmental organizations such as ourselves.

Nevertheless, we can use what we know about transportation in the United States to look ahead at the direction this country is headed under current policy. The broad direction is, quite literally, already paved with the billions of dollars of asphalt and concrete that this country has poured into automobile supportive infrastructure in the past 40 years. The conformity provisions mandated by the Clean Air

Act Amendments (CAAA) of 1990 and the new flexibilities in the Intermodal Surface Transportation Efficiency Act (ISTEA) of 1991 offer hope that future development patterns and infrastructure spending will support a shift to alternative travel modes, at least in urban areas. However, new development alters only a small fraction of the settlement patterns already laid down, and so the geographic determinants of travel demand will only be transformed over rather long time frames of 30 to 40 years or more.

Neither the Alternative Motor Fuels Act (AMFA) of 1988 nor the Energy Policy Act (EPACT) of 1992 will make much of a difference in the rising trend of U.S. transportation petroleum use over the next 20 years. The Clinton administration's Clean Car Initiative has a lofty goal but is restricted to research; it does nothing to affect the fuel consumption of the millions of vehicles to be sold and used while the research is being pursued. A major gap remaining in U.S. energy policy today is the absence of measures for meaningful control of rising gasoline use. The Climate Action Plan announced in October 1993 begins to take some new steps through the proposed parking subsidy reform and some accelerated transportation demand management efforts. While meaningful, the effects of these measures will be limited, as is acknowledged in the administration's Climate Plan follow-up process, which explicitly articulates a focus on how to control greenhouse gas emissions from personal transportation vehicles. As policymakers turn their attention to this issue, they will be looking for assurance that the strategy they choose will make a meaningful difference within the next 20 years or so.

Figure 10-1 shows light-vehicle fuel economy, vehicle-miles of travel (VMT), and oil use in the United States since 1970, along with current policy projections through 2010. Behind these projections are economic growth and oil price projections of the Energy Information Administration (EIA 1993). Gasoline prices are assumed to rise slowly, reaching about $1.50 per gallon by 2010 (neglecting here the possibility of another oil crisis like the two and a half we have had since 1973). Without policy change, our best projection is for frozen rated fuel economy of new light-duty vehicles (DeCicco 1992), as will be elaborated below.

The top curve in Figure 10-1 shows the past new light-vehicle average fuel economy, with the total light-duty stock average given as the line just below. We can see that currently there is very little gain in stock fuel economy from turnover of the stock, since new-vehicle fuel economy peaked five years ago. Thus light-vehicle oil consumption will soon again be rising in lockstep with VMT. The question we address here is, What is the potential for pricing policies to alter the course sketched in Figure 10-1?

Figure 10-1

U.S. Light-Vehicle Fuel Economy, Vehicle-Miles of Travel, and Fuel Consumption: Historical Statistics 1970–1993 and Current Policy Projections Through 2010

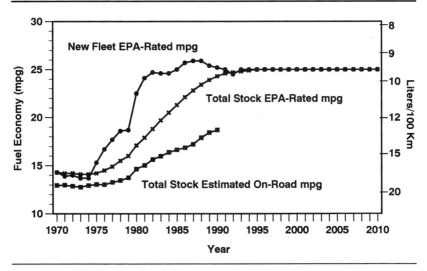

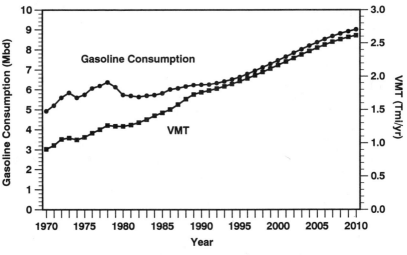

Source: EPA-rated average fuel economy of cars and light trucks through 1993 is from Murrell et al. (1993) for new fleet and from the ACEEE stock model for total light-vehicle stock. Stock on-road mpg estimates, vehicle-miles of travel (VMT), and gasoline consumption (million barrels per day [Mbd]) through 1990 are based on S.C. Davis and Strang (1993).

Note: Projections are based on VMT growth averaging 2 percent per year through 2010 and an assumption of frozen rated new-vehicle fuel economy.

The recent policy debate on light-vehicle energy consumption is characterized by a polarization between those who favor higher fuel taxes and those who place greater emphasis on regulating new-vehicle fuel economy. The former point of view is represented, for example, by Leone and Parkinson (1990), CRA (1991), DRI (1991), and congressional testimony by auto industry representatives, who emphasize the efficiency of market forces and the broad influence afforded by fuel taxation. The other point of view is taken by the environmental and energy conservation advocacy community (including the authors), who emphasize the importance of regulatory incentives directed specifically toward new-vehicle fuel economy. Market incentives in the form of vehicle pricing interventions—such as the gas guzzler tax—have also been long discussed (Difiglio 1976; W.B. Davis and Gordon 1993; DeCicco et al. 1993; and others). Of course, many point out the need for a combination of approaches, differences often being ones of degree and emphasis on a given policy.

The Efficiency Gap

Answering the question of policy choice depends on first answering some questions about goals. Why should we care about reducing oil use? How much should it be reduced? A number of reasons are cited, since oil use entails environmental damage, including greenhouse gas emissions, risks to national security, a chronic component of the U.S. trade deficit, and other economic losses. Here, we focus on the last reason, namely, economic losses other than various externalities and the trade imbalance. Since the present degree to which our transportation system relies on the petroleum resource is very much a status quo, it is perhaps clearer to say "foregone opportunities" (for greater economic welfare in terms of national income and employment) rather than "losses." Thus, behind the polarization of views on how to address rising transportation oil consumption lie differing answers to a question about the efficiency of current market conditions. To the extent that there is an "efficiency gap," closing the gap provides a rationale for how much we should seek to reduce light-vehicle energy consumption. The concept of an efficiency gap relates the technical (physical) and economic notions of efficiency.

Technical efficiency, for motor vehicles, is the ratio of the useful transportation of a vehicle's occupants and cargo to the energy available in the fuel. Technical efficiency may be defined in a number of ways, but for our purposes, fuel economy (e.g., miles per gallon) is a suitable measure of technical efficiency. Increasing fuel economy without sacrificing the ability to transport occupants and cargo clearly raises the technical efficiency of transportation. This chapter therefore focuses on policy instruments for improving fuel economy. Further support for this focus will be revealed below, when we review estimates of the potential for travel demand reductions (which can involve higher vehicle occupancy) as compared with the potential for vehicle efficiency improvements.

Economic efficiency is a measure of the extent to which resources are allocated optimally. The concept of Pareto optimality is used to judge economic efficiency: an allocation of resources is economically efficient if no one can be made better off without making someone else worse off. For the case at hand, the United States spends a certain amount of money on vehicle technologies, which has resulted in a light-vehicle stock averaging about 20 miles per gallon (mpg) on-road and having numerous other attributes valued by consumers and society (S.C. Davis and Strang 1993). We also spend a certain amount of money for the approximately 6 million barrels per day (Mbd) of gasoline consumed by those vehicles. It is possible, however, to transform our resource allocations to spend relatively more on technology for technical vehicle efficiency so that we might spend less on fuel. Such transformations do not happen overnight, of course, since the vehicle stock takes about 10 to 12 years to turn over. Moreover, the process by which one resource allocation can be transformed to another can itself involve costs. Nevertheless, if such a transformation can be made at net benefit to the country, then there is an efficiency gap, rooted in the untapped potential for increasing the technical efficiency of motor vehicles. Among the implications of such a gap are foregone opportunities for economic growth and job creation; for example, Geller et al. (1992) projected a net gain of up to 250,000 U.S. jobs if new light-vehicle fuel economy is improved to an average of 45 mpg by 2010.

The magnitude of the efficiency gap is partly estimated by engineering analysis of the potential for improving light-vehicle fuel economy. To be most useful, such an analysis must identify the direct costs of improving technical efficiency. Changes in other vehicle attributes must also be accounted for. Most analysts find it convenient to examine the potential for fuel economy improvement while holding constant such key attributes as size and acceleration ability. In Figure 10-2, per-vehicle cost is plotted against degree of automobile fuel economy improvement to arrive at estimates of the potential to improve technical efficiency. Clearly, there is a range of estimates possible depending on one's judgment of engineering possibilities. However, that discussion is outside the scope of this chapter (see OTA 1991; Ross et al. 1991; SRI 1991; Greene and Duleep 1992; NRC 1992; DeCicco and Ross

181

Figure 10-2

Estimated Cost of U.S. Automobile Fuel Economy Improvement for Varying Assumptions Regarding Technology Availability and Effectiveness

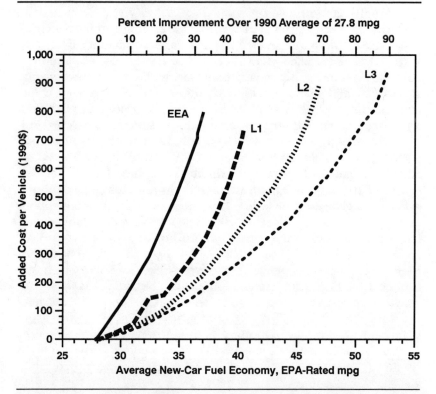

Source: Curves L1-L3 represent increasing levels of optimism regarding the availability and feasibility of improved technologies, as estimated by DeCicco and Ross (1993); the EEA (Energy and Environmental Analysis, Inc.) curve is based on Greene and Duleep (1992) and is similar to other recent DOE estimates.

1993). For reasons described by DeCicco (1992), we assume here the upper range of the estimates of potential fuel economy improvement. Allowing for stock turnover, the resulting 30 to 70 percent improvement in fuel economy would imply a 20 to 40 percent reduction in fuel consumption per mile driven.

The fuel economy "supply curve" of Figure 10-2 makes the efficiency gap quite apparent. But if there is such a gap, why does the market not close it, at least eventually? A partial answer is given in Figure 10-3, which puts the cost of fuel economy improvement in con-

Figure 10-3

U.S. Costs of Fuel and Fuel Economy Improvement in the Context of the Total Costs of Owning and Operating a Car

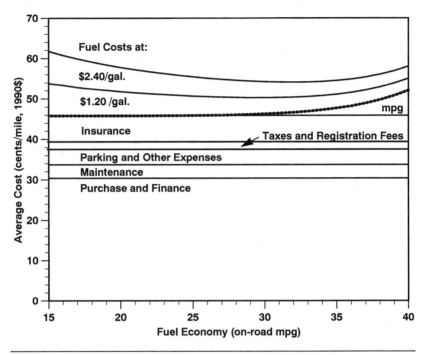

Source: Automobile expense statistics are from MVMA (1992); fuel economy improvement (mpg) cost estimates are from DeCicco and Ross (1993).

text. This graph is an update of one developed by von Hippel and Levi (1983); it is notable that when this illustration was first published, gasoline prices were 40 percent higher than they are today. Even if consumers were rational, cost-minimizing utility maximizers, the cost advantage of choosing higher fuel economy is relatively small in the context of the total cost of owning and operating a car. That the few pennies of price difference, which are quite visible at the gasoline pump and lead to such political sensitivity, seem so less relevant in new-car showrooms, where the cost of a nicer radio or fancier trim might equal a year's worth of fuel costs, should come as no surprise.

Even if consumers do not demand greater fuel economy in the showroom, citizens and policymakers can take a broader view of the situation (Kempton 1991). As long as the costs of making such an im-

183

provement in technical efficiency are lower than the value of the fuel saved, the country would be better off to undertake such change in resource allocation. This would amount to steering in a different direction on the graph of nationwide oil consumption. The curve of Figure 10-1, which shows light-vehicle oil consumption increasing to nearly 9 Mbd by 2010, could be pulled down, perhaps so as to show no net increase over the current level. For the sake of argument, we will use a target of cutting 2 to 3 Mbd from the level of light-vehicle oil consumption otherwise projected for 2010. This is of historical note, since a savings target of 2 Mbd was prominent in the discussions leading to the Energy Policy and Conservation Act (EPCA) of 1975 (Nivola 1986). This was the last major policy decision the United States made to substantially control transportation oil consumption. Quantitatively, the combined effects on U.S. oil consumption of AMFA (1988), CAAA (1990), ISTEA (1991), EPACT (1992), the $.043-per-gallon gasoline tax hike enacted in 1993, and the VMT reduction incentives of the 1993 Climate Action Plan are much lower than the 2 Mbd savings level discussed here as a "substantial" impact over the next 20 years or so.

Policy Options

The crisis mentality following the 1973 oil embargo provided a sense of urgency for taking substantive action. The 1975 EPCA established Corporate Average Fuel Economy (CAFE) standards, which took effect in 1978 for automobiles and 1979 for light trucks. These standards require manufacturers to sell a mix of vehicles over the course of a model year that averages to a predetermined level of fuel economy (mpg). Failure to achieve the standard results in a financial penalty. The CAFE standards ramped up to 27.5 mpg in 1985 for cars, with lower standards being administratively set for light trucks. Automobile standards for 1986–1989 were rolled back by the Reagan administration, and attempts to substantially increase the standards in recent years have been unsuccessful. As shown in Figure 10-1, the fuel economy of new vehicles has not increased since dropping slightly below the 1978–1988 peak. There is no indication that current market forces will pull new-fleet fuel economy above the present levels, which hover just above the level set by CAFE standards. This prognosis of essentially flat fuel economy is confirmed by the industry's own statements in hearings on fuel economy in recent years.[1] Raising

---

[1] For example, presentations by Chrysler, Ford, and General Motors representatives to the Workshop and Committee Meeting, Committee on Fuel Economy of Automobiles and Light Trucks, National Research Council, Irvine, Calif., July 1991.

CAFE standards is one option for increasing new-vehicle fuel economy that has received serious attention in recent years.

Today's cars and light trucks are more fuel-efficient than those of the early 1970s, with the average rated fuel economy of new light vehicles being 65 percent higher in 1990 than it was in 1975 (Murrell et al. 1993). It is challenging to sort out cause and effect among the many dramatic changes in fuel availability, fuel price, outlook, and policy that occurred in response to oil crises of 1973 and 1979. However, the lags in technology change and the persistence of the efficiency improvements achieved indicate that CAFE standards have had a binding effect on new-fleet fuel economy (Greene 1990). Moreover, most of the efficiency improvement was obtained by improving technology, with little change in vehicle size and a net increase in acceleration performance (U.S. DOE 1989; Williams and Hu 1991; Murrell et al. 1993). Nationwide oil savings from the standards now exceed 2.5 Mbd (DeCicco 1992). However, as established in 1975 and subsequently administered, CAFE standards have not been sufficient to check growth in light-vehicle fuel use, whereas VMT continue to grow. Contributing factors include the fact that light trucks have been more leniently regulated than automobiles while their market share has doubled and the fact that the "shortfall" between the rated and average on-road fuel economy of vehicles has grown (it is now estimated at about 20 percent) (Westbrook and Patterson 1989; Mintz et al. 1993).

The other policy developed to affect motor vehicle fuel economy is the gas guzzler tax. This federal excise tax on certain new cars was enacted in 1978 and first took effect in 1980. The threshold fuel economy, below which cars are subject to the tax, was ramped up to 22.5 mpg by 1986 and has since stayed constant. The tax schedule, which increases linearly with fuel consumption below 22.5 mpg, is given in 1 mpg steps, with the maximum tax on cars rated below 12.5 mpg being $7,700 (in effect since rates were doubled beginning in January 1991). The gas guzzler tax applies to a relatively small portion of the automobile fleet and not at all to light trucks. No estimate of the fuel savings directly attributable to the gas guzzler tax is available. There is evidence that the tax has had some effect on market choices, pulling up the average fuel economy of the least efficient portion of the new-car fleet (Ledbetter and Ross 1992; DeCicco et al. 1993; Khazzoom 1993).

More extensive guzzler tax and rebate schemes had been considered. For example, Difiglio (1976) examined a temporary guzzler tax imposed in 1977–1981, ramping up to $1,000 (1975$, or $2,300 in 1990$) on automobiles rated below 15 mpg and covering automobiles up to 24.5 mpg (about half the fleet in 1980–1981). He projected a 13 percent reduction in fleetwide fuel use by 1985. Rebates on vehicles more efficient than average were also considered. But rebates were not enacted because of concerns that the program would favor imported models at the expense of domestic models. Interest has revived in using an expanded gas guzzler tax or fee and rebate ("feebate") program as a way to steer the vehicle market to lower fuel consumption. A number of feebate or guzzler tax bills have been introduced in recent years at the federal and state levels; see W.B. Davis and Gordon (1993) and DeCicco et al. (1993) for reviews.

Thus, aside from the relatively limited role of the gas guzzler tax, U.S. policymakers have relied on regulation to address light-vehicle oil consumption. A tension exists between the market forces that result from low fuel prices and the market constraints imposed by fuel economy regulation. There have been persistent calls to address the problem, perhaps exclusively, through fuel taxation. The politics of this debate have evolved slowly. Nivola (1986) pointed out the strong popular sentiment that views gasoline as a necessity and a gasoline tax as an inequitable burden on consumers who have little ability to respond without disruptive lifestyle sacrifices; this political analysis remains largely true today (AAA 1993). By contrast, a number of studies have suggested superior economic efficiency for fuel taxation compared with vehicle regulation (Leone and Parkinson 1990; CRA 1991; DRI 1991; Miles-McLean et al. 1993). Support has also increased for energy taxation as a means to address environmental externalities, particularly greenhouse gas emissions (Dower and Zimmerman 1992). Externality considerations also provide a rationale for vehicle taxation (Koomey and Rosenfeld 1990). To sort out the likely effectiveness of pricing interventions, we will review the ways in which fuel and vehicle pricing changes might affect the average fuel economy realized in the marketplace.

Mechanisms of Market Change

The major difficulty in sifting through the evidence regarding the effects of pricing policies is understanding the mechanisms of change in the complex of interacting markets that determines transportation energy consumption. Many factors have been at work over the years that shape both technology and behavior. Understanding the mechanisms is crucial for guiding policy development.

Consider the recent debate on the effects of a broad-based energy (or Btu) tax. The range of opinions expressed was quite wide. Some opinions appeared to be based on a view that energy use was essentially inelastic. The tax would then be a direct drag on consumers and businesses, and very damaging to those for whom energy costs are a large share of their total expenditures and who have no ability to pass the costs on. Others expressed the opinion that there was some ability to respond by improving the efficiency of energy use or, more generally, by substituting other factors for energy. Some noted, however, that there are market barriers to efficiency improvement, so that the burden of the tax could be alleviated only if other steps were taken to overcome these barriers.

This range of views suggests a question: how and to what extent are there market barriers that inhibit the ability to respond to pricing changes? Figure 10-3 illustrates the relatively small role of fuel cost in the economics of vehicle ownership and use in the United States. That even this small share of fuel costs is remote at the time of vehicle purchase is an example of an added informational context barrier that can inhibit the ability of the market to respond to fuel price changes, particularly gradual changes as would likely be enacted by policymakers (versus oil supply disruptions).

Time Frames

A key issue is how long it takes for the effects of policy changes to be reflected in market outcomes. Some divergence in opinions about policy mechanisms can be traced to different assumptions about the relevant time frame. There are no generally accepted definitions of how many years constitute the "long term" as opposed to "short term." Mechanisms of short-term response may be considered as part of the long-term response. To set a context for discussion, we present working definitions of the time frames, shown in Table 10-1. Underlying cycles of physical stocks are used to guide these definitions.

It makes sense to define short term as essentially immediate—one year or so. In the context of the light-vehicle market, a short-term effect is one that is observable in the year following a change in the factor causing the effect. New-vehicle regulatory policies have a clear

Table 10-1

Time Frames for Effects of Transportation Energy Policies

Term	Years	Rationale
Short	1–2	Immediate changes, largely behavioral, some technological
Medium	15–20	Light-vehicle stock turnover
Long	30+	Infrastructure and land use transformation

short-term effect. For example, the new federal Tier I tailpipe emissions standards start to take effect in 1994. By the end of 1994, all model-year 1994 vehicles are in use, and there will be a definable impact related to the expected usage of those vehicles. Light vehicles up to a year old account for about 10 percent of vehicle-miles driven (S.C. Davis and Strang 1993), so the short-term effect of a policy will amount to about 10 percent of the change in characteristics relative to the overall vehicle stock.

Pricing policies also have a short-term effect, on both vehicles and behavior. For consistency when talking about time frames, we term a short-term behavioral response as one observable within a year from the change. For example, it is clear that the oil embargo of 1973, which constrained our fuel supply, precipitated a short-term response. VMT dropped in 1974 after increasing by nearly 5 percent annually for the previous two decades (FHWA 1991).

Rather than just distinguish long term from short term, it makes sense to define an intermediate, medium-term time frame. A physical basis for such a time frame is the turnover of the vehicle stock. Vehicle lifetimes may differ regionally, of course, and lifetimes have increased over the past decade, but these appear to be second-order effects from an energy use perspective (though not when criteria emissions are concerned). As determined by statistics from S.C. Davis and Strang (1993), the average automobile lifetime is about 12.5 years. Vehicles more than 12 years old account for less than 5 percent of VMT, and those more than 15 years old account for less than 2 percent. If we also factor in an average design lead-time of 4 to 5 years and recall the fact that not all models are changed every year, the result is a roughly 15- to 20-year horizon over which the physical characteristics of the vehicle fleet can essentially be transformed.

Finally, the lifetimes of transportation infrastructure and land use patterns provide a basis for long-term response. These are on the order of human generations, i.e., 30- to 40-year time frames. Settlement patterns, relating the location of residences and jobs, production sites and markets, do continuously evolve. However, at any given time, new development makes only marginal changes in the overall pattern. If, for example, we were to change pricing and other policies to favor a less automobile-oriented land use, new locational decisions would be made, affecting new development. One might even affect choice of residence and location of business. But so many such locations are like sunk costs, especially if one dismisses rapid, draconian changes in the relevant policies, which are politically unrealistic. Thus, the geographic transformations that might have a significant impact on transportation patterns and the resulting energy consumption can be expected to take a generation or so. Of course, this limitation is less applicable in any circumscribed region, particularly regions that are growing. For example, changes in transportation-related land use policy and changes in fuel and road pricing could have an impact in shaping new growth— e.g., in the San Francisco Bay area—over even the next decade. The odds of consistent changes happening contemporaneously throughout all major growth areas of the country is quite small, however. Therefore, a 30- to 40-year time frame seems realistic for observing such long-term effects on oil consumption and CO_2 emissions.

These divisions into short, medium, and long time frames are somewhat arbitrary, of course, since the factors that influence response largely operate on a continuous basis. The time frames are clearly hierarchical, in that the long-term response is inclusive of the effects that happen over shorter time frames. The divisions are useful, however, when it comes to discussing particular policy goals, such as target years for reductions in oil use or greenhouse gas emissions. The intermediate time frame is of particular interest for greenhouse gas emissions goals that might be set for 2000, prior to when a full medium-term response can be reached, and 2010, by which time vehicle stock can be essentially replaced.

Fuel Pricing Effects

The effect of fuel pricing is captured through the elasticity of fuel consumption with respect to fuel price. For small changes, the elasticity is approximately the percent change in fuel consumption associated with a percent change in fuel price. The response to changes in gasoline price involves a number of mechanisms affecting gasoline demand. Reported estimates of the elasticity of vehicle fuel consumption to fuel price vary by a factor of 5, from around –0.2 to –1 (Bohi and Zimmerman 1984; Chandler and Nicholls 1990). There is some consensus that the lower end of the range is the short-term response and that the upper end of the range represents the long-term response. However, questions exist regarding how to interpret the factors that have bearing on responses in both the short and long term. The total response can be split into two components: the effect on travel demand and the effect on vehicle efficiency. The magnitude of the total response is the sum of the magnitude of these two components.

Effect on Travel Demand

Of recent analyses that separately examined the travel demand and vehicle efficiency components, the estimated or implied elastici-

189

ties of travel demand (VMT) with respect to gasoline price are in the range of –0.05 to 0.1. Results given in EIA (1991) imply a short-term VMT elasticity of –0.06 for a $.10-per-gallon price increase to –0.08 for a $.50-per-gallon price hike, immediately applied rather than phased in. The VMT response is lower in the long term or for a phased-in price increase because of offsetting increases in vehicle efficiency. The transportation module of EIA (1990) uses a fuel price elasticity of –0.07 to model VMT growth. Theoretical considerations suggest an upper bound of less than –0.1 for the elasticity of travel with respect to fuel price when accounting for likely medium- and long-term responses of vehicle efficiency and land use (Greene 1993a). Under current conditions, the elasticity appears to be about –0.05, but the response is likely to increase as the fuel cost share of total transportation costs increases.

These estimates are also consistent with results from regional transportation modeling studies. A set of model runs, based on transportation models developed for the San Francisco Bay Area, was used to simulate gasoline price increases of $.75 to $1.50 per gallon as part of a broad transportation demand management strategy (UCS et al. 1991). A breakout of the fuel price-only part of the response implied an elasticity of –0.06. This degree of response appears to be a consensus view among urban and regional transportation analysts, who expect that vehicle efficiency improvement would be the larger component of the response to a fuel price increase and who generally turn to other strategies to control travel demand as part of regional transportation plans (Harvey 1993; Williams 1993).

Figure 10-4 summarizes the likely effects of gasoline price increases on VMT, using projected gasoline price and VMT levels for the year 2010. EIA (1993) projects an average retail gasoline price of about $1.50 per gallon in 2010. Assuming such slowly rising gasoline prices and modest economic growth, the average VMT growth rate for 1990–2010 is likely to be about 2 percent per year (UCS et al. 1991; EIA 1993). This growth rate results in a projection of 2.6 trillion (10^{12}) miles of light-duty-vehicle travel, a 48 percent increase over the 1990 level, shown as the dot in Figure 10-4. The response to changes in gasoline price is illustrated using an elasticity range of –0.05 to –0.15. The midrange effect is that a doubling of gasoline prices (as might be effected by a $1.50-per-gallon tax increase) would imply a 7 percent decrease in VMT.

Effect on Vehicle Efficiency

Most studies suggest that the larger part of the response to an increase in fuel prices will be increased vehicle fuel economy. Recent work by the U.S. Department of Energy (DOE), as reflected in the Na-

Figure 10-4

Projected U.S. Light-Duty Vehicle (LDV) Miles of Travel (VMT) in 2010 as a Function of Gasoline Price, for Varying Values of Price Elasticity

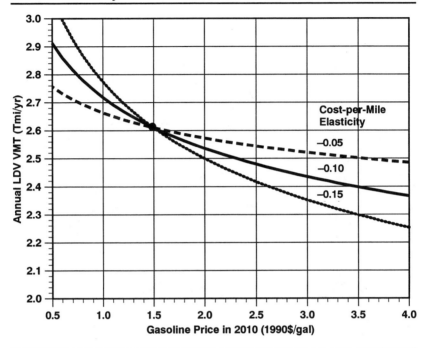

Note: Based on a nominal projection of 2.610 × 10¹² miles per year (trillion miles per year) at a gasoline price of $1.50 per gallon (1990$).

tional Energy Strategy and Annual Energy Outlook projections (EIA 1993), assumes that fuel economy will rise continuously as gasoline prices rise above current levels. The rise in new-car fuel economy projected in EIA (1993), for example, corresponds to an implied elasticity of about 0.8. This effect is based on a technological response to market demand for greater fuel economy, working from a "supply curve" of costs and benefits of various engineering measures for improving fuel economy (similar to the "EEA" curve in Figure 10-2). The validity of this response model is open to question, however, since the DOE projections of new fleet fuel economy rising for several recent years have not been borne out by data, which show new-vehicle fuel economy as flat or declining since 1988.

191

A different approach is embodied in the work of Train (1986), which examines car buyer response using a disaggregate model of household vehicle choice (noted below in a discussion of vehicle pricing policies). This work suggests a smaller response of fleet average fuel economy to fuel price, with implied elasticities on the order of 0.2 to 0.4. Some recent results of Greene (1993b) also suggest an elasticity of 0.2 to 0.3 for fuel economy with respect to fuel price. These estimates are consistent with a value of about –0.4 for the overall response of fuel consumption to fuel price, including the smaller VMT response component.

Fuel prices in most European countries range from $2.60 per gallon to over $4.00 per gallon (EIA 1991). Schipper et al. (1992) made comparisons of international data (Western Europe, Japan, and the United States) for 1973–1988 on vehicle fuel intensity (the inverse of fuel economy) and fuel price. Their results suggest an elasticity range of 0.2 to 0.3 for new-vehicle fuel economy with respect to fuel price. These results are thus broadly consistent with the previously cited analyses of the U.S. market alone. Schipper et al. also note that many countries have vehicle taxation policies, some of which place quite substantial taxes on vehicles of different sizes or engine types. Their gasoline price analysis did not factor in possible effects of vehicle taxation. To the extent that nonfuel vehicle taxes are positively correlated with decreasing fuel economy, the sensitivity of fuel economy to fuel price would tend to be overstated.

Figure 10-5 shows a plausible range of response for new light-vehicle fuel economy to increases in fuel price, for an elasticity range of 0.2 to 0.4. The projections work from recent conditions, with a gasoline price of $1.20 per gallon and new light-vehicle average fuel economy of 25 mpg (EPA rated). The midrange curve, with elasticity of 0.3, implies that it would roughly take a tripling of gasoline prices to yield a 40 percent increase in new-vehicle fuel economy (to an average of 35 mpg for new cars and light trucks).

One limitation of this type of analysis is that it does not account for the effect of fuel economy standards. This is also a limitation of the aggregate estimates of the gasoline price effect that show even higher degrees of responsiveness than suggested here. Sweeney (1979a, 1979b) pointed out that when fuel economy standards are binding, raising gasoline taxes will have little or no effect on vehicle efficiency. Under such conditions, the market equilibrium fuel economy (what it would be in response to fuel price alone, in the absence of standards) is very difficult to estimate. Sweeney (1979b) analyzed the effect of CAFE standards in terms of an "equivalent tax" on gasoline—i.e., the gasoline tax increase needed to raise fuel economy from its price-only

Figure 10-5

Estimated U.S. New Light-Vehicle Fuel Economy as a Function of Gasoline Price, for Varying Values of Price Elasticity

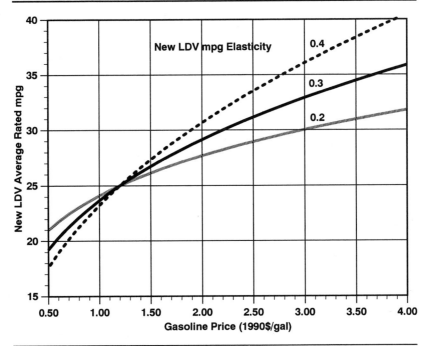

Note: Based on a nominal estimate of 25 mpg (EPA-rated city/highway mpg, average of cars and light trucks) at a gasoline price of $1.20 per gallon (1990$). Assumes adequate lead time for changes in manufacturer product planning in response to changes in fuel price.

equilibrium value to the level resulting from the regulations. As long as a new gasoline tax is less than the equivalent tax, average fuel economy will not improve beyond the level set by the standard. Sweeney derived theoretical estimates of the equivalent tax for a range of discount rates. His conservative (6 percent discount rate) projection for what it would have taken to induce a fleet average equal to the 27.5 mpg standard set for 1985 was an added tax of $.79 per gallon (1979$, or $1.39 in 1990$).

The fact that new-vehicle fuel economy has been hovering at or barely above the standards level in recent years suggests that CAFE standards are still binding on most manufacturers. This is corroborated by the rising share of light trucks in the overall light-duty market. Figure 10-6 illustrates the constraining effect of fuel economy

193

standards. Although we do not know exactly how large the effect is, for illustrative purposes we show a 2 mpg effect. The solid line represents the hypothetical response of new-vehicle fuel economy to fuel price in the absence of CAFE standards. Here we assume an elasticity of 0.3, the midrange value shown in Figure 10-5. The dashed curve in Figure 10-6 goes through the current new-fleet average of 25 mpg and runs parallel to the solid curve. The dashed curve response is what might be projected without accounting for the effect of CAFE standards, which is what most recent studies of a gasoline tax have done.

With a CAFE constraint, initial increases in gasoline price will have little or no effect on fuel economy. This is the "region of poor and uncertain response" shown in Figure 10-6, similar in concept to Sweeney's "equivalent tax." Under the stated assumptions, this region extends to an increase of up to $.30 per gallon. If the underlying response is more elastic, the region of poor response is smaller. For example, with an elasticity of 0.4, the full response would start after an increase of about $.15 per gallon. These values are much smaller than those suggested by Sweeney's pre-1980 analyses; however, Sweeney (1979a, 1979b) derived his equivalent tax estimates based only on the consumer (demand) response, without considering the automaker (supply) response of technology improvement. Since we know that the supply response is dominant, an equivalent tax much smaller than Sweeney's early estimates is implied.

Though largely conceptual, these analyses strongly suggest that energy taxes amounting to less than $.10 per gallon, as recently proposed, will have no effect on fleet average fuel economy. Although some economists differ with this view, many noneconomists are likely to agree with it as a matter of common sense. The effect of small gasoline tax increases is almost surely limited to the smaller travel demand response. A further implication is that raising CAFE standards would further weaken or even neutralize the fuel economy component of the response to fuel price. This conclusion is quite broad. As Sweeney (1979a, p. 15) noted in reference to gasoline taxes, gas guzzler taxes, and efficient vehicle procurement measures, "No policy option will increase mean efficiency unless that option provides strong enough incentives to increase mean efficiency above the standards even in their absence." On the other hand, the gap between the regulated fuel economy level and that which would be the fuel price-only market outcome can be viewed as a degree of tension imposed by the standards. (Some economists might also ascribe a "deadweight loss," from reductions in consumer and producer surplus, to this gap.) If fuel economy standards are raised, then raising fuel taxes would serve to ease this

Figure 10-6

Possible Effect of U.S. Fuel Economy Standards in Holding New Light-Vehicle Fuel Economy Above the Level Induced by Gasoline Price Alone

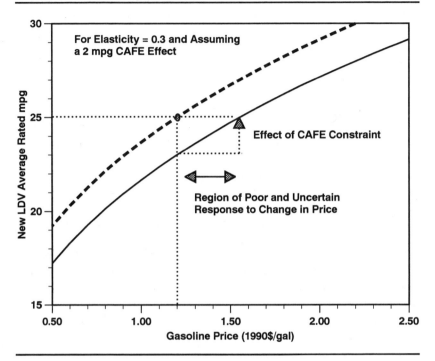

tension, although the results shown here suggest that fuel price increases would have to be quite high to eliminate it.

Combined Effects

Separate estimates of the travel demand and vehicle efficiency components yield magnitudes of 0.05 to 0.15 and 0.2 to 0.4, respectively, for the elasticity with respect to higher gasoline prices. Summing these estimates suggests a combined elasticity magnitude of 0.25 to 0.55 (midrange 0.4).

There has been extensive aggregate analysis of the likely overall effects of higher gasoline prices in the United States. Bohi and Zimmerman (1984) reviewed elasticities of demand in all of the major energy-using sectors. Their findings for transportation energy indicated a range extending higher than that suggested here. A number of post-1973 econometric studies suggest combined gasoline consumption elasticities with magnitudes in excess of 0.5, with some estimates reaching a unit elasticity response of 1 (i.e., that the sector can respond to fuel price increases alone so as to keep fuel expenditures constant). Chandler and Nicholls (1990) also reviewed the literature on gasoline demand, indicating an elasticity magnitude range of 0.2 (short term) to 0.7 (long term).

Much of this work, however, fails to account for factors other than price that influenced the response to the 1973 and 1979 oil crises. These nonprice factors include actual fuel shortages, rationing, accompanying fears of ongoing shortages and much higher future prices, the national consensus to address the energy crisis, and resulting public policies such as fuel economy standards. The failure of many economic analyses to account for the effect of fuel economy standards in raising vehicle efficiency is a particularly serious flaw, since the more detailed work all suggests that vehicle efficiency improvement is the dominant part of the response to higher gasoline prices. Attributing vehicle efficiency improvement to price alone rather than fuel economy standards (or other nonprice factors that influence automaker product planning) yields inflated estimates of the elasticity. Greene (1990) showed that when fuel economy standards and price are examined together for their effect on vehicle efficiency over the 1978–1989 period, standards are found to be the dominant factor and that the price effect is only marginally significant.

Careful studies, using more disaggregate data, have generally shown combined effects on gasoline consumption within the lower elasticity magnitude range of 0.3 to 0.5. A high-fuel-price scenario by Train (1986) yielded an implied elasticity of –0.32. An earlier analysis by Greene (1979), which examined differences in gasoline consumption among U.S. states, obtained a gasoline price elasticity of –0.34. Thus, the earlier stated range of roughly 0.3 to 0.5 appears to be a reasonable estimate of the expected response to higher gasoline prices. This can be considered a medium-term response, since it will take a vehicle stock turnover cycle to fully realize the fuel economy improvement component of the response. The short-term response would be even smaller, with an elasticity on the order of –0.1, based on the travel demand component of the response.

The evidence for a larger long-term response—e.g., from changes in geographic factors of land use and transportation infrastructure—is unclear. Econometric work has generally failed to find such a response. On the other hand, a broader look at the effect of land use on fuel consumption suggests the possibility of substantial changes in per capita gasoline consumption from changes in land use (Newman and

Kenworthy 1989). However, even though higher gasoline prices are correlated with lower rates of fuel consumption, it is far from clear that fuel price itself is any more of a factor than is suggested by the low short-term travel demand elasticities noted above. A reason that fuel price alone may be insufficient to induce a larger long-term response is that the dominant medium-term response of higher vehicle efficiency will hold down the cost per mile driven in spite of higher fuel prices, thus dampening the incentive for long-term changes in geographic factors. Of course, other policy changes, perhaps in concert with higher fuel prices, could result in substantially different land use and travel demand.

Vehicle Pricing Effects

Fewer published analyses are available on the effects of differential vehicle pricing related to fuel economy. The main sources of information are experience with the existing U.S. gas guzzler tax, international experience with price differentials correlated to fuel economy, and econometric studies of vehicle choice. Common sense suggests that a fee and rebate scheme ("feebate") related to fuel economy should shift the decisions of both consumers and automakers, but quantifying this effect is difficult. Among the many factors that go into pricing, manufacturers presumably price cars so as to help meet CAFE targets. This means cutting prices of efficient vehicles, which means low margins on these vehicles. Conversely, standards can increase the per-unit profitability of inefficient cars. The result is a cross-subsidy tending to benefit buyers of the more fuel-efficient vehicles within the two regulatory categories of cars and light trucks. Although some analysts have examined this issue (e.g., Greene 1991), the magnitude of CAFE-induced price differentials is not publicly known and may vary among automakers according to their favored segments and market strategies.

Government intervention in vehicle pricing could mitigate some or all of this pressure to modify the vehicle pricing for the sake of compliance with CAFE standards. Thus, a pricing-induced increase in demand would make efficient vehicles more profitable. In principle, a subsidy proportional to the extent that a vehicle exceeds a standard could motivate ongoing technological improvements in efficiency. On the other hand, if a binding regulatory constraint is in place, the response to a feebate could be weakened analogously to the weakened response to the fuel price increases illustrated in Figure 10-6. To the extent that CAFE standards involve cross-subsidy of vehicles based on fuel economy, a feebate would only induce a further response if the feebate differentials were greater than the hidden price differentials induced by the regulatory regime. An added noneconomic response might result from associating a sticker price difference with fuel economy information, but such a consumer-only response is likely to be small and possibly transient.

Gas Guzzler Tax

Feebates can be viewed as an extension of the gas guzzler tax. A look at the past record and fuel economy distribution of the automobile fleet provides evidence that the gas guzzler tax does have an effect. Figure 10-7 plots the gas guzzler tax threshold along with the average fuel economy of low-mpg cars (vehicles rated at less than 21 mpg prior to the onset of the gas guzzler tax) and that of other cars

---

Figure 10-7

U.S. Gas Guzzler Tax Thresholds and the Average Fuel Economies of New Low-mpg Cars Versus Other Cars, 1980–1987

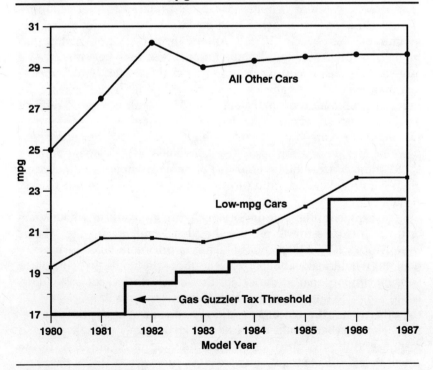

Source: From Ross et al. (1991).

from 1980 through 1987. It can be seen in this figure that the gas guzzler tax has acted to bring up the less efficient part of the fleet, even while improvement of the rest of the fleet has slowed down.

Figure 10-8 presents a scatter plot of fuel consumption versus new-car price for the 1990 fleet. The bulk of the fleet shows a definite positive correlation, but the points level off along the 22.5 mpg line, corresponding to the gas guzzler tax threshold. Few models cross that line, putting a turn in an otherwise linear trend. Another view of this same phenomenon is given by the cumulative distribution of vehicle sales with respect to fuel economy (see Heavenrich et al. 1991, Table 2). A kink occurs at 22.5 mpg, above which the sales fraction rises

Figure 10-8

U.S. Fuel Consumption Versus Vehicle Price for 1990 New Cars

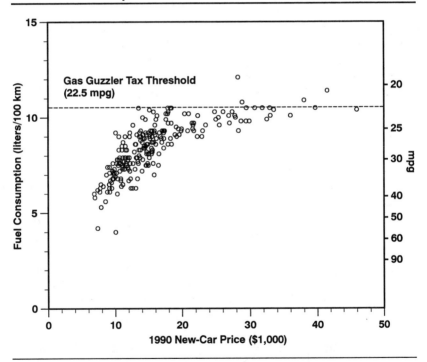

Source: Based on nameplate average fuel economy from Williams and Hu (1991); prices estimated as the median of the base Manufacturer's Suggested Retail Price (MSRP) listings for each name-plate, rounded to the nearest $100, from Automotive News (1990).

Note: For the vehicles in our database, the estimated 1990 average new-car price was $15,100, slightly lower than the $16,000 average 1990 new-car transaction price reported by MVMA (1992). The estimated average price of 1990 new light trucks was $13,200, and the overall 1990 light-duty-vehicle average was $14,500.

rapidly. Khazzoom (1993) reported finding strong evidence for the effect of the gas guzzler tax in his econometric analyses of factors relating to fuel economy and safety.

Thus, it seems clear that the gas guzzler tax is having an effect on the market, through some combination of decisions by both consumers and manufacturers. Because of the aforementioned effect of CAFE standards (as noted by Sweeney 1979a), however, it is not likely that the gas guzzler tax is resulting in higher fleet average fuel economy. Manufacturers meeting a CAFE standard constraint are probably balancing fewer sales of guzzlers with fewer sales of their most efficient cars.

International Experience

Internationally, vehicle taxes are often related at least indirectly to vehicle fuel consumption rates (Dolan et al. 1992; Schipper et al. 1992). Taxes specifically related to emissions or fuel economy have been enacted in Austria, Denmark, Germany, and Sweden. Austria's new tax program took effect in January 1992; it applies a scale ranging from 0 to 14 percent, with 0 percent tax for cars averaging less than 3 liters per 100 km on European driving tests (a fuel economy better than 80 mpg). In many countries, tax schedules traditionally have been based on weight, engine displacement, or power (IEA 1991). Vehicle tax rates are thereby linked to fuel consumption rate, since these attributes are correlated with fuel consumption. Further analysis of this issue is given in Chapter 11 of this book (Schipper and Eriksson 1995).

In 1989, the Province of Ontario established a gas guzzler tax consisting of a four-tier tax schedule applicable to cars having a highway fuel consumption above 9.5 liters per 100 km—i.e., an adjusted highway fuel economy of less than 19 mpg (Millyard 1991). In 1991, the guzzler tax was expanded, increasing the maximum tax level and providing a rebate of $100 for vehicles using less than 6 liters per 100 km (adjusted highway fuel economy greater than 36 mpg). Termed the Tax for Fuel Conservation, this program set a precedent for feebates in North America. The Ontario program is designed to generate revenue, estimated at $30 million to $35 million in 1991, which is dedicated to other environmentally related transportation programs. An expansion of the program to cover all light-truck classes and provide rebates up to $250 was proposed in April 1992 but not enacted. An evaluation of the effects of this program on vehicle choice has not yet been reported.

Von Hippel and Levi (1983) graphed various countries' vehicle purchase and registration taxes, reduced to equivalent cents per mile, against vehicle fuel consumption rate, revealing a general association of higher tax rates with higher fuel consumption rates. Tax rates reported at that time often went up substantially at consumption rates greater than 10 liters per 100 km (lower than 23.5 mpg). Dolan et al. (1992) tabulate a number of vehicle tax schedules, which might be used to further analyze the correlations shown by Schipper et al. (1992) relating vehicle fuel consumption to fuel price. Since so little analysis relating these vehicle taxation policies to national fleet average fuel economy has been reported, this remains a promising area for research.

Vehicle Market Analyses

Extensive econometric analysis has been pursued regarding consumer decision making in the light-vehicle market. The most sophisticated analyses reflect the disaggregate nature of consumer decision making that characterizes durable goods markets, such as that for automobiles. Qualitative choice models—which treat choice among exhaustive, finite, and mutually exclusive options—provide a useful way to describe and estimate automobile demand (Train 1986). Such models have been applied to analyze the potential consumer acceptance of alternatively fueled vehicles and the response to changes in fuel taxes and other vehicle-related policies. A DOE-sponsored study (discussed below) is using qualitative choice methods to analyze feebates (W.B. Davis et al. 1993).

Aggregate analyses have generally concluded that the consumer response to feebates is relatively small, on the order of a 1 mpg response for a vehicle pricing differential of $300 per mpg (based on one of the authors' analyses of the proposed California DRIVE+ program—see Gordon and Levenson 1989). Greene (1991) examined short-term pricing strategies for improving fuel economy. Although feebates were not directly addressed, he concluded that beyond small shifts (less than about 1 mpg), it is difficult to improve fleetwide fuel economy through consumer-side sales shifts alone; he did not analyze manufacturer responses. Response to a feebate would exhibit short- and medium-term characteristics analogous to those described earlier in discussing response to a gasoline tax. The short-term response represents no more than a one-time reordering of consumer choice. A larger response can be expected after manufacturers have had time to make product changes in response to fuel economy-related tax differentials.

Unfortunately, manufacturers' responses to feebates are the area about which the least information is publicly known. A strong manufacturer response could yield a large fleetwide fuel economy improvement if automakers add efficient technologies to new vehicles and downplay technology applications, such as acceleration performance enhancements, which are detrimental to fuel economy. Estimation of manufacturer response to feebates can be guided by a technology cost model such as those developed by Energy and Environmental Analysis, Inc. (EEA 1985, and later work—e.g., Greene and Duleep 1992) or ACEEE (DeCicco and Ross 1993). However, as when used to model response to fuel price, this technology cost framework faces limitations because other factors influencing manufacturer decision making (such as CAFE standards) may not be adequately accounted for. The technology cost rationale assumes that automakers will improve fuel economy up to the point where the marginal cost of improvement matches the feebate rate.

Using an updated technology cost model based on EEA (1985) and an updated consumer demand model based on Train (1986), W.B. Davis et al. (1993) estimated the overall response for a variety of feebate formulations. The principal case analyzed is a feebate roughly equivalent to a front-loaded $.50 per gallon gasoline tax, or $60 per mpg for cars and $110 per mpg for light trucks at current new-fleet average fuel economy levels. Preliminary results of Davis et al. indicate improvements of about 11 percent by 2000 and 14 percent by 2010 in average new light-duty fleet fuel economy relative to their baseline, which itself had new light-vehicle fuel economy improving 32 percent over the 1990 level. They therefore predict a roughly 50 percent improvement in new light-vehicle fuel economy by 2010 with the feebate in place. The Davis et al. model also indicates that the technology improvement component is dominant by far, with the manufacturer response contributing 13 percent and the consumer response contributing only 1 percent to the 14 percent overall response they project for 2010. This is a substantial response for feebates that appear to average 1 to 2 percent of new-vehicle price on a fleet average basis. Feebates for some models would be larger; the Davis et al. scenario has maximum rebates of $760 for cars and $920 for trucks, or 5 to 6 percent of the $14,500 average new light-vehicle price in 1990.

Feebate Response Possibilities

Thus, although the medium- to long-term fuel economy improvement that might be induced by a feebate could be substantial, it remains quite uncertain. Clearly, the response of both consumers and manufacturers to a feebate is related to the magnitude of the fees and rebates. As just noted, preliminary modeling results of W.B. Davis et al. (1993) suggest that feebate magnitudes averaging 1 to 2 percent of vehicle price could induce a substantial response. A big issue is the effect of unmodeled factors that might weaken the response, such as binding CAFE standards or strong consumer and manufacturer preferences for applying technologies for performance and other vehicle amenities besides fuel economy. Sweeney (1979a) projected that the guzzler tax would have no impact on fleet average fuel economy in the presence of CAFE standards. The feebate scheme analyzed by Davis et al. is much broader in coverage (it includes light trucks and rebates on efficient vehicles), but somewhat weaker in leverage (average feebate as a percentage of price) for the vehicles that the existing guzzler tax does cover. However, Davis et al. did not attempt to simultaneously model feebates with CAFE standards, and so, with the information at hand, it is difficult to say what the effect of a feebate system would be in the presence of either current or strengthened CAFE standards.

DeCicco et al. (1993) suggest that feebates averaging 5 to 10 percent of vehicle price might be needed to obtain a substantial fuel economy improvement. Manufacturer sales rebates typically fall in the range of 5 to 10 percent of price, which is coincidentally close to the average feebate magnitude of 8 percent of vehicle price that would be obtained by extending the current U.S. gas guzzler tax (DeCicco et al. 1993). A feebate or guzzler tax can be linked to a schedule of increasing fuel economy standards, as proposed by the Energy Conservation Coalition (ECC 1992) and DeCicco and Geller (1992). This combined approach would provide a greater degree of predictability because manufacturers would be constrained by the standards. It may not initially improve average fuel economy beyond the standards level. However, if standards become fixed at some point in time, feebates might eventually pull the fleet average above the standards level if advances in automotive engineering yield technologies for ongoing efficiency improvements at low cost.

At present, the uncertainty regarding the response to vehicle taxation appears to be greater than that to fuel taxation. However, the influence of feebates on the vehicle market is clearly more direct than that of fuel taxes. According to the technology cost rationale and the preliminary results of W.B. Davis et al. (1993), feebates might begin to close the efficiency gap discussed earlier. The resulting induced fuel economy improvements could be in line with estimated technically feasible levels well above the 1990 new-fleet average, depending on what one believes about technology effectiveness and costs. For example, the preliminary Davis et al. projection of a 2010 new-fleet average fuel economy roughly 50 percent higher than the 1990 level is well into the range of 30 to 80 percent potential improvement identified in

Figure 10-2. Clearly, such improvements could be achieved with greater certainty if feebates are used in combination with strengthened fuel economy standards.

Policy Implications

Although the responses to fuel taxation and vehicle pricing policies are not fully certain, the uncertainty does not appear to be so large as to preclude some policy conclusions. For the sake of argument, we will examine what it would take to hold U.S. light-vehicle gasoline consumption to the 1990 level of roughly 6 Mbd in 2010. As noted earlier, without policy changes, gasoline consumption is likely to increase to 8 to 9 Mbd by 2010. Policies adequate to achieve consumption reductions of 2 to 3 Mbd—i.e., savings of 25 to 33 percent relative to expected growth—would therefore be required.

A range of estimates for the required increase in fuel price can be obtained by examining two bounding cases: (1) low growth (25 percent cut needed) with high elasticity (–0.55) and (2) high growth (33 percent cut needed) with low elasticity (–0.25). The resulting requisite price increase is by factors of 1.7 to 5. The midrange estimate is that fuel prices would have to rise by a factor of 2.4, to about $3.00 per gallon (1990$) in order to obtain a 30 percent cut in light-vehicle fuel consumption. This estimate does not fully account for stock turnover time, for a likely phase-in of the tax increase, or for the region of poor price response due to the CAFE constraint. Thus, an even higher tax level would probably be needed to return fuel consumption to the 1990 level by 2010.

Compared with fuel prices, vehicle taxation will more directly affect fuel economy, which, as noted earlier, is the principal component of response. With unadjusted projections of VMT growth, achieving 25 to 33 percent cuts in gasoline use by 2010 implies a need for 30 to 50 percent increases in stock fuel economy by that time. This is within the range noted earlier as potentially achievable assuming a technology cost model for the manufacturer response to feebates of adequate magnitude. W.B. Davis et al. (1993) suggest that vehicle tax differentials averaging only 2 percent of new-vehicle price could achieve a substantial degree of fuel economy improvement. DeCicco et al. (1993) propose that higher feebates, averaging 5 percent or more of new-vehicle price, might be needed. In any case, this range of vehicle pricing changes is certainly much smaller than the range of fuel pricing changes needed to achieve similar effects.

If gasoline prices are stable or rise only slowly (without major fuel tax increases) and if a feebate causes fuel economy to rise more than fuel price, the cost per mile of driving will fall. The resulting rebound effect of increased VMT will follow curves like those shown earlier in Figure 10-4. Thus vehicle-oriented fuel economy policies, such as feebates or stronger CAFE standards, might usefully be complemented with fuel tax increases sufficient to keep the cost of driving from falling. In such a scenario, a gasoline tax increase could be phased in at a rate chosen to match to rate of stock (all vehicles, new and used) fuel economy improvement. For example, offsetting a 40 percent improvement in stock average fuel economy achieved over 20 years would involve a fuel tax increase of 2 percent per year (about $.025 per year) in real terms and would not increase the average gasoline tax burden. From a fiscal policy perspective (federal and state), such tax increases would be needed to avoid erosion of this revenue source due to the increased fuel economy. Of course, other policies to hold down VMT, such as transportation demand management, greater provision of alternative modes, and pay-as-you-drive insurance, would also counteract a fuel economy rebound effect.

The combined impact of fuel price and vehicle fuel economy policies can be calculated from their estimated effects on VMT and stock average fuel economy. Figure 10-9 gives a contour plot of projected 2010 light-vehicle gasoline consumption, showing the separate effects of stock fuel economy and fuel price. The curves present a gasoline consumption "surface," which slopes downward for both increasing gasoline price and increasing fuel economy. Superimposed is an estimated locus of the medium-term response of fuel economy to fuel price (assuming a fuel economy-versus-gasoline price elasticity of 0.3, the midrange value of Figure 10-5). The intersection of the dotted lines represents forecast gasoline consumption in absence of policy change, with gasoline price at $1.50 per gallon and stock fuel economy rising only marginally, to about 26 mpg. The resulting consumption level is 8.4 Mbd (between the plotted "level curves" for 8 Mbd and 9 Mbd).

Following the fuel economy response locus up to the 6 Mbd-level curve indicates what is required to achieve this degree of oil consumption control with fuel taxation; the implied fuel price is about $3.50 (1990$) per gallon. (This accounts for stock turnover, but not tax phase-in or likely nonequilibrium of the current fuel economy market.) The region above the fuel economy-versus-fuel price locus represents possibilities obtainable with vehicle taxation policies inducing a greater degree of fuel economy improvement. For example, if fuel taxes are not increased and the 2010 fuel price is $1.50 (1990$) per gallon, extending the vertical dotted line up to the 6 Mbd contour gives the requisite 2010 stock fuel economy, roughly 37 mpg (average of

Figure 10-9

Projected U.S. Light-Vehicle Gasoline Consumption in 2010 as a Function of Gasoline Price and Stock Average Fuel Economy

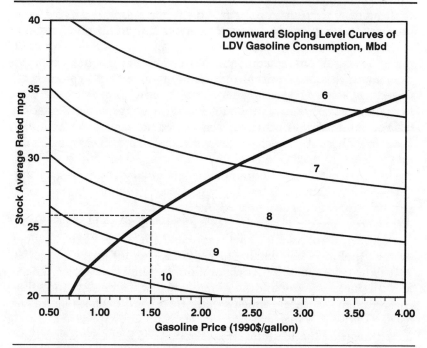

Note: Assumes nominal projections of 2.61 × 10^{12} miles per year vehicle-miles of travel (VMT) and $1.50 per gallon gasoline, fuel price elasticities of –0.10 for VMT and 0.30 for mpg, and 20 percent shortfall between rated and on-road fuel economy. Level curves (contours) of projected gasoline consumption are shown in millions of barrels per day (Mbd).

both cars and light trucks, new and used; this does account for the rebound effect). One can interpolate results of stock model analyses to find the new-vehicle fuel economy trajectory needed to achieve a given degree of stock improvement. For example, scenarios of continuous improvement from 1994 to 2010 suggest that new-fleet CAFE improvements of 30 percent by 2001 and 60 percent by 2010 would yield a stock average of approximately 37 mpg by 2010 (DeCicco 1992), provided there are proportional improvements in light trucks and that the light-truck market share stabilizes at 33 percent.

Within the plausible range of elasticity estimates, it appears that increasing U.S. fuel taxes to levels comparable to those in Europe might be sufficient to substantially curtail growth in U.S. light-vehicle oil consumption. After adjusting for the medium-term response, such a policy would represent an increase in taxation of roughly $140 billion. Annual U.S. federal individual income tax receipts are now approximately $400 billion. Therefore, effectively controlling light-vehicle fuel consumption (and CO_2 emissions) through fuel taxation would entail not only a major energy policy challenge, but a profound transformation of the U.S. taxation system.

Compared with gasoline tax increases amounting to a 100 to 200 percent change in fuel price, vehicle tax differentials averaging 5 to 10 percent of new-vehicle price would appear to be less politically intimidating. Since a feebate can be revenue-neutral, such a policy can also be implemented without the need for major tax reform. Politics and practicality are surely not wholly ignorant of economics, and economics can be informed by both. Nevertheless, the obvious practical contrast between these two policy approaches was apparently lost on the authors of one recent study sponsored by the U.S. Environmental Protection Agency (DRI 1991), which found raising the gasoline tax to be the superior option in terms of "economic efficiency."

It goes without saying that the "error bars" on an analysis such as that presented here are quite large, since it involves extrapolations well beyond the observed ranges of response for mpg and VMT. The synthesis shown in Figure 10-9 is clearly illustrative rather than definitive. Other analysts could develop other scenarios based on different assumptions for the key parameters. However, the policy implications would not differ greatly for other reasonable values of the elasticities as reviewed here. It appears that a combination of policies would be most effective to achieve the degree of control over U.S. gasoline consumption examined in this chapter. Vehicle-directed policies, such as feebates or CAFE standards, appear to be essential. A fuller accounting of the costs of such actions is beyond the scope of this chapter, as is a further revisiting of the arguments as to why such a degree of control would be desirable. Greater understanding of the mechanisms and effectiveness of vehicle pricing policies is required if they are to complement or replace the regulatory approach. Nevertheless, the need for a vehicle-directed approach means that policymakers should not delay actions to fill the current void in U.S. energy policy that leaves rising light-vehicle oil use unaddressed.

The automotive industry has a crucial role to play in the policy development effort needed to formulate workable vehicle taxation policies. All indications are that the greatest response to any policy change will be the effects on manufacturer product planning. Government and independent analysts can only hope to approximately estimate the industry's response. In addition, vehicle pricing interventions must address the difficult area of intermanufacturer equity, which again can only be treated with the industry's help. One response by the industry might be to deny that there are serious problems associated with the rising light-vehicle fuel consumption. Another response might be to parry responsibility by stating that the only appropriate intervention is through fuel tax increases. Such responses will ensure ongoing political battles, resulting in policies that satisfy neither side and only set the stage for future controversies. There may be progress, but it will be intermittent and painful.

We envision a different type of response, however. To start, there would have to be a process of building consensus about common goals and setting the framework for vehicle taxation-based policies. But if this process succeeds, the industry and government can together change the rules of the marketplace so that fuel economy improvement becomes part of the game. Progress is a key to survival—ongoing improvements in cars and light trucks are part of a competitive business strategy. Today, raising fleet average fuel economy is not part of that improvement strategy. Establishing a meaningful price advantage for more efficient vehicles would change the rules so that fuel economy gets the ongoing attention of the substantial design and engineering talents that the industry can marshal. Developing a policy structure that is equitable and effective and that allows adequate time for improvements is a challenge that cannot be met without good-faith participation by the industry. If this challenge is met, we can look ahead to a time when cars and trucks will be continually improved in many ways, including fuel economy. The United States will have then succeeded in steering itself down a road of decreasing transportation oil consumption.

Conclusion

Raising the average fuel economy of light vehicles is a most important aspect of controlling transportation oil use and its associated economic and environmental problems for the United States. Market conditions in recent years and as expected over the next decade or so entail relatively low oil prices, rising slowly in real terms and possibly punctuated by transient disruptions related to political instabilities in supply regions. Little if any improvement in fuel economy is expected in the absence of policy change.

From an engineering perspective, fuel economy could be improved 30 to 70 percent through technology changes costing less than the value of fuel saved, even at low oil prices. This potential to improve fuel economy implies an efficiency gap, representing a foregone opportunity to improve economic efficiency by improving the technical efficiency of the transportation system. If fully realized, this level of fuel economy improvement is likely to be adequate to avoid net growth in U.S. light-vehicle gasoline consumption by 2010 relative to the 1990 level, yielding environmental as well as economic benefits. What one believes regarding the extent of such an efficiency gap partly determines the degree of policy intervention justified to improve automotive fuel economy.

Past U.S. policy has relied on fuel economy regulation—CAFE standards—as the primary means to control light-vehicle fuel consumption. Tension between regulatory requirements and market forces is inevitable. However, if it becomes too extreme and is in disagreement with political thinking, such tension is destabilizing from a public policy perspective, leading to unsteady and inadequate policy guidance. Shifts in policy thinking are manifest in the CAFE standard rollbacks of 1986–1989 and the political hurdles faced by attempts to renew and strengthen fuel economy regulation. Market-based policies offer hope of addressing the issue in a way that results in less tension while achieving comparable goals. Fuel taxation and efficiency-related vehicle taxation are two proposed market-based policy options for replacing or complementing fuel economy regulation. This chapter has explored the potential and limitations of such pricing policies for reducing light-duty-vehicle fuel consumption.

Existing information on the response of the vehicle and travel demand markets indicates that dramatic increases in fuel price would be needed to stabilize light-vehicle fuel consumption in the United States. Although there is uncertainty in the response, even the most optimistic suggest at least a doubling of fuel prices would be needed. On the one hand, price levels in excess of $3.00 per gallon would be on a par with those of most Organisation for Economic Cooperation and Development (OECD) countries and therefore need not be considered unreasonable if phased in. On the other hand, achieving such price levels would entail a truly radical change in U.S. taxation policy, amounting to a transfer equivalent to about one-third of present personal income tax revenues. Much smaller tax increases, on the order of $.10 per gallon or less, as recently discussed, fall inside an area of great uncertainty of response; although such small increases might have some tiny (probably unobservable) effect on travel demand, it is most likely that their effect on fuel economy would be nil.

Less information is available about the response to efficiency-based vehicle pricing policies, such as an expanded gas guzzler tax or feebates. There is clear evidence that the existing U.S. gas guzzler tax, even though it touches a relatively small fraction of the fleet, is bolstering the fuel economy of the least efficient automobile classes. The more extensive experience with similar vehicle taxes in OECD countries has yet to be analyzed in a way that permits quantitative extrapolation to the U.S. market. Vehicle choice modeling does offer some guidance, suggesting that vehicle pricing approaches could induce fuel economy improvement approximately equal to the technical potential for improvement, which, as noted earlier, is likely to be sufficient to stabilize light-vehicle oil consumption. Studies also indicate that the dominant part of the response is through manufacturer product improvements, with a much smaller response through changes in consumer product choices. Although the magnitude of the required tax differentials is uncertain, modeling results and other evidence (existing gas guzzler tax and manufacturer sales rebates) suggest that average tax differentials amounting to 5 to 10 percent of vehicle price could accomplish a substantial fuel economy improvement.

Compared with a fuel pricing approach, adequate control of rising light-vehicle gasoline consumption through vehicle taxation would require a much less radical change in existing fiscal and economic policies. Fuel economy regulation will increase the certainty with which a given (standards) level of fuel economy improvement would be obtained. However, the existence of a binding regulatory constraint weakens the fuel economy response to either feebates or fuel taxes. In particular, given the low elasticity of fuel economy to fuel price, it is possible that fuel taxation will never be an effective way to raise fuel economy in the U.S. context as long as reasonably strong vehicle-directed policies (either regulation or feebates) are in place. Nevertheless, increased fuel taxes will be a valuable complement to fuel economy policies at least because higher taxes can offset a "rebound" effect by keeping the cost per mile of driving from falling. Other policies to control travel demand can also address the rebound effect; there may also be other good reasons to raise the gasoline tax.

In short, if the U.S. hopes to steer light-vehicle fuel consumption through pricing interventions, policymakers should focus on vehicle stickers rather than on gasoline pumps. Given goals based on either stabilizing light-vehicle oil consumption or closing the apparent efficiency gap, fuel taxation may be helpful but is far from sufficient. Although vehicle taxation shows great promise, a much greater understanding is needed of the industry's response and the conditions necessary for the effectiveness of such an approach. It would therefore be imprudent to abandon the trying but tried-and-true regulatory approach for the current round of policymaking. However, adding a feebate or expanded gas guzzler tax to strengthened standards would provide an opportunity to develop and refine this type of market approach. Vehicle pricing policies are likely to be the key to a long-term strategy for obtaining substantial ongoing improvements in fuel economy, perhaps without the need to periodically agonize over strengthening the regulatory standards. A concerted and rational policy development effort, in which industry must play a crucial role, is needed if the country is to avail itself of a promising new approach to addressing the problems associated with rising transportation energy consumption.

References

American Automobile Association (AAA). 1993. Press release on results of a public opinion poll regarding proposed increases in energy and gasoline taxes. Washington, D.C. February

Automotive News. 1990. *1990 Market Data Book*. Detroit: Crain Communications.

Bohi, D.R., and M.B. Zimmerman. 1984. "An Update on Econometric Studies of Energy Demand Behavior." *Annual Review of Energy* 9: 105–154.

Chandler, W.U., and A.K. Nicholls. 1990. *Assessing Carbon Emissions Control Strategies: A Carbon Tax or a Gasoline Tax?* ACEEE Policy Paper No. 3. Washington, D.C.: American Council for an Energy-Efficient Economy. February.

Charles River Associates (CRA). 1991. *Policy Alternatives for Reducing Petroleum Use and Greenhouse Gas Emissions*. Report prepared for the Motor Vehicle Manufacturers Association by Charles River Associates. Boston, Mass. September.

Davis, S.C., and S.G. Strang. 1993. *Transportation Energy Data Book*. 13th ed. ORNL-6743. Oak Ridge, Tenn.: Oak Ridge National Laboratory. March.

Davis, W.B., and D. Gordon. 1993. *Using Feebates to Improve the Average Fuel Efficiency of the U.S. Vehicle Fleet*. LBL-31910. Berkeley: Lawrence Berkeley Laboratory, Energy Analysis Program. January.

Davis, W.B., M.D. Levine, K. Train, and K.G. Duleep. 1993. "Feebates: Estimated Impacts on Vehicle Fuel Economy, Fuel Consumption, CO_2 Emissions, and Consumer Surplus." Preliminary results of a study forthcoming from the Energy Analysis Program, Lawrence Berkeley Laboratory. Presented at the Conference on Transportation and Energy Strategies for a Sustainable Transportation System, Asilomar, Calif., August 22–25, 1993.

DeCicco, J.M. 1992. *Savings from CAFE: Projections of the Future Oil Savings from Light Vehicle Fuel Economy Standards*. Washington, D.C.: American Council for an Energy-Efficient Economy. May.

DeCicco, J.M., and H.S. Geller. 1992. *A Size-Based Feebates Approach for Increasing Light Vehicle Fuel Economy*. Washington, D.C.: American Council for an Energy-Efficient Economy. January.

DeCicco, J.M., H.S. Geller, and J.H. Morrill. 1993. *Feebates for Fuel Economy: Market Incentives for Encouraging Production and Sales of Efficient Vehicles*. Washington, D.C.: American Council for an Energy-Efficient Economy. May.

DeCicco, J.M., and M. Ross. 1993. *An Updated Assessment of the Near-Term Potential for Improving Automotive Fuel Economy*. Washington, D.C.: American Council for an Energy-Efficient Economy. November.

Difiglio, C. 1976. *Analysis of Fuel Economy Excise Taxes and Rebates*. Special Report 169, pp. 40–46. Washington, D.C.: Transportation Research Board, National Research Council.

Dolan, K., B. Anderson, H. Nishimaki, L. Schipper, R. Steiner, and W. Tax. 1992. "Policies Affecting Automobile Attributes in Western Europe and Japan." Draft. International Energy Studies Program, Lawrence Berkeley Laboratory, Berkeley, Calif. January.

Dower, R.C., and M.B. Zimmerman. 1992. *The Right Climate for Carbon Taxes: Creating Economic Incentives to Protect the Atmosphere*. Washington, D.C.: World Resources Institute. August.

DRI (DRI/McGraw-Hill, Inc.). 1991. *An Analysis of Public Policy Measures to Reduce Carbon Dioxide Emissions from the U.S. Transportation Sector*. Report prepared for the U.S. Environmental Protection Agency, Office of Policy, Planning, and Evaluation. January.

Energy and Environmental Analysis, Inc. (EEA). 1985. *Documentation of the Characteristics of Technological Improvements Utilized in the Technology Cost Segment Model (TCSM)*. Report prepared for the U.S. Department of Energy. Arlington, Va. June.

Energy Conservation Coalition (ECC). 1992. *Combining Consumer and Manufacturer Incentives with Stronger Fuel Economy Standards*. Takoma Park, Md. April.

Energy Information Administration (EIA). 1990. *Transportation Energy Demand Module for the PC-AEO Spreadsheet Model*. Washington, D.C.: U.S. Department of Energy, Energy Information Administration.

———. 1991. *Studies of Energy Taxes*. Service Report SR/EMEU/91-02. Washington, D.C.: U.S. Department of Energy, Energy Information Administration.

———. 1993. *Annual Energy Outlook 1993*. Washington, D.C.: U.S. Department of Energy, Energy Information Administration.

Federal Highway Administration (FHWA). 1991. *Highway Statistics 1990*. Report FHWA-PL-91-003. Washington, D.C.

Geller, H., J.M. DeCicco, and S. Laitner. 1992. *Energy Efficiency and Job Creation: The Employment and Income Benefits from Investing in Energy Conserving Technologies.* Report. Washington, D.C.: American Council for an Energy-Efficient Economy. October.

Gordon, D., and L. Levenson. 1989. *DRIVE+: A Proposal for California to Use Consumer Fees and Rebates to Reduce New Motor Vehicle Emissions and Fuel Consumption.* Berkeley: Lawrence Berkeley Laboratory. July.

Greene, D.L. 1979. "State Differences in the Demand for Gasoline: An Econometric Analysis." *Energy Systems and Policy* 3 (2): 191–212.

———. 1990. "CAFE or Price? An Analysis of the Effects of Federal Fuel Economy Regulations and Gasoline Price on New Car Mpg, 1978-1989." *Energy Journal* 11 (3): 37–57.

———. 1991. "Short-Run Pricing Strategies to Increase Corporate Average Fuel Economy." *Economic Inquiry* 29 (1): 101–114.

———. (Oak Ridge National Laboratory). 1993a. Personal communication. February.

———. 1993b. "Effect of a Gasoline Tax on Fuel Economy and Gasoline Consumption." Presentation to the SAE Government/Industry Meeting, Washington, D.C., May 7, 1993.

Greene, D.L., and K.G. Duleep. 1992. *Costs and Benefits of Automotive Fuel Economy Improvement: A Partial Analysis.* ORNL-6704. Oak Ridge, Tenn.: Center for Transportation Analysis, Oak Ridge National Laboratory. March.

Harvey, G. (DHS Associates, Berkeley, Calif.). 1993. Personal communication. January.

Heavenrich, R.M., J.D. Murrell, and K.H. Hellman. 1991. *Light-Duty Automotive Technology and Fuel Economy Trends Through 1991.* EPA/AA/CTAB/91-02. Ann Arbor, Mich.: U.S. Environmental Protection Agency, Office of Mobile Sources. May.

International Energy Agency (IEA). 1991. *Fuel Efficiency of Passenger Cars.* Paris: International Energy Agency, Organisation for Economic Cooperation and Development (OECD).

Kempton, W. 1991. "Automobile Efficiency and Behavior: Lessons from Utility Energy Efficiency." Presentation to the Workshop and Committee Meeting, Committee on Fuel Economy of Automobiles and Light Trucks, National Research Council, Irvine, Calif. July.

Khazzoom, J.D. 1993. *An Econometric Model of Fuel Economy and Single-Vehicle Highway Fatalities.* Report. Department of Economics, California State University at San Jose. May.

Koomey, J., and A.H. Rosenfeld. 1990. "Revenue-Neutral Incentives for Efficiency and Environmental Quality." *Contemporary Policy Issues* 8 (July): 142–156.

Ledbetter, M., and M. Ross. 1992. "Light Vehicles: Policies for Reducing Their Energy Use and Environmental Impacts." In *Energy and Environment: The Policy Challenge*, edited by J. Byrne. University of Delaware Energy Policy Studies, Vol. 6. Newark, Del.: Transaction Books.

Leone, R.A., and T. Parkinson. 1990. *Conserving Energy—Is There a Better Way? A Study of Corporate Average Fuel Economy Regulation*. Report prepared for the Association of International Automobile Manufacturers (AIAM). Washington, D.C. May.

Miles-McLean, R., S.M. Haltmaier, and M.G. Shelby. 1993. "Designing Incentive-Based Approaches to Limit Carbon Dioxide Emissions from the Light-Duty Vehicle Fleet. In *Transportation and Global Climate Change*, edited by D.L. Greene and D.J. Santini. Washington, D.C.: American Council for an Energy-Efficient Economy.

Millyard, K. 1991. *Brief on the Ontario Tax for Fuel Conservation*. Ottawa: Friends of the Earth.

Mintz, M.M., A.R.D. Vyas, and L.A. Conley. *Between EPA-Test and In-Use Fuel Economy: Are the Correction Factors Correct?* Paper No. 931104. Transportation Research Board. Washington, D.C. January. 1993.

Motor Vehicle Manufacturers Association (MVMA). 1992. *MVMA Motor Vehicle Facts and Figures 1992*. Detroit, Mich.

Murrell, J.D., R.M. Heavenrich, and K.H. Hellman. 1993. *Light-Duty Automotive Technology and Fuel Economy Trends Through 1993*. EPA/AA/CTAB/93-01. Ann Arbor, Mich.: U.S. Environmental Protection Agency, Office of Mobile Sources. May. 1993.

National Research Council (NRC). 1992. *Automotive Fuel Economy: How Far Should We Go?* Report of the Committee on Fuel Economy of Automobiles and Light Trucks. Washington, D.C.: National Academy Press. April.

Newman, P.W.G., and J.R. Kenworthy. 1989. *Cities and Automobile Dependence: A Sourcebook*. Aldershot, England: Gower Technical.

Nivola, P.S. 1986. *The Politics of Energy Conservation*. Washington, D.C.: Brookings Institution.

Office of Technology Assessment (OTA). 1991. Improving Automobile Fuel Economy: New Standards, New Approaches. Report OTA-E-504. Washington, D.C.: U.S. Congress, Office of Technology Assessment. October.

Ross, M., M. Ledbetter, and F. An. 1991. *Options for Reducing Oil Use by Light Vehicles: An Analysis of Technologies and Policy*. 1991. Washington, D.C.: American Council for an Energy-Efficient Economy. December.

Schipper, L., and G. Eriksson. 1995. "Taxation Policies Affecting Automobile Characteristics and Use in Western Europe, Japan, and the United States." *In Transportation and Energy: Strategies for a Sustainable Transportation System*, edited by D. Sperling and S. Shaheen. Washington, D.C.: American Council for an Energy-Efficient Economy.

Schipper, L., S. Meyers, R.B. Howarth, and R. Steiner. 1992. *Energy Efficiency and Human Activity: Past Trends, Future Prospects*. Cambridge, England: Cambridge University Press.

SRI. 1991. *Potential for Improved Fuel Economy in Passenger Cars and Light Trucks*. Report prepared for the Motor Vehicle Manufacturers Association by SRI International, Menlo Park, Calif. July.

Stobaugh, R., and D. Yergin, eds. 1979. *Energy Future: Report of the Energy Project at the Harvard Business School*. New York: Random House.

Sweeney, J.L. 1979a. "Effects of Federal Policies on Gasoline Consumption." *Resources and Energy* 2: 3–26.

———. 1979b. "New Car Efficiency Standards and the Demand for Gasoline." *Advances in the Economics of Energy and Resources* 1: 105–133.

Train, K. 1986. *Qualitative Choice Analysis*. Cambridge, Mass.: MIT Press.

Union of Concerned Scientists (UCS), Alliance to Save Energy, American Council for an Energy-Efficient Economy, and Natural Resources Defense Council. 1991. *America's Energy Choices: Investing in a Strong Economy and a Clean Environment*. Cambridge, Mass.: Union of Concerned Scientists. December.

U.S. Department of Energy (U.S. DOE). 1989. *Energy Conservation Trends: Understanding the Factors That Affect Conservation Gains in the U.S. Economy*. DOE/PE-0092. Washington, D.C. September.

von Hippel, F., and B. Levi. 1983. "Automobile Fuel Efficiency: The Opportunity and the Weakness of Existing Market Incentives." *Resources and Conservation* 10: 103–124.

Westbrook, F., and P. Patterson. 1989. "Changing Driving Patterns and Their Effect on Fuel Economy." Paper presented at the 1989 SAE Government/Industry Meeting, Washington, D.C., May 1989.

Williams, J. (Metropolitan Council of Governments, Washington, D.C.). 1993. Personal communication. January.

Williams, L.S., and P.S. Hu. 1991. *Highway Vehicle Mpg and Market Shares Report: Model Year 1990*. ORNL-6672. Oak Ridge, Tenn.: Oak Ridge National Laboratory. April.

Taxation Policies Affecting Automobile Characteristics and Use in Western Europe, Japan, and the United States, 1970–1990

LEE SCHIPPER AND GUNNAR ERIKSSON

Transportation (travel behavior) is influenced by cultural attitudes, infrastructure design and supply, geographical distributions, fiscal policies, and the very characteristics of vehicles themselves. However, the relationships these factors establish are reciprocal, which complicates the question of what influences travel behavior. For example, not only do cultural attitudes influence the choice and use of vehicles, but vehicles and their uses also influence these attitudes. Existing infrastructures are both a response to the previous demand and an influence on future use. Because of how they are distributed, housing, commercial businesses, services, and recreational destinations determine transportation demand, but at the same time, all these factors influence the supply of transport infrastructure and its services. Because of these interactions, it is impossible to describe and analyze all conceivable interrelationships in a quantitative manner. Thus, we focus here on tax structures alone and their direct influence on the transport market as served by individual vehicles.

This chapter presents a description of automobile taxation programs and some preliminary results of our analysis. Outlined are the current taxation schemes and related incentives and disincentives that have been implemented in eight European nations (Denmark, France, the former West Germany, Italy, the Netherlands, Norway,

Sweden, and the United Kingdom), Japan, and the United States.[1] We illustrate the impact of these taxation schemes on a sample of cars sold in the United States that represent typical values for cost, weight, power, and fuel consumption. Although we include some of the features of taxation as applied to diesel vehicles, the focus of our analysis is on gasoline-powered automobiles. Other important factors that contribute to the kinds and use of cars found on the road—land use planning policies that address parking and public transit requirements, regulatory mechanisms that influence emissions with accompanying enforcement policies, and fees applied to use of transport infrastructures like roads and bridges—are not discussed here.

Why Tax Cars? The Deadly Sins

A recent study carried out for the American Academy of Arts and Sciences (Johnson 1993) points to a number of problems and externalities related to the automobile that we label the "deadly sins of the automobile." They include safety problems, air pollution, parking shortages, increased asphalt, urban sprawl, congestion and access problems, disposal of hulks, increased noise, CO_2 levels, and energy use. Table 11-1 itemizes these problems along with an indication of whether each depends strongly (S) or weakly (W) on fuel consumption, distance traveled, time travel takes place, or location where travel takes place. We have listed these alleged sins without particular prejudice as to their possible order of importance, whether in a heuristic sense, a political one (as determined by the outcome of elections or the content of laws), or, suitably monetized, as an economic analysis. What matters for the present discussion is that most of the various tax schemes are *not* aimed at specific sins or externalities, in the Pigouvian sense, but are simply designed to raise revenue or change behavior without reference to a particular sin.

It could be argued that the high fuel taxes in Europe, coupled with the modest (but sometimes high) taxes on car acquisition, more than offset the possible social costs of automobile use there. However, few of the taxes levied in Europe are actually aimed at the sins identified in Table 11-1. Historically, European governments have taxed cars and drivers for revenue purposes. As a result, the response of car buyers or car users to these taxes may be far from optimal because neither own-

---

[1] Much of the information about specific countries was taken from the appendix of a longer version of this chapter published as a Lawrence Berkeley Laboratory report (Schipper and Eriksson 1993).

Table 11-1

The Deadly Sins of the Automobile

	Influencing Factors			
"Sin"	Fuel Consumption	Distance Traveled	Time of Travel	Location of Travel
Safety problems	–	S[a]	W[b]	S
Air pollution	S	S	W	S
Spatial issues: parking, asphalt, sprawl	–	–	W	S
Congestion, access	–	–	S	S
Hulks	–	–	–	S
Noise	–	S	S	S
CO_2 emissions	S	S	–	–
Energy use	S	S	W	S

[a]S = "Sin" strongly dependent on listed factor.
[b]W = "Sin" weakly dependent on listed factor.

ership nor use is taxed to the point at which the marginal tax equals the estimated marginal external cost.

We have recently quantified the main parameters of automobile use in European countries (Schipper et al. 1993a, 1993b), showing how the differences in fuel use could be divided into roughly equal multiplicative components of car ownership, yearly car use in kilometers, and fuel use per kilometer. Whatever the reasons for taxing automobiles and their use, western and northern Europeans use 25 to 33 percent less fuel, per capita and per year, than do North Americans. Three factors—motorization (car ownership), mobility (travel), and macho (the characteristics and fuel economy of cars)—share roughly equally in explaining the three-to-one difference between per capita fuel use in the United States and that in Europe (Figure 11-1).

If Americans had driven the European fleet of vehicles in 1990, per capita fuel use would have been about 25 percent lower than it was, as the second column suggests; if, instead, Americans had driven their cars the distances Europeans drive, fuel use would have been about 30 percent lower, as the third column shows. The fourth column presents the impact on U.S. fuel use of combining these effects, while the last column—actual per capita fuel use for cars in Europe—also reflects lower car ownership there.

Across the ten countries studied, economic and administrative regulation of the automobile is universal. Most countries began taxing

Figure 11-1

Per Capita Energy Use by Automobiles in the United States and Europe, 1990

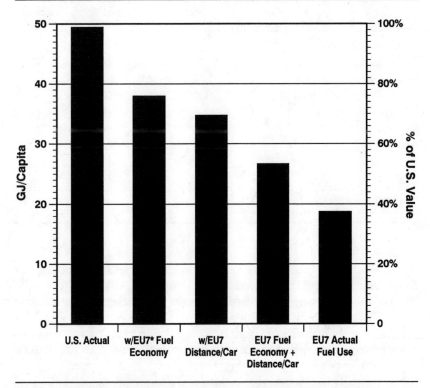

*EU7 = West Germany, France, Italy, the United Kingdom, Norway, Sweden, and Denmark.

Source: Schipper et al. (1993b), p. 8.

cars and fuel before 1973 as a means of raising revenues and funds for highway development and maintenance. Following the oil crisis, many raised these charges to keep pace with changes in the market. At present, the degree and methods of taxation vary widely among countries. Very high purchase taxes and other fiscal schemes have been particularly effective in restraining car size in Denmark, Norway, and Italy and have restrained ownership as well in Denmark. High fuel prices also restrain per capita distance traveled in automobiles in Europe to roughly two-thirds of the U.S. figure.

Few of the taxation schemes we review are aimed at the externalities arising from using motor vehicles. As a result, the impact on these problems has been indirect. From this we conclude that taxation schemes designed to affect fuel use through their impact on automobile ownership, characteristics, or use must be blunt—i.e., effectively increasing the cost of moving a kilometer or buying a car using 1 liter per 100 km of fuel more at the margin. Taxation schemes aimed directly at fuel (fuel taxes) or driving (kilometer taxes) will have a more profound impact on fuel use than those aimed primarily at new-car purchases or other attributes of cars related to fuel use.

Taxation Patterns

Taxation of cars and fuel has a profound impact on the transportation market. The cost of new cars is raised from slightly under 10 percent of the pre-tax price in the United States to over 200 percent in Denmark and Norway. The price of fuel is raised from 30 percent of the pre-tax price in the United States to 300 percent in Italy. Taxes are placed on the cost of insurance, yearly registration, and other items directly related to owning or using a car.

Revenues from the overall system are huge. In 1991, for example, the Italian government collected 64,000 Bn LIT, or approximately $1,000 per capita (1985 U.S.$),[2] by far the highest tax burden on motoring. The Danish government took in 19 Bn DKK (approximately $550 per capita, 1985 U.S.$) from registration, annual commercial vehicle taxes, and taxes on fuel, insurance, and license plates. This income is dominated by new-car taxes (8.3 Bn DKK), with virtually no company cars, although many individuals register cars with their private firms. France collected approximately $550 per capita (1985 U.S.$); the United Kingdom, approximately $475 per capita (1985 U.S.$); and West Germany, 135 Bn DEM ($420 per capita, 1985 U.S.$). To gauge these total taxes, recall that total private gasoline expenditures, *including taxes*, in the United States lay at around $400 per capita (1985 U.S.$) in 1991.

Every nation except the United States taxes fuel significantly. Most countries, again with the exception of the United States, also tax cars moderately or heavily. Taxation of cars varies almost inversely with the importance of the automobile industry. In general, the taxes on fuel are the largest component of the total income, followed by value-added taxes on cars purchased. However, in Denmark and Norway, new-car taxes are so high that this component provided more than 40 percent of the total tax burden.

---

[2] The monetary values are converted from nominal currency in the country denomination to real 1985 U.S.$, using each country's consumer price index and 1985 purchasing power parities.

Do any patterns emerge? Many subtle signs indicate that these taxes have clear impacts on both the characteristics of automobiles and their use. Where tax rules define clear boundaries between tax regimes (e.g., based on engine capacities or weights), company buyers, individual purchasers, and even car manufacturers cluster the number of cars available at the upper end of each range. In France, for example, where the tax is based on engine displacement and no company car benefits exist, cars tend to have low power. In West Germany, where volume is taxed, cars tend to have high compression ratios. In Denmark, high taxes reduce the number of cars, extend their lifetime, and, perversely, encourage the importation of inexpensive but poorly built cars from Eastern Europe. In the United States, where taxes on all these aspects of motoring are low, cars are large, heavy, and powerful and use more fuel per kilometer than cars in European fleets.

Fuel costs in the United States are one-third of the average. Not surprisingly, cars are driven more in the United States than in Europe. Within Europe, differences in yearly driving depend not only on fuel prices and incomes but also on the number of cars in the stock and the number of company cars for which drivers do not pay for fuel. Thus the distance per car per year is highest in Denmark and the United Kingdom, the countries we studied with the fewest cars per capita. Driving distances are high in Sweden (roughly 15 percent company cars) and the United Kingdom (roughly 30 percent company cars).

Not all policies increase the cost of owning or using cars. Company car taxation policies in the United Kingdom, the Netherlands, Sweden, and West Germany have had the opposite effect on both ownership and size, offsetting the effect these kinds of policies would have had for as many as two-thirds of new-car drivers. Most European countries permit some kind of tax relief for commuting costs. Sweden even permits commuters to deduct the cost of commuting if they can show the car saving at least one-half hour of time each way compared with transit. The treatment of parking or other benefits related to using cars varies among countries. These policies significantly raise car ownership, size, and driving. Complementary policies provide for tax deductions or even subsidies for commuting expenses. If we estimate the value of these major subsidies, however, they are still small compared with the total taxation of fuel and motor vehicles.

Taxation Schemes

National and local governments levy a variety of taxes and fees on transportation. We classify these taxes and fees according to whether they are levied at acquisition, on ownership, or on various use parameters, such as driving or parking. In general, the present value of ownership taxes is less than that of use or acquisition taxes. However, in addition to the direct, revenue-raising effect, taxes clearly discourage consumers from purchasing too much of what is taxed.

In addition to taxes, there are tax rules and other conditions of great importance. Company car policies and allowances for deducting some commuting costs are examples. Factors of these kinds are not included in the calculations.

Acquisition or "Fixed" Taxes

All countries levy fees on car acquisition and yearly registration. We denote these as fixed costs since they are payable once only. Neither the taxation schemes for cars nor their outcomes are uniform across the countries studied. Moreover, the relationship between fixed costs, yearly costs, and variable costs is not uniform.

For our purposes, what matters is not only the level of this taxation, but also whether the tax is higher or lower than that on other (or all) goods and services. Equally important, we examine taxation schemes for discontinuities. These occur either because the tax is defined in terms of intervals (such as weight or volume classes) or because the tax rate changes discontinuously at certain values of the taxed parameters.

Acquisition taxes are commonly related to vehicle price. Value-Added Tax (VAT) in the European countries adds roughly 20 percent to the vehicle price. In effect since the late 1960s and early 1970s, VAT has both declined and increased during the past two decades. For example, in France in 1986, VAT was equal to 33 percent; in 1994, it stands at 22 percent. In Denmark (10 percent in 1967) and Sweden (4 percent in the 1960s), VAT is now 22 percent and 25 percent, respectively. In most cases, VAT on cars is similar to that on other goods and services.

In most countries, governments can also link taxes to a number of other features—i.e., car weight, cylinder volume, motor horsepower, or fuel use. The Italian VAT ranges from 19 percent to 38 percent, depending on the engine capacity; Sweden and Japan add an acquisition tax based on a vehicle's weight. The French base tax policies upon categories of "administrative power" (or fiscal horsepower), measured in CV (*cheval fiscal*) rather than in actual power. The formula for calculating CV incorporates the engine displacement (measured in cm³), type of motor fuel (weighted such that a diesel engine of the same volume as a gasoline one has a lower CV), and transmission type. Norway even requires a deposit on new vehicles that is refunded when an aged vehicle is properly scrapped rather than resold. VAT on vehicles, as well as sales taxes, are included in our analysis.

Governments also extract supplemental fees in many of the European countries: one-time license plate fees (Sweden), insurance taxes (Denmark, France, and Italy), one-time registration taxes (West Germany), point-of-purchase taxes (the Netherlands), and special car taxes (the United Kingdom).

All countries (or states, in the case of the United States) place VAT or a sales tax on the value of new cars. Many even charge some turnover tax on the sale of used cars. France charges a higher VAT on cars than on other goods and services. While the United Kingdom charges an additional 10 percent of the value of the car, the Netherlands and Denmark increase the tax rate if the price exceeds a certain amount, which for Denmark is a low threshold.[3] Italy taxes displacement and increases the VAT rate on cars with displacement larger than 2,000 cc.

Over a decade ago, the United States imposed a special sales tax on gas-guzzling automobiles—i.e., those with a fuel economy rating below a specified threshold. Since volume and weight both are indirectly related to fuel economy, the taxes on these attributes resemble taxes on test fuel economy, but they are normally small.

Fiscal stimuli also extend to emissions controls. In Denmark, for instance, excise taxes on cars with the most advanced emissions controls are significantly lower (by approximately $650, 1985 U.S.$) than taxes on cars that meet the present U.S. standards. Similar policies exist in Sweden and West Germany. In Sweden, buyers of cars with slightly higher emissions than the present U.S. standards pay approximately $650 (1985 U.S.$) more. A price differential can be particularly effective if a country's taxation scheme causes the overall price of a new car to be substantial. Under this circumstance, any price differential becomes an effective incentive to buyers.

Ownership Taxes

Every country (states or even local authorities, in the case of the United States, but not the federal government) imposes some yearly fees for registration, inspection, and even, in some cases, taxes on au-

---

[3] For cars priced under 19,750 DKK ($1,380) in 1990, the car is taxed at 105 percent. Cars priced above this amount are taxed at 105 percent up to 19,750 DKK and then at 180 percent for their remaining value. Tax deductions are offered for some safety technologies like antilock brakes, seatbelts for the back seats, security equipment, radio, halogen headlights, right side mirrors, and rear window wipers. "Environmentally sound" cars (as defined within their tax code) are also tax deductible. Electric cars are exempt.

tomobile insurance to contribute to national health insurance. The annual registration fees are usually related to value, weight, or displacement and decline as the vehicle ages. In Italy, ownership tax is progressive, rising out of proportion to engine size, and is higher for diesel cars than gasoline ones (to offset the lower price of diesel fuel). In Denmark, the fee is significant (as a fraction of all costs) and rises progressively with the weight of the vehicle. Japan charges a lower annual tax for minicars, those with displacement under 600 cc.

Taxes on ownership are annual. In a few cases (Norway, Italy, and the United Kingdom), a flat rate is charged, but ownership tax is more commonly related to vehicle characteristics: age, weight, cylinder volume, or engine displacement. Ownership tax is generally independent of the use of the car, with the only exceptions being the Danish, French, and Italian taxes on automobile insurance. Such taxes can be high; in Denmark the cost of automobile liability insurance is taxed at 50 percent; French and Italian rates are 17 percent and 21.5 percent, respectively. When insurance rates are related to driving distance, these taxes have an element of use taxation; however, we have classified them as taxes on ownership.

West Germany employs a complex system for taxing different types of vehicles. The annual license fees for motorcycles and passenger vehicles with standard piston engines depend upon the engine displacement. All other vehicles are taxed according to total weight and number of axles. This tax is subdivided into three classes (Blum and Rottengatter 1990), as shown in Table 11-2.

Tax exemptions are applied to vehicles identified as having low emissions (to begin on the day of the first licensing for a limited extent of time). Criteria to determine whether the car qualifies for a tax exemption include (1) engine type (spark-ignition or rotary); (2) engine displacement size (in cubic centimeters); (3) emissions level as compared with national and European Community standards; and (4) the date when the vehicle was first classified to have low emissions.

A subsidy of 550 DEM ($160, 1985 U.S.$) is offered to the owner of a vehicle if (1) the vehicle was not tax exempt, (2) the vehicle was first registered by the end of 1990, and (3) the vehicle was retrofitted with a catalytic converter between January 1990 and the end of July 1992. The subsidy is granted once per vehicle. Upon retrofitting, the vehicle is treated as a low-emissions vehicle and thus entitled to a limited tax exemption.

The subsidy is raised to 1,100 DEM ($310, 1985 U.S.$) if the car is retrofitted with a three-way catalytic converter that regulates the oxygen-to-fuel ratio so as to control hydrocarbon, carbon monoxide, and NO_x emissions. It is further increased to 1,200 DEM ($340, 1985

Table 11-2

West German Vehicle Ownership Taxes

Class	Taxation Rate
Emission-reduced engines	
Gasoline	13.2 DEM/100 cm³ ($4, 1985$)
Diesel	21.60 DEM/100 cm³ ($7, 1985$)
Non-emission-reduced engines licensed before 1986	
Gasoline	18.80 DEM/100 cm³($6, 1985$)
Diesel	35.20 DEM/100 cm³ ($10, 1985$)
	(prior to July 1991: 27.20 DEM/100 cm³ ($8, 1985$)
Non-emission-reduced engines licensed in 1986 and after	
Gasoline	21.60 DEM/100 cm³ ($7, 1985$)
Diesel	38.00 DEM/100 cm³ ($11, 1985$)
	(prior to July 1991: 30.00 DEM/100 cm³ ($9, 1985$)

Source: Blum and Rottengatter (1990).

U.S.$) if the vehicle is retrofitted with the above technology as well as an evaporative filter for the reduction of hydrocarbon emissions. Electric vehicles have a tax reduction of 50 percent. However, they are tax exempt if their engine size is equivalent to a 1,000 cc car.

In general, the ownership taxes on these characteristics of cars are smaller than those imposed on the value. But the existence of various intervals or levels of taxation, particularly in intervals of motor displacement, often leads to the appearance of cars with characteristics just inside the maximum permitted for a given tax. In this sense, these taxes have an effect quite out of proportion to their monetary impact on the price of a new car.

Use Taxes

The most important taxes on vehicle use are indirect, through taxes on fuel. Additionally, there are the so-called kilometer taxes based on distances diesel-fueled cars are driven in Sweden and Norway. These charges, which expired in 1993, were aimed at offsetting the low taxes on diesel fuel. Finally, CO_2 taxes were instituted in the Scandinavian countries in 1991. Other taxes, such as those levied on parking, bridge tolls, and city tolls, are not considered here.

European countries have taxed fuel for decades. The International Energy Agency publishes these taxes (and prices) on a quarterly basis (IEA *Energy Prices*). Conversely, fuel is not heavily taxed in the United

States for a number of reasons (see Sweeney 1993 for a full discussion).

Table 11-3 compares total fuel prices (fuel plus tax) in the countries studied for 1991. The price of diesel fuel has remained low relative to that of gasoline in most countries because of the importance of

Table 11-3
Gasoline and Diesel Prices per Liter, 1991

Country	Currency	Total Price	CPI[a]	1985 Local Price	PPP[b]	1985 U.S.$	Tax as a % of Total Price	Tax as % of Fuel Price
GASOLINE								
Denmark	DKK	6.06	1.24	4.89	9.05	$0.54	68	210
France	FFR	5.36	1.2	4.47	6.5	$0.69	75	300
Germany	DEM	1.44	1.107	1.30	2.2	$0.59	68	209
Italy	LIT	1536.00	1.401	1096.36	1196.00	$0.92	76	317
Japan	YEN	127.00	1.104	115.04	217.00	$0.53	46	84
Netherlands	DFL	1.87	1.077	1.74	2.38	$0.73	70	233
Norway	NOK	7.25	1.4	5.18	9.4	$0.55	67	207
Sweden	SEK	6.8	1.478	4.60	7.8	$0.59	68	209
United Kingdom	UKL	0.49	1.412	0.35	1.412	$0.25	66	194
United States	USD	0.3	1.266	0.24	1.266	$0.19	33	40
DIESEL								
Denmark	DKK	2.65	1.24	2.14	9.05	$0.24	21	26
France	FFR	3.12	1.2	2.60	6.50	$0.40	54	119
Germany	DEM	0.94	1.107	0.85	2.20	$0.39	53	112
Italy	LIT	954.00	1.401	680.94	1196.00	$0.57	64	177
Japan	YEN	77.00	1.104	69.75	217.00	$0.32	35	54
Netherlands	DFL	0.98	1.077	0.91	2.38	$0.38	46	84
Norway	NOK	2.84	1.4	2.03	9.40	$0.22	24	32
Sweden	SEK	4.15	1.478	2.81	7.80	$0.36	30	44
United Kingdom	UKL	0.38	1.412	0.27	1.41	$0.19	57	130
United States	USD	0.3	1.266	0.24	1.27	$0.19	34	52

Note: The price in local currency is in nominal currency. This price is converted to real 1985 currency, then converted to 1985 U.S.$ purchasing power parities (PPP) (published by the OECD) that give currencies in terms of U.S.$. The tax as a percentage of "total price" refers to the tax as a share of the total purchase price, the sum of the fuel cost, and tax. The tax as a percentage of "fuel price only" is calculated by dividing the amount of tax by the price of the fuel minus any tax.

[a] CPI = Consumer Price Index.
[b] PPP = purchasing power parities.

Table 11-4

Emissions Taxes per Liter on Motor Fuels, 1991

Country	Currency	Leaded Price	CIP[a]	1985 Local Price	PPP[b]	1985 U.S.$
Denmark	DKK	2.9	1.24	2.34	9.05	$0.26
Norway	NOR	3.23	1.4	2.31	9.4	$0.25
Sweden	SEK	2.42	1.478	1.64	7.8	$0.21

[a] CPI = Consumer Price Index.
[b] PPP = purchasing power parities.

diesel fuel for trucks. Many countries—namely Denmark, West Germany, the Netherlands, Norway, and Sweden—have levied additional annual taxes on diesel-powered cars as a means of offsetting the cheaper diesel prices. However, the relatively low price of diesel fuel appears to have raised the popularity of diesel cars, particularly since 1985, when the importance of diesel fuel to automobiles began to rise significantly in France, West Germany, and Italy (Schipper et al. 1993a). However, fluctuations in diesel and gasoline prices and taxes from year to year have caused sales of diesel cars to oscillate.

Differences in pricing were used by almost every European country to encourage the use of unleaded fuels. Taxes on unleaded gasoline were lowered by as much as 10 percent of the total price, compared with the price of leaded gasoline. Not surprisingly, the buying public responded quickly.

In 1991, Norway and Sweden levied an environmental tax on the usual carbon dioxide emissions and lead content of fuels. These countries imposed a fee equivalent to 0.60 DKK per liter, based on the carbon content in fuel. Part of the fee imposed in Sweden offset a reduction in other taxes. These prices are shown in Table 11-4.

Subsidies

European policies tend to influence the cost of owning and operating a car by raising fuel prices as well as the costs of acquiring new cars. The impact of these policies is often reduced because many nations provide subsidies as well. Given the high marginal income tax rates in some countries, such give-backs have become a standard form of income.

Company cars and tax deductions for commuters using public transportation are two examples of such give-back policies. Any automobile that is partly or fully financed by a business firm for the use of the employee, including mileage allowances, is considered a company car. The beneficiary pays income tax for the privilege of using the car. However, the tax is almost always less than what would have been paid on the income the beneficiary needed to purchase the car privately. And most company car schemes do not tax free fuel, insurance, and maintenance if these are provided by the employer. Consequently, company car schemes reduce the marginal cost of driving to almost zero.

The Swedes have devised an elaborate scheme for the use of company cars, which are pervasive, reflecting a response to taxation policies on employees' disposable income. Between 1980 and 1985, the share of company cars to total new registrations in Sweden varied between 30 percent and 38 percent, with an additional 7 percent to 8 percent attributed to personal businesses. The number of company cars varies from year to year because of changes in the tax structure. Beginning January 1, 1991, Sweden adjusted its company car policies to accommodate five categories of company cars, including old luxury cars and partly financed company cars. For all categories, the car's value is determined and adjusted for age or additional features and then added to the employees' pre-tax salaries.

In the United Kingdom, the company car motorists have been identified as the United Kingdom's "privileged polluters" (Rowell and Fergusson 1991). Company cars make up the major component of the United Kingdom's automobile fleet (20 percent of the total stock), and the benefits of use (company-assisted financing, free fuel—even, in some cases, complete coverage of all expenses) can make up 13 percent of an employee's total salary. With scale charges based on just three sizes of engines, manufacturers have responded with engine capacities that fall just below the thresholds, thereby avoiding the higher charges. However, larger cars are assessed as a basis for income tax at lower rates—61 percent versus 88 percent for smaller engine sizes. Scale charges on mileage are a function of kilometers driven, again with the rates lower for a greater number of kilometers driven.

Many of the Organisation for Economic Cooperation and Development (OECD) countries allow commuters tax exemptions, usually based on distance, for using public transportation. For example, in Denmark, commuters deduct 0.83 DKK ($.05, 1985 U.S.$) per kilometer of daily travel for distances between 20 and 55 km. (The deduction decreases to 0.22 DKK for distances greater than 55 km.) In Germany, commuting costs are fully deductible—a practice in force since 1920!

In Denmark, a commuter can deduct 0.83 DKK ($.05, 1985 U.S.$) per kilometer traveled daily at distances between 20 and 55 km. The deduction is 0.22 DKK ($.01, 1985 U.S.$) per km for distances over 55 km. If a commuter must travel more than 55 km per day, has no access to public transportation, and uses a private vehicle, 0.78 DKK ($.05, 1985 U.S.$) per km can be deducted after the first 20 km. The annual subsidy for the use of public transit, 250 DFL ($70, 1985 U.S.$) per person, is available for those who commute over 30 km.

In Sweden, a commuter qualifies for a commuting deduction of 12 SEK per 10 km ($1, 1985 U.S.$) if he or she lives at least 5 km from work and can prove that driving, rather than public transport, saves the commuter more than one hour each way. A commuter can disregard the two-hour limitation under two conditions: first, if the car is driven for business purposes for at least 60 days a year and covers a minimum of 3,000 km, a commuter can deduct 12 SEK per 10 km for each day the car is used for business purposes. Second, if the car is used for business purposes for more than 160 days of the year, and again covers a minimum of 3,000 km, a commuter can deduct 12 SEK per 10 km for the total annual business days.

Subsidies for commuting, such as tax deductions for commuting costs or light tax treatment of employer-subsidized commuting costs, were instituted for two reasons. First, they promote labor mobility by reducing the constraint of home location on searching for a job. Second, they provide some kind of offset for company car policies. Even when commuting subsidies can be applied to driving to work (if the distance exceeds a certain threshold, or the time saved relative to taking collective transit is more than a certain amount), these subsidies could be seen as providing benefits for those whose taxes support transit but cannot use transit, such as workers who commute tangentially to work or who do not live in major population centers where transit systems are readily accessible. Almost all of these subsidies act through tax deductions.

Comparison of Taxation Across Countries

Any given tax scheme defies description and analysis of the total tax burden. We need a method to add acquisition, ownership, and use taxes. It is not difficult to carry this out for a self-consistent set of representative parameters that describe both costs and characteristics that are taxed directly, as well as those that influence taxation, such as fuel economy.

To make comparisons possible, the same assumptions should be used for all countries. We calculate the total lifetime taxation on a given car using current tax schemes, assuming a vehicle lifetime of ten years, a real discount rate of 5 percent, and an annual driving distance of 14,000 kilometers. However, it is important to keep in mind that those factors vary in the real world. The calculations we show are not descriptions of actual taxation in all countries. All taxes have been translated to 1985 U.S.$ according to 1985 purchase power parities.

Three caveats are in order. First, a particular combination of base price and characteristics does not necessarily describe a given car as sold in all countries. The most important attributes of cars—price, weight, displacement, horsepower, and so on—differ from country to country since manufacturers vary the combinations in response to taxation plans and consumer interest. Second, the overall mix of cars purchased varies greatly from country to country since consumers respond to car prices after taxation through their choices of car features and prices. This affects the average tax burden profoundly. Finally, it is not correct to assume that cars differing greatly in price and characteristics will be driven the same distance in a year. Nevertheless, by selecting a set of parameters, we obtain a first-order comparison of the impact of each tax scheme on various cars.[4]

Figure 11-2 shows automobile taxation in 1990 for four types of cars: subcompact, compact, intermediate, and luxury. Table 11-5 describes the parameters of these cars. The definitions of car types are based on statistics about vehicles sold in the United States in 1990; the most common categories have been chosen. The low U.S. taxation is striking. (Sales tax, lying between 6 and 8 percent, depending on the state, was estimated at 7 percent.) The Danes and the Norwegians tax automobiles heavily and tax fuel highly as well. The figure also shows that the differential between the subcompact and luxury car is largest in these two countries because of the importance of the ad valorem taxes. In most countries, the tax burden differs considerably among the types of automobiles, not least in Denmark and Norway, where the vehicle price is the most important determinant of acquisition taxes. Indeed, the tax burden in Denmark is so large that the pre-tax selling price of new cars must be lowered significantly.

The average tax burden in 1990 (shown in Figure 11-3) is calculated as an average of the burden on each type of vehicle, weighted according to market share in the U.S. market. This means that the real tax burden in Europe is lower than shown because the new-car market is weighted toward less power, weight, fuel intensity, and presumably

---

[4] In further work we will explore how the tax scheme influences in turn the actual mix of cars purchased, as well as how cars are used. See Schipper and Johansson (1994), for example, for some estimates of how taxation affects ownership, use, and fuel economy.

cars with slightly lower base prices. The total tax is divided into acquisition, ownership, and use taxes. To put these taxes into perspective,
Figure 11-4 shows the untaxed car prices (and fuel prices as well)
below the dotted line above the x-axis. Once again the hefty Norwegian and Danish taxation is clear: the acquisition tax is by far the most

Figure 11-2

Automobile Taxation, 1990

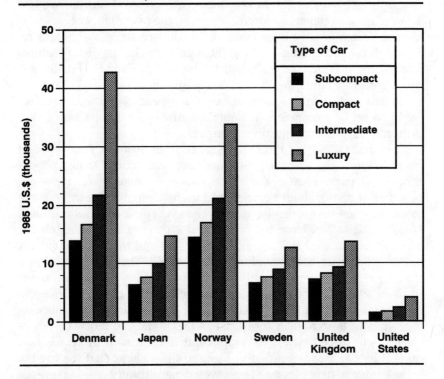

Table 11-5

Description of Cars Chosen for Analysis in This Study

Car Type	Real Price (1985 U.S.$)	Horsepower	Displacement (cc)	On-Road Weight (kg)	Intensity (1/100 km)	Market Share in U.S. (% km)
Subcompact	7,750	90	1,600	1,200	9.9	12.4
Compact	9,300	110	2,300	1,300	11.5	15.5
Intermediate	11,200	140	3,100	1,600	12.9	16.1
Luxury	24,500	180	4,000	1,800	15.0	7.6

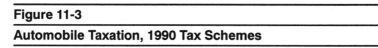

Figure 11-3

Automobile Taxation, 1990 Tax Schemes

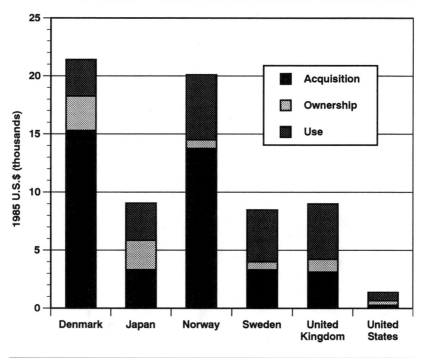

important component. The Japanese have a relatively high tax on car ownership. One also notices the well-known pattern of automobile-producing countries (United States, Japan, the United Kingdom, and Sweden) with comparably low acquisition taxes.

The total tax burden has changed over time. New taxation schemes are an obvious reason, but inflation is of major importance as well. Figure 11-5 shows how the total tax burden has changed, given the above-mentioned car types and weighted average. For this calculation, we start with the given cars and the taxation schemes valid in the year shown, taking into account changes in yearly taxes and fuel prices thereafter and discounting all of these back to the same starting year.

In most countries, the tax burden appears stable. Nominal tax increases and inflation seem to have counterbalanced each other, but a major tax reduction in Japan is apparent. This occurred when the very high tax on luxury cars was abandoned at the beginning of the 1970s. Recall, however, that we use the U.S. mix to calculate the total burden

Figure 11-4

Automobile Taxation, 1990 Tax Schemes

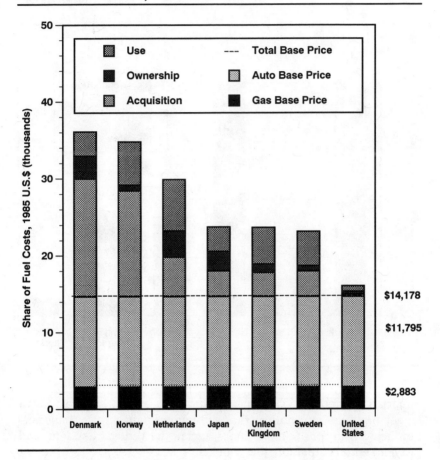

on the average car. Of course, the luxury vehicles that were subject to the heavy tax in Japan were not common at that time. But taxes on other classes of cars have been lowered as well. Therefore this picture gives a good indication of the variation of taxes on motoring over time.

It should be clear that these taxes have a profound impact on the cars actually bought in each country. Figure 11-6 shows country taxation in Europe applied to the same car. (We leave the United States out of this comparison because the burden is small compared to that of European countries.) The high taxes applied in Denmark have depressed market conditions so that the price before taxes has been lowered as much as possible. Given this taxation, it is not surprising that

Figure 11-5

Total Tax Burden

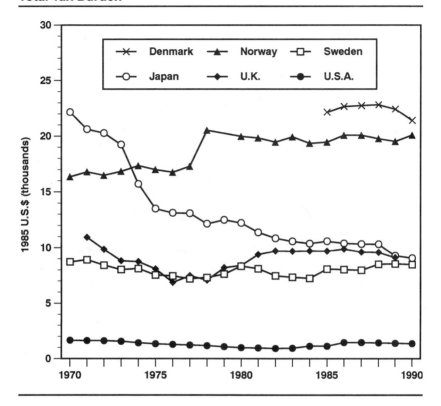

there are fewer cars in Denmark or England than in the other countries shown.[5]

When we examine Figure 11-4, another important facet of taxation is clear. In Norway and Denmark, acquisition taxes dominate the total tax burden, and acquisition dominates the total picture of costs shown.[6]

In the case of Denmark, this has suppressed car ownership to less than 325 cars per 1,000 people and extended the time a car is kept running to well over 15 years (Vibe-Petersen 1991); in Norway, the average car life is 14.9 years (Eriksen and Johansen 1991). In these countries, the

[5] The fact that the tax on this car is highest in Norway is troubling because Norwegian car ownership is higher than that of the United Kingdom or Denmark.

[6] More detailed analysis of the Danish and Norwegian situations that include other costs confirms that our figures are representative of the overall cost picture—i.e., including insurance and other costs. See COWIconsult (1992) or Eriksen and Johansen (1991).

Figure 11-6

The Cost of an Opel Kadett in 1990 (1.4-liter LS three-door)

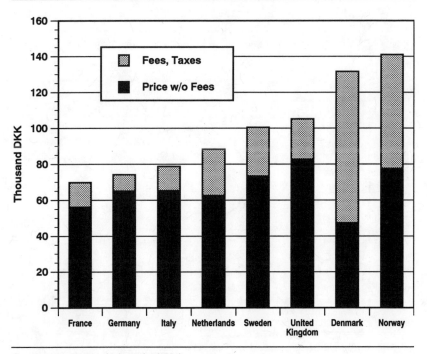

Source: *Vejtransporten i tal og tekst* (1991).

rationale for high acquisition taxes has been the fear that high imports would hurt balance-of-payments considerations. More recently, however, analysts in Denmark have voiced concern that high taxes on fixed costs, relative to those on variable costs, slow down the turnover of the stock, with the consequence that consumers keep older cars, which pollute more and use more fuel than newer ones, longer than otherwise. A shift from fixed to variable taxation could more clearly address the current concerns over traffic, exhaust emissions, and CO_2.

Conclusions

Taxation on cars and fuel has a profound impact on the transportation market. With overall huge revenues, the tax systems also indirectly affect car characteristics, but important policies partially offset heavy tax burdens.

Two important patterns emerge: (1) taxes on cars are greatest in the countries without domestic car industries (Denmark, Norway, and the Netherlands); (2) taxes on ownership (acquisition and yearly fees) dominate in Japan, the Netherlands, Denmark, and Norway and tend to discourage ownership.[7] (Although Japan's tax burden on ownership is heavy, it must be seen in a broader economic context: everything in Japan is expensive!)

The brief analysis presented here does not quantify the exact magnitude of the impact of taxes on automobile ownership, characteristics, or use, although Schipper and Johansson (1994) show that taxation does affect these parameters. They found that taxes on automobile value (or other characteristics) have only a small impact on fuel use and that fuel prices affect fuel intensity the most, distance driven somewhat less, and car ownership only weakly. The conclusion from that investigation, which is reinforced here, is that where taxes are used to offset the generation of externalities, the taxes should be applied to attributes of motoring that directly affect the externalities. Only a small fraction of the revenue raised from the taxes studied here is related to externalities or earmarked for roads or other transportation services. This means that the taxation of cars and motoring, however large or small, is not economically efficient relative to either externalities or public goods associated with cars and motoring. The revenues from motoring are an important source of income for most European countries. Perhaps it is time for those revenues to be more closely matched to the "deadly sins" facing the car and other parts of the transportation system. However, the more subtle impacts of the kinds or analytical forms of taxation await further study.

This question has not gone unnoticed in policy circles. The Nordic countries want to maintain revenues from motoring but are seeking ways of transferring some of the burden from fixed costs to variable costs. This is particularly true in Denmark, where cars have a very long lifetime. The cost of fuel, for example, is only 16 percent of the total costs shown for Denmark. But among the other countries, there is no clear relationship between the share of total costs fuel plays and driving per capita or per car.

Congestion and revenue requirements prompted erection of toll rings around Norway's major cities and a profound debate on road pricing for infrastructuring financing in Sweden, the United Kingdom,

---

[7] We believe that the oil boom in Norway supported the rapid rise in car ownership there in spite of heavy taxes.

and West Germany (in Japan, France, and Italy, the motorways already require tolls.) One of the authors was surprised in Stockholm by a parking ticket with a price tag of more than $75 (1985 U.S.$). Some governments see benefits in using fiscal instruments both for fiscal policy and to achieve environmental goals as well.

Since few of the taxation schemes we reviewed were aimed at the externalities arising from using motor vehicles, the impact of taxation on these problems has been indirect. Taxation schemes aimed directly at fuel (fuel taxes) or driving (kilometer taxes) will have a more profound impact on fuel use than those aimed at new-car purchases or other attributes of cars only indirectly related to fuel use. In other words, taxation schemes designed to affect fuel use through their impact on automobile ownership, characteristics, or use must be blunt, effectively increasing the cost of moving a kilometer or buying a car using 1 liter per 100 km of fuel more at the margin. Policies aimed at reducing congestion or overall driving should also be aimed at these problems directly. By adjusting taxation to match perceived externalities and other costs, governments could probably maintain their revenues from the transportation sector and reduce the magnitude of these problems at the same time.

References

COWIconsult. 1992. *Afgifter som styringsinstrumenter. Incitamenter i afgifts- og beskatningsforholdene for vejtransport* [Fees as policy instruments: Incentives in the fee and taxation schemes for road transport]. Copenhagen: Danish Energy Agency.

Eriksen, K., and K. Johansen. 1991. *Alternative avgiftssystemers. Effekt på bilhold, bilutskiftning og utslipp* [Alternative fee systems: Effects on car ownership, scrappage, and emissions]. Report 0963/1991. Oslo: Norwegian Centre for Transport Research.

Johnson, E., ed. 1993. *Avoiding the Collision of Cars and Cities*. Report of a study sponsored by the American Academy of Arts and Sciences.

International Energy Agency (IEA). *Energy Prices and Taxes of IEA Member Countries*. Published quarterly. Paris: Organisation for Economic Cooperation and Development, International Energy Agency.

Schipper, L., and G. Eriksson. 1993. *Taxation Policies Affecting Automobile Characteristics and Use in Western Europe, Japan, and the United States, 1970–1990*. LBL-35222. Berkeley: Lawrence Berkeley Laboratory.

Schipper, L., M. Figueroa, L. Price, and M. Espey. 1993a. "Mind the Gap: The Vicious Circle of Automobile Fuel Use." *Energy Policy* 18 (12): 1173-1189.

Schipper, L., and O. Johansson. 1994. "Measuring Long-Run Automo-

bile Fuel Demand and Policy Implications Through Separate Esti-
mations of Vehicle Stock, Mean Fuel Intensity, and Distance Driven per Car per Year." Draft report. Berkeley: Lawrence Berkeley
Laboratory.

Schipper, L., R. Steiner, M.J. Figueroa, and K. Dolan. 1993b. "Fuel
Prices and Economy: Factors Affecting Land Travel." *Transport
Policy* 1 (1): 6–20.

Sweeney, J., 1993. "Gasoline Taxes: An Economic Assessment." Prepared for the U.S. Office of Technology Assessment. Palo Alto,
Calif.: Stanford University, Department of Engineering and Economic Systems.

Vejtransporten i tal og tekst [Road transport in figures and text]. 1991.
33. Hellerup, Denmark: Automobil-Importørernes Sammenslut-
ning [Danish Automobile Importers Association].

Vibe-Petersen, Johs. 1991. *Nye bilers energiforbrug og sikkerhed* [New automobile energy use and safety]. Report 68. Aarhurs: University
of Aalborg, Institute of Development and Planning.

Bibliography

Denmark

Lamont, Norman, Chancellor of the Eschequor. 1991. *Written Answer
to the House of Commons*. London: Her Majesty's Stationery Office.
December 2.

Magnusson, J., and M. Brandel. 1991. "Energi och miljö i Norden—
avändning av skatter och avgifter som miljöpolitiska styrmedel"
[Energy and environment in the Nordic countries: Use of taxes
and fees as instruments in environmental policy]. *Nord* (Copenhagen) 1991: 23.

Vejtransporten i tal og tekst [Road transport in figures and text]. 1989.
31. Hellerup, Denmark: Automobil-Importørernes Sammenslut-
ning [Danish Automobile Importers Association].

Vejtransporten i tal og tekst [Road transport in figures and text]. 1991.
33. Hellerup, Denmark: Automobil-Importørernes Sammenslut-
ning [Danish Automobile Importers Association].

France

Barrier-Lynn, Christiane, Yiannakis Geeorgiades, and Jacques Lam-
bert. 1989. "Les Industries Automobiles Françaises et Allemandes
Face aux Nouvelles Normes Anti-pollution" [French and German
auto industries and pollution control standards]. *Les Cahiers Scien-
tifiques du Transport* 20: 11–30.

Département Économie Statistiques. 1990. "Les Dépenses de Motorisation: Évolution de 1980 à 1989" [Motoring costs from 1980 to 1989]. December 5.

Lamont, Norman, Chancellor of the Eschequor. 1991. *Written Answer to the House of Commons.* London: Her Majesty's Stationery Office. December 2.

Italy

Lamont, Norman, Chancellor of the Eschequor. 1991. *Written Answer to the House of Commons.* London: Her Majesty's Stationery Office. December 2.

Japan

Hughes, Peter. 1991. "Travelling Green: Reducing Pollution from Personal Travel." *Town and Country Planning.* October.

JAA. 1990. *1990 Handbook of the Japan Automobile Association.* Tokyo. April.

McShane, Mary, and Masaki Koshi. 1984. "Public Policy Toward the Automobile: A Comparative Look at Japan and Sweden." *Transportation Research* 18A (2): 97–109.

Netherlands

Lamont, Norman, Chancellor of the Eschequor. 1991. *Written Answer to the House of Commons.* London: Her Majesty's Stationery Office. December 2.

Norway

Magnusson, J., and M. Brandel. 1991. "Energi och miljö i Norden—avändning av skatter och avgifter som miljöpolitiska styrmedel" [Energy and environment in the Nordic countries: Use of taxes and fees as instruments in environmental policy]. *Nord* (Copenhagen) 1991: 23.

Sweden

Bilismen i Sverige [Road traffic in Sweden]. 1990. Stockholm: Association of Automotive Producers.

Cardebring, Peter. 1987. "Company and Personal Business Car Ownership." Report 305A. Linköping, Sweden: Swedish Road and Traffic Institute.

———. 1989. "A Note on Company and Personal Business Car Ownership in Sweden." *Traffic Engineering & Control.* February.

McShane, Mary P., Masaki Koshi, and Olof Lundin. 1984. "Public Policy Toward the Automobile: A Comparative Look at Japan and Sweden." *Transportation Research-A* 18A: 97–109.

Olsson, Lars Olov. 1987. "Motor Vehicle Pollution Control and Regulations for Sweden." In *Motor Vehicle Pollution Control: A Global Perspective*, pp. 85–91. SP-718.

Swedish National Tax Board. 1992. *Löntagare deklarationsupplysningar 1992, inkomståret 1991* [Information on wage-earner income tax return 1992, income year 1991].

United Kingdom

Griffiths, John, and Simon Holberton. 1991. "Company Car Policy Goes in for a Rethink." *Financial Times* (London). May 10.

Hillman, M., and Anne Whalley. 1983. "Energy and Personal Travel: Obstacles to Conservation." London: Institute for Policy Studies Report No. 611.

Hughes, Peter. 1990. "Transport Emissions and the Greenhouse Effect." Ph.D. thesis. Universities Transport Studies Group Conference, Energy and Environment Research Unit, the Open University.

———. 1991a. "Traveling Green: Reducing Pollution from Personal Travel." *Town and Country Planning*. October.

———. (Open University.) 1991b. Personal communication. November 25.

Lamont, Norman, Chancellor of the Eschequor. 1991. *Written Answer to the House of Commons*. London: Her Majesty's Stationery Office. December 2.

Mogridge, M.J.H. 1985. "The Effect of Company Cars upon the Secondhand Market." Contractor Report 10. Crowthorne, Berks: Department of Transport, Transport and Road Research Laboratory.

Motor Industry of Great Britain 1990 World Automotive Statistics. 1990. London: Society of Motor Manufacturers and Traders Ltd.

Potter, Stephen. 1991a. "Company Cars: The Case for Abolishing the Fiscal Incentives for Company-Assisted Motoring." Briefing from Transport 2000, Earth Resources Research, Transport & Environment Studies, Friends of the Earth, London Amenity & Transport Association. January.

———. 1991b. *The Impact of Company-Financed Motoring on Public Transport*. 1991 Public Transport Symposium, Newcastle Upon Tyne, April 9–11, 1991.

———. 1991c. "Company Car Report: What the Company Car Costs the Households of the United Kingdom." Draft report. July 2.

———. 1991d. *Integrating Fiscal and Transport Policies*. Independent Advisory Group on Labour Transport Policy, Funding, Investment, Fiscal, Integration Working Group. September.

————. 1991e. (Open University.) Personal communication. December 2.

Rowell, A., and M. Fergusson. 1991. "Company Car Report." Draft. London: Earth Resources Research. February.

Whitelegg, John. 1984. "The Company Car in the United Kingdom as an Instrument of Transport Policy." *Transport Policy Decision Making* 2: 219–230.

United States

Davis, S., and M. Morris, eds. 1992. *Transportation Energy Data Book.* 12th ed. ORNL 6710. Oak Ridge, Tenn.: Oak Ridge National Laboratory. March.

Gordon, D. 1991. *Steering a New Course: Transportation, Energy, and the Environment.* Cambridge, Mass.: Union of Concerned Scientists.

New York Times. 1991. August 4. Source: American Petroleum Institute.

Senate Bill, State of Maryland, 1992.

Tax Foundation, Inc. 1989. *Monthly Tax Features.* Washington, D.C. June.

U.S. Council of Economic Advisers. 1992. "Economic Report of the President." Washington, D.C.: USGPO. February.

West Germany

Blum, U., and W. Rottengatter. 1990. "The Federal Republic of Germany." In *Transport Policy and the Environment: Six Case Studies,* edited by Jean-Philippe Barde and Kenneth Button. London: Earthscan, pp. 61–92.

Hauntzinger, H. 1991. (Institut für Angewandte Verkehrs und Tourismusforschung E.V. [Institute for Applied Traffic and Tourism Research], Heilbronn.) Personal communication. June 12.

Lamont, Norman, Chancellor of the Eschequor. 1991. *Written Answer to the House of Commons.* London: Her Majesty's Stationery Office. December 2.

Other

ACEA. 1992. *Tax Guide: Motor Vehicle Taxation in the European Community.* Brussels: Association des Constructeurs Européen des Automobiles.

International Energy Agency, OECD (IEA). 1992. *Energy Prices and Taxes, Fourth Quarter 1991.* Paris.

International Energy Studies. 1991. Berkeley: Energy Analysis Program, Lawrence Berkeley Laboratory.

Chapter Twelve

Technology, Economics, and the ZEV Mandate: A Vehicle Manufacturer's Perspective

DEAN A. DRAKE

1993 marked the hundredth anniversary of the arrival of the motor vehicle in the United States. This century of the automobile began with a wide variety of powerplants—internal combustion engines of all sorts, steam engines, and electrics—competing with each other for market dominance. By the end of World War I, however, the gasoline-powered vehicle had driven electric and steam vehicles from the market. Today, the state of California is attempting to revive the electric vehicle through the use of production mandates. Before encouraging California to embark on a very expensive public policy experiment, the proponents of the zero-emission vehicle (ZEV) mandate must first provide convincing answers to the question, Why should electric vehicles fare any better in today's market than they did 80 years ago?

History of the Electric Vehicle

In the beginning of the automotive age, electric and steam-powered vehicles were the dominant forms of private transportation. In 1900, for example, steam-powered vehicles took 40 percent of the market, electrics 38 percent, and gasoline-powered vehicles only 22 percent (Shacket 1978).

There are a number of reasons why electric vehicles were preferred over gasoline-powered vehicles in 1900. Compared with gasoline-powered vehicles, electric vehicles were easier to operate, particularly in starting (which, for the gasoline-powered vehicle, meant hand-cranking) and in shifting while driving (the gasoline-powered vehicle required the use of a clutch). Electric vehicles had good driveability, required little maintenance, and had sufficient range for most driving requirements. Above all, the electrics were quiet and nonpolluting. At the time, W. C. Durant, who later went on to create General Motors, commented that gasoline-powered cars were "noisy and smelly, and frighten the horses" (Durant 1983).

Yet, by the end of World War I, just 18 years later, the electric vehicle industry was dead, largely because gasoline-powered vehicle technology had advanced faster than electric vehicle technology. Charles Kettering's invention of the electric starter overcame the need to hand-crank the car, and advances in carburation and ignition significantly improved driveability (although the popular dry plate clutch still made driving a gasoline-powered vehicle a skill, a shortcoming later overcome by the development of the automatic transmission). Also, by improving engine efficiency, increasing the number of cylinders in the engine, and later, using rubber engine mounts, manufacturers reduced vibration to an acceptable level. Finally, mass production lowered the cost of gasoline-powered vehicles more than it did the cost of electrics (because of the batteries), making gasoline-powered vehicles affordable for the masses.

Compared with the rapid progress being made in gasoline-powered vehicle technology in the early part of the century, electric vehicle technology proceeded at a snail's pace. Little could be done to lower the cost or improve the performance of the most expensive part of the electric vehicle—the batteries. Furthermore, development of the remainder of electric vehicle hardware—motors and controllers—had already matured for nonmobile uses, and further progress was limited until semiconductors were invented in the 1950s.

Outside of the vehicle itself, society changed. In 1900, vehicles were used almost exclusively for travel within cities; thus the electric car's short range, long recharge time, low speed, and need for an electric infrastructure were not a problem. By 1915, however, motor vehicles had become the primary means of rural transportation from farm to city, and even city people occasionally used their vehicles to travel to another city. As the intercity road system developed and gasoline stations began to dot the landscape, it became evident that gasoline-powered vehicles had essentially an infinite range and could be used everywhere, whereas electrics were tethered to major cities by their need for electricity, their 100-mile range, and their overnight recharging time.

The Revival of the Electric Vehicle

The current revival of interest in electric vehicles began in the late 1960s, when the automotive industry was being challenged to make major reductions in tailpipe emissions. It was widely speculated both inside and outside the industry that in order to meet the 90 percent reduction in tailpipe emissions mandated in the 1970 amendments to the Clean Air Act, some new powerplant would be required. General Motors, like other automobile manufacturers, made an extensive evaluation of alternative powerplants, which included building prototype electric, electric-gasoline hybrid, and electric-fuel-celled vehicles.

Unfortunately for alternative powerplants, however, advances in gasoline-powered vehicle emission control technology—most notably the development of the catalytic converter for mobile applications—permitted achievement of the mandated emission levels at a lower cost than for any of the alternative powerplants evaluated.[1]

As a result of these evaluations, it was concluded within the industry that (1) the economics of electric vehicle production and the inherent technical limitations prevented mass merchandizing, but (2) given the right combination of circumstances, there might be a niche market for electric vehicles. For there to be such a market, however, there had to be some advantages for the electric vehicle customer that would compensate for the vehicle's inherent liabilities.

One possible use in which electric vehicles could have a comparative advantage would be as small delivery vans in densely populated urban areas. Thus, in the mid-1980s, GM's Bedford Division in England manufactured 600 small electric vans. Demand, however, was not enough to justify production (market research had indicated that GM could have expected to sell 10,000 electric vans, not 600).

Another possible scenario giving electric cars an edge would be one in which the price of gasoline skyrocketed, which did occur after the December 1973 decision of the Organization of Petroleum Exporting Countries (OPEC) to shut off the supply of oil to the United States.

---

[1] According to the U.S. Bureau of Labor Standards, the average cost of emission controls on 1975 model-year passenger cars (the first year catalytic converters were introduced) was $412 (1991$), and the total cost of emission controls on a 1992 model-year vehicle was $1,560 (1991$). When compared with the estimated costs for pure electric vehicles discussed later in this chapter, emission controls on gasoline-powered vehicles, while expensive, are far less costly than electric vehicles.

Anticipating that gasoline prices would steadily increase, GM began the design of a small electric vehicle it intended to market in the mid-1980s. By the mid-1980s, however, a world oil surplus had emerged, and gasoline regained the dubious distinction of being the lowest-cost liquid other than water. That, combined with problems in achieving the necessary battery durability, led to the project's cancellation.

The most recent chapter in electric vehicle development—the GM Impact electric vehicle—has been prompted by environmental concerns and advances in technology (such as the technologies developed for the solar-powered Sunraycer electric vehicle). Rather than hope for a superbattery (which has eluded engineers for the better part of a century), the Impact is able to achieve its outstanding performance through sophisticated technologies that minimize weight and drag and maximize the utilization of available energy. Using an amount of energy equivalent to 1.5 gallons of gasoline, the Impact can accelerate from 0 to 60 mph in 8 seconds and travel 70 city and 90 highway miles between charges while meeting applicable government safety standards. It also includes customer amenities, such as air conditioning and stereo entertainment.

Can Electric Vehicles Succeed Today?

Electric vehicles still retain some of the advantages they once had over the gasoline-powered vehicle. They are still smoother and quieter (although the gap has narrowed considerably). They require almost no maintenance and, with home recharging, can always be "fully gassed up" for the morning commute. They are not tied to petroleum for a fuel and so are nearly impervious to interruptions in the oil supply. And even with the improvements made in gasoline-powered vehicle emission control, electric vehicles potentially can pollute less (and if the electricity is generated from nuclear or solar sources, electric vehicles are true zero-emission vehicles).

Furthermore, the electronics revolution has made possible more efficient motors and controllers and allows features such as regenerative braking, all of which helps increase performance. But will those advantages be enough to overcome the electric vehicle's two biggest handicaps: higher costs and limited range between recharges?

Electric Vehicle Costs

It is generally agreed that the very first electric vehicles will be expensive. Industry sources estimate the ZEVs marketed in California in

1998 (the first year they are mandated) will cost $10,000 to $30,000 more than a comparable gasoline-powered vehicle.[2]

In spite of the high initial costs, the ultimate cost of electric vehicles as compared with gasoline-powered vehicles is controversial. One viewpoint assumes that the cost of the earliest electric vehicles will be extremely high but will fall to the level of gasoline-powered vehicles with mass production. Another position asserts that electric vehicles have an inherent cost disadvantage over gasoline-powered vehicles and will always cost more unless internally subsidized by the manufacturers or explicitly subsidized by the government.

In the automotive industry, two primary elements outside of overhead dominate the cost of producing a vehicle after sufficient production volume is reached over which to amortize the cost of tooling. The first is the cost of labor used in assembling the vehicle and fabricating its components; the second is the cost of the materials used in constructing the vehicle. If the materials are commonly available, large-scale production will lower the cost of the vehicle (there will be economies of scale). But if the materials themselves are scarce, mass production could actually drive up the cost per vehicle by driving up the cost of the materials used (for example, a titanium or gold vehicle would have negative economies of scale).

If it is assumed that there is little difference in the labor required to build a gasoline-powered versus an electric vehicle, the question of cost can be analyzed by comparing the cost of materials used. Gasoline-powered vehicles are made primarily of iron (and steel, an iron derivative), plastic, glass, and rubber—all common materials. Electric vehicles begin with a high mass for energy storage (the GM

---

[2] The very first electric vehicles built by manufacturers are likely to be very small-volume models. Although 2 percent of California production (the amount required in the first years of the mandate) represents a large volume of a manufacturer's California sales (GM, for example, has only five passenger car models that represent in excess of 2 percent of its California passenger car sales), it is a very small percentage of total production (for GM, the mandated production of electric vehicles in California for 1998 represents only 0.16 percent of total U.S. production of GM passenger cars and light trucks, making it a very limited production item). This is one paradox of the ZEV mandate: at the local level, the mandated amount dictates a mass-market, low-cost vehicle from a marketing perspective, but because the product is desirable only in a limited area, it is a small-volume vehicle from a manufacturing perspective. One of the more thorough analyses of the cost of electric vehicles was done by Sierra Research and Charles River Associates in 1994. They estimated that, in the early years, electric vehicles will cost $25,299 more than comparable gasoline vehicles, with the price dropping to $12,588 to $21,034 over the comparable gasoline-powered vehicle with economies of scale (depending upon whether the electric vehicle is sold in volume nationally or just in California) (Sierra Research/Charles River Assoc. 1994, p. 5).

Impact, for example, contains over 800 pounds of lead-acid batteries), which is compensated for by the use of extremely low-weight construction (usually aluminum or composite).

Both the materials used in the batteries and those used in the body construction of electric vehicles are more expensive than the common materials used in gasoline-powered vehicles, suggesting an inherent cost disadvantage, even after economies of scale are considered. Also, even though some electric vehicle drivetrain components may be less expensive than gasoline-powered vehicle components, the extremely efficient auxiliary devices used on an electric vehicle are more expensive (for example, heating and air conditioning on the Impact are provided by a heat pump system that is far more complex than the comparable system on a gasoline-powered vehicle).

A recently released report of the incremental costs of low-emission vehicles prepared by Sierra Research and Charles River Associates projects the incremental additional cost of a zero-emission vehicle at $21,034 for California, or $12,588 nationwide, on a net present value basis taking into account "learning curve" cost improvements (Sierra Research/Charles River Assoc. 1994).

In short, even though a precise determination of the ultimate cost differential between gasoline-powered and electric vehicles would take a complex quantitative analysis, qualitatively it can be expected that electric vehicles will always cost some premium over comparable gasoline-powered vehicles in a free (unsubsidized) market. The incremental difference used in the rest of this analysis ($10,000) appears to be at best a conservative estimate.

Electric Vehicle Range

There are three dimensions to the range question surrounding electric vehicles: (1) average range, (2) range variation, and (3) refueling time.

The average range of electric vehicles on a full charge is well established to be about 80 miles under normal driving conditions,[3] compared with a range of 300 to 400 miles for the typical gasoline-powered vehicle before refueling is required. The average daily driving on the typical urban car is about 25 miles. Electric vehicle proponents use these figures to support the argument that electric vehicles

---

[3] The Impact, for example, is viewed as representing state-of-the-art performance for a purpose-built electric vehicle intended for sale in the 1998 model year. The range of the latest generation Impact vehicle is 70 miles in the city and 90 miles on the highway using the EPA test cycle and an 85 percent battery discharge.

will satisfy a normal customer's requirements. Industry marketing experience suggests that people do not buy vehicles to satisfy their average needs, but rather their 99th-percentile needs. For example, people rarely have passengers in the back seat, yet two-seat commuter cars are shunned by purchasers (even in multicar families). Similarly, trunk space is hardly ever fully utilized but remains a consideration in purchasing decisions. For this reason, there is concern that a few bad experiences with limited range (e.g., the time a person leaves on a short trip with an electric vehicle but needs to extend the trip for unforeseen circumstances) will give electric vehicles a bad reputation among consumers. This scenario is even more likely in an environment in which sales mandates force the use of subsidies that encourage people who should not be driving electric vehicles to buy them in spite of the vehicle's limitations.

Similarly, the electric vehicle's extreme range variation leads to concern. In a normal gasoline-powered vehicle, the energy contained in the fuel is independent of temperature, and the energy expended for auxiliary functions such as heating, cooling, and electrical components is a small percentage of total energy consumption. This is not the case, however, in an electric vehicle. Depending on the battery type, range may be reduced because of cold weather. Air conditioning and heating have a significant impact on range, as do lights and windshield wiper operation. Whether consumers can preplan around these variables remains to be seen.

Finally, the electric vehicle's refueling time will be a critical factor in its success or failure. Although progress has been made on quick-charge systems, the technology available for 1998 production will require hours to fully charge the vehicle.

Before any vehicle manufacturer commits hundred of millions of dollars to mass-producing electric vehicles, more needs to be known about public acceptance of these range limitations.

The Market Effects of a ZEV Mandate

According to California regulation, any vehicle manufacturer with California sales of 35,000 units a year or more must make 2 percent of its 1998 through 2000 model-year production zero-emission vehicles (i.e., electric). This percentage increases to 5 percent in model years 2001 and 2002 and jumps to 10 percent in model-year 2003.

When California adopted the ZEV mandate, it expected that the mandate would force manufacturers to develop electric vehicles and put them into production. Further, since manufacturers would have to sell ZEVs, they would have the incentive to develop vehicles that customers would want. In the event customers did not want electric vehicles at a price that made them profitable, California anticipated that manufacturers would lower the price of electric vehicles and increase the price of gasoline-powered vehicles until the dealers' lots were cleared of ZEVs.

In terms of one of California's intended outcomes—encouraging those large vehicle manufacturers not investing in electric vehicle research and development to do so—the ZEV mandate was successful. Regarding the remainder of California's vision, however, there are significant reasons to believe the outcome will be far less desirable than expected.

If, come 1998, manufacturers have developed electric vehicles that overcome the performance limitations described above, at a cost that permits compliance with the 2 percent mandate without taking a loss on each electric vehicle sold, then the mandates will present no problem. But is such an outcome likely?

First, any electric vehicle produced for sale in 1998 would have to begin development soon and must incorporate technology that is proven by 1995 and that works with the infrastructure that can be anticipated in the next several years. Thus, the electric vehicles likely to be offered for sale will be similar to the prototypes under evaluation today.

Second, electric vehicles with basic lead-acid batteries may cost $10,000 more than a comparable gasoline-powered vehicle even after available subsidies are considered. Manufacturing experience and economies of scale may reduce this cost beyond what Sierra Research and Charles Rivers Associates thought was possible, but even then, the inherent cost penalties of the premium materials required will likely result in the electric vehicle costing more than a comparable gasoline-powered vehicle. These costs, coupled with range limitations, make it doubtful that manufacturers could charge a premium for electric vehicles. Finally, electric vehicles incorporating advanced batteries will have an even higher cost differential.

For these reasons, it is important to analyze what could happen if the industry cannot sell the mandated 30,000-plus electric vehicles in 1998[4] at a price that recovers the cost of production. This scenario

---

[4] According to R. L. Polk, there were 1,278,600 passenger cars and light trucks produced by companies subject to the mandate and registered in California in 1991. If we assume a 2.5 percent growth rate, 1998 sales can be estimated at 1,519,863 units. Since 2 percent of these vehicles must be electric, the result is an estimated 30,400 electric vehicles in 1998.

leaves the manufacturers with a number of theoretical choices. The first would be to price electric vehicles at cost, sell fewer than the mandated number, and then either ration the sales of gasoline-powered cars accordingly or pay the fine on the difference. Alternatively, a manufacturer could cut the price of California ZEVs and boost the price of California gasoline-powered vehicles to compensate (thereby subsidizing the sale of ZEVs).

Neither paying the fine nor sales rationing would be an acceptable option for most manufacturers, thus leaving subsidies as the logical choice. If we assume a cost differential of $10,000 in the year 2003[5] and a manufacturer with 10 percent of its U.S. sales occurring in California,[6] the price of a gasoline-powered car in California would go up well over $1,000 if the subsidies are taken just on California sales, or over $100 if the subsidies are spread out over the entire United States (according to GM economists, the former pricing policy would cost the company less than the latter).

Although economies of scale would tend to reduce the cost of electric vehicles over time, other factors would work to cancel out the economies of scale, such as increased use of scarce materials for batteries driving up the price of those materials. Thus, for the purpose of the qualitative analysis that follows, it is assumed that the degree of subsidy required to sell electric vehicles in the 1998–2003 timeframe remains constant.

First, by increasing the price of vehicles that people prefer (gasoline-powered vehicles) to subsidize the sales of vehicles people do not want at cost, there would likely be an overall decrease in new-car sales in California. This would be true of any cross-subsidization scheme, such as Corporate Average Fuel Economy (CAFE), feebates, or mandates such as the ZEV mandate.

Second, since new cars would be more expensive, used cars would become more valuable and expensive in California. This would lead to an aging fleet and the increased importation of used cars from out of state. Although California's smog impact fee might slow this trend somewhat, it would be unlikely to stop it.

Third, the "near new" category of gasoline-powered vehicles

---

[5] The $10,000 figure is based on the best-case assumptions by Sierra Research and Charles River Associates (1994, p. 5) even after the learning curve and economies of scale are taken into account and is rounded for the sake of simplicity.

[6] Actual industry sales of passenger cars in California, based on R. L. Polk registration data, are about 14 percent of production. Sales of domestic makes are about 9 percent of total production. For purposes of this analysis, a typical manufacturer is assumed to sell 10 percent of its total U.S. sales in California.

(current-model-year cars with 7,500–10,000 miles on them) would become an important player in the California market. A person buying a new gasoline-powered car outside of California may be able to put 7,500 miles on it and then sell it in California for more than was paid for it, even after the smog impact fee is considered.[7]

Fourth, electric cars may not stay in California very long. Under the above scenario, the electric vehicle could be expected to be sold to a California resident for $10,000 less than its cost elsewhere (most manufacturers' distribution systems will permit them to offer electric vehicles nationwide, where there will be some limited demand even at a price that reflects true cost). Since a "used" California electric vehicle would therefore be much less expensive than a new electric vehicle outside of California, economic pressures may lead to the export out of state of some of the electric vehicles being produced to comply with the mandate. Thus the number of electric vehicles remaining in California may be far less than the number mandated.

Fifth, the cost penalty imposed on manufacturers with California sales of 35,000 or more vehicles could reduce the market share of manufacturers subject to the mandate and increase the share of manufacturers not subject to the mandate (about 18 percent of the California market in 1991). Although the degree of market shift depends on a number of factors, some shift would likely occur at price differentials of $1,000 per vehicle. This shift would decrease the total number of vehicles sold in California by manufacturers subject to the mandate, and thus the number of electric vehicles sold in California as well. Although comparatively small, this is a factor that could diminish the air quality benefits otherwise anticipated because of the ZEV mandate and thus should be taken into account.

If you add up the effect of the decreased number of new, clean gasoline-powered California cars sold as a result of mandates and the increased number of older cars—many with federal emission control systems—plus the diminished number of electric vehicles that stay in California, it is possible that the ZEV mandate may harm the environment and create significant distortions to the California new-vehicle market.

If electric vehicles are desirable and can be marketed and sold at a fair price in the volumes mandated, then mandates are not needed for

---

[7] Certain highly desirable models would depreciate less than $1,000 even after 7,500 miles, and thus the seller could make a net profit. On all models, a near-new California car (with about 3,000 miles on it) with a $1,000 electric vehicle subsidy premium would be less desirable than an identical out-of-state car with 7,500 miles on it selling for $1,000 less.

electric vehicles to become a reality. If electric vehicles are not marketable, mandates could create distorted markets with significant adverse unintended consequences. Further, as a result of forced massive investments in tooling of a potentially unmarketable technology, money and expertise would be diverted from the essential research necessary to create a marketable product.

The Future of the Electric Vehicle

One of the big fears of many, including those who believe that the electric vehicle has a future, is that the early introduction of an uncommercial product forced by unrealistic mandates will poison the market for an improved product later on. James Baldwin, technology editor of the *Whole Earth Review*, wrote in *Garbage* magazine that "the hasty adoption of the ZEV standard has had the effect of slowing the development of some of the better [electric vehicle] designs, which might contribute less overall environmental damage—and which people might be more likely to buy" (Baldwin 1993). He also observed in the same article that "designing a radically improved car is a difficult challenge and a dangerous game: If customers don't like your eco-righteous car, you're out of the market . . . or out of business."

Clearly, the number one question is whether the current generation of electric vehicles will satisfy enough of the customers' needs and have enough advantages over gasoline-powered vehicles that they can be profitably sold in the mandated quantities. In cases in which no technology exists for customers to evaluate, typical marketing research efforts are not satisfactory. Rather, electric vehicles must be put in the hands of potential customers for evaluation. GM is doing so with the Impact in its PrEView program, building a fleet of 50 Impacts in order to gauge public reaction. (There is a historic precedent for this approach: in the mid-1960s, Chrysler built a fleet of 50 turbine-powered cars to determine if customers would view the attributes of the turbine worth the extra price.)

If the current generation of electric vehicles is not acceptable to consumers, then additional research is necessary to widen the electric vehicle's appeal and minimize the cost penalty. The domestic automobile industry has addressed these issues with two consortia—one on batteries and one on electric vehicle component technology.

Conclusion

Historically, the free market has favored gasoline-powered vehicles over electric vehicles. Although substantial progress has been made in electric vehicle technology, there exists no evidence to suggest that electric vehicles, even in mass production, will ever occupy more than a market niche. Given the history of electric vehicles as compared with gasoline-powered vehicles, it is incumbent upon electric vehicle advocates to prove that electric vehicles are acceptable in today's market. This is what is being attempted in the electric vehicle field demonstrations currently under way.

If the results of these evaluations indicate that electric vehicles cannot be marketed without continuous subsidies (either internal manufacturer subsidies or external government subsidies), then the appropriateness of mandates as sound public policy needs to be re-examined.

If electric vehicles can make a positive contribution to society, their ultimate success should not be destroyed by premature mandates in the absence of demonstrated consumer acceptability. If the government wants to encourage the development of technologies that will result in a cleaner environment, it should consider policies such as appropriate energy taxes or emissions trading. These policies could internalize the pollution cost of all activities and technologies, sending price signals to customers regarding which transportation mode best fits their needs, which trips to take and when, and how much fuel should be consumed. A strong argument can be made that only by utilizing market mechanisms can a truly efficient sustainable transportation system be developed.

Mandates, while being an appropriate policy instrument in some situations, can lead to unacceptable unintended consequences when applied in other situations. Given the number and potential severity of the possible unintended consequences of the ZEV mandate and the serious concerns about the market acceptability of ZEVs, the mandate may be the wrong policy instrument to encourage the development of the electric vehicle.

References

Baldwin, James. 1993. *Garbage*. June/July.
Durant, W.C. 1983. *Automotive News*. September.
Shacket, S.R. 1983. *The Complete Book of Electric Vehicles*. Domus Books.
Sierra Research/Charles River Associates. 1994. "The Cost Effectiveness of Further Regulating Mobile Source Emissions." Report prepared for American Automobile Manufacturers Association. February 28.

Chapter Thirteen

How Government and Industry Can Cooperate to Promote Fuel Conservation: An Industry Perspective

PAUL MCCARTHY

Fuel conservation has been an expressed goal of public policy for over 20 years. At first, energy conservation was seen as one leg of a strategy to establish independence from foreign sources of oil, especially the Middle East. These strategic concerns were broadly consistent with the cold-war focus on the relative balance of power between the West and the East that dominated foreign policy from 1945 until the beginning of the 1990s. At the same time, emerging concern about the environment led some to believe that the energy crisis was a signal of the beginning of a widespread collapse that would occur as human population exceeded the earth's carrying capacity. The latter view, expressed in the Club of Rome's *Limits to Growth* (Meadows et al. 1972), maintained that the absolute quantity of remaining resources, including oil, were not sufficient to support rapidly expanding use and would be exhausted within a few decades, leading to a catastrophic collapse in the world economy. The inevitability of such an apocalyptic outcome does not hold up to careful economic scrutiny, however (see Nordhouse [1992] for a thorough review).

The large decline in the real price of oil since 1981 (from $53 per barrel to around $17 per barrel in 1992$) has also played a role in the unwinding of the energy crisis over the course of the 1980s, and a 50 percent increase in proved oil reserves has resulted in a more sanguine view of the future availability of oil, at least in the near term (API 1993). There remains, however, the potential for future oil price shocks that will generate costly adjustments for the economy.[1] In the wider political context, energy security concerns have been largely superseded by emerging worries about accumulating CO_2 emissions from the fossil fuel combustion and their potential influence on global climate.

In spite of the change in focus of economic policymaking from energy security to global warming, there has been little change in the policies and policy instruments used to reduce oil consumption in the transportation sector. The United States has relied on a single approach to energy conservation in the transportation sector—a regulatory standard for corporate average fuel economy (CAFE). Demand for energy has not been addressed directly; rather, the policy approach has been one of regulating the characteristics of the new-vehicle fleet and waiting for fleet turnover to increase the efficiency of the vehicle stock.

The history of past U.S. efforts to raise new-vehicle fuel economy lacks successful examples of industry and government working together. Standards were established in a contentious political process, and subsequent efforts to modify the standards, both upward and downward, have been similarly polarized. This failing has been recognized both in and out of government as a barrier to development of a sound policy addressing fuel consumption.

Today, however, cooperative research efforts among the Big Three are advancing the rate of technical progress in materials and technologies with direct application to improving the fuel efficiency of vehicles. Increasingly these research efforts also involve linking the research and development expertise of the auto industry with the technical and scientific capabilities of the federal laboratories. The most important of these new cooperative initiatives is the Partnership for a New Generation of Vehicles (PNGV), which expressly aims to develop the technologies necessary to build an affordable vehicle with up to three times the fuel efficiency of today's average car.

There are significant ongoing barriers to more effective technical cooperation between industry and government, and it is hoped that

---

[1] For a discussion of the nature and extent of the present energy security threat and the opportunities to reduce it through energy conservation, see Bohi and Toman (1993), who find that energy security threats are minimal and do not justify expensive policy responses, and Greene and Duleep (1992), who argue that the risks are substantial.

the PNGV program will serve as a model of cooperative research. Barriers to cooperation are even more evident when broad policies to reduce fuel consumption—such as higher fuel economy standards, subsidies and requirements for alternative fuels, or higher fuel taxes—are being contemplated. Overcoming the long history of mutual distrust between industry and government will require a sustained commitment to working together. Progress is difficult when both sides perceive that arguments are being exaggerated to improve the chances for a desired political outcome. On the other hand, communication is facilitated when both parties resist taking strategically motivated positions on public policy issues and instead try to maintain the best standards of objective analysis. Many useful insights can still be gained from constructive inquiry despite more than 20 years of public debate about fuel economy and energy conservation.

USCAR

Since 1989, Chrysler, Ford, and General Motors have formed a number of consortia to carry out collaborative precompetitive work on individual projects. The umbrella organization assisting the various consortia is the United States Council for Automotive Research (USCAR). The establishment of this organization and the projects it manages was enabled by three important pieces of legislation: (1) the 1984 National Cooperative Research and Development Act, which allows companies to work together on precompetitive technologies; (2) the 1989 National Competitiveness Technology Transfer Act, which allows federal laboratories to establish cooperative research agreements with industry; and (3) the 1993 National Cooperative Research and Production Act, which facilitates cooperative production programs. The USCAR mission calls for the organization to create, support, and direct cooperative research and development (R&D) in a manner responsive to the needs of the environment and society in general. Such R&D is to include the appropriate public and private stakeholders; its aim is to support domestic automobile manufacturers in their efforts to establish global leadership in technology through cooperative, precompetitive research and development, thereby strengthening the U.S. industrial base and providing jobs for U.S. workers.

Eight of the thirteen cooperative research initiatives undertaken to date are directly or indirectly related to improving the fuel efficiency of vehicles (see Table 13-1). In some instances, government participation in these efforts is contemplated or taking place, either as a source of leveraged finance or directly in the form of active participation by technical laboratories and government researchers. By far the largest federal involvement has been in the U.S. Advanced Battery Consortium (USABC), which in 1994 had a budget of $265 million to support grants to develop important storage battery technology.

Table 13-1
USCAR Consortia Developing Environmental Technologies

USCAR Consortia	How Consortia Relate to Partnership for a New Generation of Vehicle (PNGV) Goals
Auto/Oil Air Quality Improvement Research Program	Develops data on potential vehicle emissions improvements from reformulated gasoline, alternative fuels, and new automotive technology
Computer-Aided Design (CAD) / Computer-Aided Manufacturing (CAM) Partnership	Promotes and applies feature-based technology to reduce the complexity and cost of product and process design and tool manufacturing
Environmental Research Consortium	Conducts research on the environmental impact of vehicle and manufacturing emissions
Low Emissions Technologies R&D Partnership	Coordinates research and development activities in vehicle emissions technologies
Supercomputer Automotive Applications Partnership	Conducts high-performance parallel computing and communications research applied to vehicle design and development
U.S. Advanced Battery Consortium (USABC)	Pursues research and development of advanced energy systems capable of improving range and performance of electric vehicles
U.S. Automotive Materials Partnership	Conducts vehicle-oriented research and development in lightweight and other advanced materials and materials processing
Vehicle Recycling Partnership	Conducts research on recycling, reuse, and disposal of motor vehicles and vehicle components

Partnership for a New Generation of Vehicles (PNGV)

The Partnership for a New Generation of Vehicles (PNGV), a new technology initiative announced by President Bill Clinton on September 29, 1993, is the basis for an innovative program joining the federal government and USCAR in a unique research and development effort representing a fundamental change from the manner in which government and industry have interacted in the past.[2] The initiative is intended to address the nation's transportation energy goals through informed cooperation, rather than through confrontation in a political and regulatory process that emphasizes adversarial interactions between industry and government. This partnership between the government and industry will permit private and public resources to be systematically focused on achieving major technological breakthroughs, possibly making traditional technology-forcing regulatory interventions irrelevant.

Both government and industry bring unique strengths to this project. The industry partners have the capability to determine which product concepts have the highest probability of success in the market; further, their expertise in mass production for domestic and international markets is essential to convert any advanced technical idea into a practical product. Federal agencies have access to certain types of advanced technologies and research resources not generally available to private firms. For example, many technologies being developed for specific military or space applications may have direct relevance for the PNGV project. In other cases, federal funds can be used directly to fund government/industry partnerships where the technical risks are too great or the returns too distant to justify adequate funding from the private sector alone.

The PNGV Program Plan

The overall goal of the PNGV Program Plan is embodied in three independent but related research initiatives, the specific goals of which are as follows:

Goal 1: Significantly improve national competitiveness in manufacturing. Continuous and rapid improvement in manufacturing technolo-

---

[2] The following section on PNGV goals and structure is largely a condensed version of the PNGV Program Plan (PNGV 1994). Although much of the section takes language directly from this document, the interested reader should consult the complete program plan for comprehensive details.

gies is critically important to assuring competitiveness in today's marketplace, as well as being a necessary condition for successful production of a new generation of vehicles.

The pursuit of advances in manufacturing techniques includes the use of high-speed computers for efficient design and testing of products and components before they are fabricated; the development of advanced materials and material fabrication techniques; the use of efficient, flexible manufacturing equipment; and the development and use of advanced sensors and control systems to optimize the management of complex assemblies and parts. These advances in manufacturing capability are critical to developing commercially feasible vehicles that embody advanced energy-saving technology. New production technologies will enable the industry to make effective use of advanced light-weight materials by reducing production time and cost. Advanced design and simulation have numerous applications, from optimizing aerodynamic performance to assuring an ability to successfully integrate and validate the performance of combined technologies.

More sophisticated computer simulation systems need to be developed for testing complex research designs as they apply to such issues as tire rolling resistance and braking characteristics and for designing analytical methods to determine strength characteristics of composite structures and other light-weight materials.

Goal 2: Implement commercially viable innovations from ongoing research on conventional vehicles. Research will focus on technologies that reduce the demand for energy from the engine and drivetrain. Throughout the research program, the industry commits to apply those commercially viable technologies resulting from this research that would be expected to significantly increase vehicle fuel efficiency and improve emissions.

Pursuit of advances that can lead to increases in the efficiency of gasoline-powered vehicles in the near term requires further improvement in the ability to model the combustion process and accurately predict energy release and pollutant formation. Other areas in which government aerospace and defense research could be reprogrammed to contribute to improving the efficiency of vehicles in the near term include advances in lubricants, and cost-effective surface treatments and component modifications that will enable more efficient, but more stressful, engine and drivetrain operating conditions.

An important existing goal 2 initiative in the cooperative effort between government and industry is the Engine Support System Technology (ESST) Program of USCAR's Low Emissions Technology R&D

Partnership (LEP). This program has placed a high priority on the development of NO_x catalysts to enable the use of lean-burn and ultra-lean-burn internal combustion engines. Other new technology areas identified include on-board vehicle diagnostic systems, enhanced air-fuel mixture preparation strategies, advanced emissions sensors, and rapid heat-up catalysts.

Goal 3: Develop a vehicle to achieve up to three times the fuel efficiency of today's comparable vehicle (i.e., the 1994 Chrysler Concorde, Ford Taurus, and Chevrolet Lumina). Such a vehicle should have equivalent customer purchase price, cost of ownership, and performance (including driving range per "refill").

Many of the early negotiations about the goals of the PNGV program have focused on clarifying this third goal, including a very specific definition of today's comparable vehicle. These definitions are an important part of the PNGV Program Plan because they structure the technology-selecting and development process and because they allow a clear distinction to be made between true efficiency enhancements and fuel economy gains that can result from compromising other value characteristics.

Some of the specific assumptions related to the up-to-three-times fuel efficiency goal are that

- the vehicle will achieve Tier II emissions levels (at 100,000 miles).

- the vehicle will meet the up-to-three-times efficiency improvement goal while meeting present and future Federal Motor Vehicle Safety Standards (FMVSS).

- the vehicle will improve recyclability to at least 80 percent, up from today's 75 percent industry average.

- a concept vehicle should be available at about the year 2000 and a production prototype approximately four years later.

The Technology Challenge

The distribution of input energy in a current midsize (family sedan) vehicle is shown in Figure 13-1, for both an urban and a highway driving cycle. Fuel efficiency improvements could be attained by reducing the input energy required by any part of the system; however, substantial increases in fuel economy will require that the system be addressed as a whole. Thus the PNGV program will be evaluating the opportunities to improve fuel economy by

- reducing vehicle weight, aerodynamic drag, and rolling resistance.

Figure 13-1

Energy Distribution in a Typical Mid-Size Vehicle

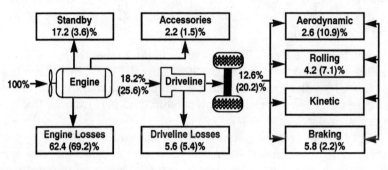

Urban (Highway) Driving Cycle

Source: PNGV (1994).

- increasing the thermal efficiency with an advanced propulsion system.
- improving the efficiency of the power transmission.
- eliminating engine standby/idling losses.
- recovering vehicle braking energy.

Propulsion and Vehicle Improvements Needed for 80 Mpg

Major advances must be made in several technologies simultaneously in order to achieve an 80-miles-per-gallon (mpg) vehicle. To shift the energy balance in favor of improved fuel economy requires a three-pronged approach: (1) convert energy more efficiently; (2) reduce the energy demand by the vehicle; and (3) implement regenerative braking to conserve energy.

Results from a parametric model used to show how these factors interact to achieve 80 mpg are shown in Figure 13-2, which illustrates the approximate "design space" for one set of alternative approaches for achieving the goal. The design space has both theoretical and practical limits. Three-times fuel economy is unlikely to be achievable by engine improvements alone, given feasible thermal efficiencies with various heat engines. The thermal efficiency needed ranges from approximately 40 to 55 percent—about twice as efficient as thermal efficiencies presently found in the market. Even with advanced fuel cells,

Figure 13-2

Design Space for Achieving Fuel Economy Target

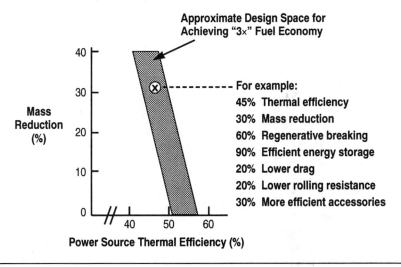

Source: PNGV (1994).

which have higher potential efficiencies than heat engines, other vehicle improvements will be needed.

Reductions in vehicle mass on the order of 20 to 40 percent from today's baseline vehicles will be required. These levels of mass reduction are beyond simple refinement of today's steel frame and body construction and will involve the introduction of entirely new classes of structural materials to the automobile.

Models show that lighter vehicles with improved engines will still require an efficient regenerative braking system to recover, store, and reuse energy currently lost in braking. Such a system will reduce the amount of energy consumed in what is normally the most inefficient step of the energy cycle.

Several other advances, though contributing less to the overall system goal, must also be made; these include reduced aerodynamic drag, reduced tire rolling resistance, and more efficient mechanical and electrical components.

As these new technologies mature to the point of commercial application, the problems shift to identifying how they can be incorporated into the vehicle fleet. The mix and degree of technological application will be optimized to minimize vehicle cost, subject to meeting the efficiency target and other program parameters.

Figure 13-3

The Three Mutually Supportive Goals of the PNGV

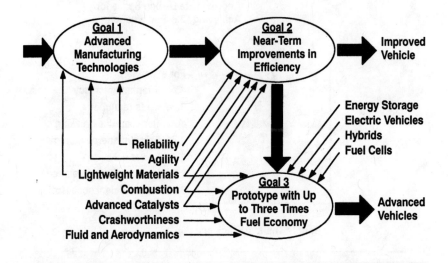

Interrelationship and Integration of Goals

The close interrelationship among the PNGV's three mutually supportive goals is illustrated in Figure 13-3. New manufacturing technologies and approaches can lead to dramatic improvements in product quality, cost, and time to market. Manufacturing productivity improvements will help assure that the cars of the future are manufactured by U.S. industry.

Organization of the Partnership

Organizationally, the PNGV partnership is a coordinated effort between the federal government and USCAR. Two primary groups comprise the organizational structure—the Operational Steering Group and the Technical Team. Each group includes representatives from both government and industry. In addition, the organization has its own legal and public affairs support.

The Operational Steering Group is the policy- and decision-making group for the initiative. The under secretary for technology chairs the government Operational Steering Group, which includes senior officials from the Department of Commerce (DOC), the Department of Defense (DOD), the Department of Energy (DOE), the

Department of Transportation (DOT), the Environmental Protection Agency (EPA), the National Aeronautics and Space Administration (NASA), the National Economic Council (NEC), the National Science Foundation (NSF), the Office of the Vice President (OVP), the Office of Science and Technology Policy (OSTP), the Office of Management and Budget (OMB), and the Office of Environmental Policy (OEP). The industry Operational Steering Group is comprised of the vice presidents from Chrysler, Ford, and General Motors, who rotate the chair responsibilities, supported by the three companies' PNGV directors.

The Technical Team, which reports to the Operational Steering Group, is also composed of government and industry units. The government Technical Task Force is comprised of technology managers from the operating agencies, plus OVP, OSTP, and OMB. At this time, the government Technical Task Force has organized its resources into panels to carry out its planning responsibilities, as follows: System Analysis, Vehicle Technologies, Advanced Design and Manufacturing, and Components Integration. The industry PNGV Technical Team is represented by senior executives from Chrysler, Ford, and General Motors. The auto industry has built its planning process around the established goals, utilizing its preexisting consortia to carry out its responsibilities. These organizational arrangements may be periodically revised based on need.

A government PNGV Secretariat has been established as a central point for storing and maintaining nonproprietary data and information, establishing and maintaining a library and reading room, disseminating government information in response to public information, and establishing and maintaining a physical facility for government support staff. The USCAR Secretariat serves as the industry administrative arm.

To accomplish the defined goals of the PNGV program, government and industry will negotiate and enter into various contracts, subcontracts, understandings, cooperative research, and development agreements as well as shared research arrangements. Participants in the project will share the costs of the enterprise using a variety of arrangements, including direct funding of research in industry or university facilities and cooperative research arrangements that combine government and private research without transfer of funds. While the relative proportions of government and private funding will vary depending on the initiative and on the specific project involved, it is envisioned that there will be significant cost sharing by industry and government. The proportion of federal funding will be higher for high-risk projects in which the outcome is uncertain, whereas industry funding will be higher for technologies with a clear near-term market application.

Barriers to Cooperation

Cooperation between industry and government is impeded by many barriers, including poor communication, differences in culture, legal constraints, and genuinely divergent objectives. All of these barriers are evident as PNGV evolves from a concept to a multifaceted research program. The government/industry cooperation emerging from the PNGV program does not exist in a vacuum. The present administration has committed to reducing the growth of U.S. greenhouse gas (GHG) emissions and is actively seeking to pursue this goal. Indeed, the PNGV program was initiated to demonstrate and expand the limits of technical improvements in vehicle efficiency that could help reduce GHG emissions in the future. The benefits of the PNGV program will arise over a period of years from the successful transfer and joint development of commercially viable new vehicle technologies.

Cooperation in matters of scientific and technical understanding is often easier when it is separated from politics. However, separation can raise the danger that the political process that generates policy may not be informed of the relevant facts about what can be achieved and how much it will cost. This information gap can lead to multiple policies with the same intent, thus diverting funds from the most promising options and raising the cost of achieving the ultimate goal. Congress has in the past contemplated changes in the corporate fuel economy standards and remains outside the PNGV formal structure. It is the view of industry that requiring vehicle manufacturers to meet stringent interim goals would be detrimental to attainment of the PNGV goal.

At the heart of the difficulties associated with industry and government cooperation at the national policy level is the adversarial nature of our political and legal system. Often it seems that the present system requires all interested parties to make the strongest case possible for the outcome that is in their best interest before the process of compromise can begin.

Representative democracy at its best establishes broad tradeoffs that reflect both the wider social interest and the needs and concerns of minority constituents. Thus one could argue that the system has worked with regard to fuel economy standards. While their imperfections are widely known, the CAFE regulations represent a political compromise that has survived considerable controversy (Crandall et al. 1986; NRC 1992). The standard was temporarily lowered in the late

1980s, instead of being repealed outright, when falling fuel prices and rising incomes shifted consumer demand toward vehicles with lower fuel economy. On the other hand, recent attempts to raise the standards have also failed to receive congressional approval. The political process will be inherently less successful at evaluating the relative commercial and scientific merits of different technical options. Success is particularly unlikely when there are vocal interests who will gain or lose by shifts in politically determined standards or regulations.[3]

The political process is ultimately responsible for the relative valuation of competing social goals. It is unrealistic to think that industry and government will ever be in complete agreement about how much energy conservation is necessary, how it should best be conserved, and who will have to pay. While consensus is not necessary, successful achievement of ambitious social goals is facilitated when there is widespread consensus about the need for, and the means to reach, a particular end.

The fundamental orientation of energy policies is also determined in a political process. Possible approaches can range from rigid specification of fuel usage or fuel economy to incentive systems that place greater reliance on the free choices of producers and consumers. Of course, most of the time the policy response is not to change policy at all. When it comes to political debate, it may be that the most that can be hoped for is understanding of what the parties have at stake, combined with a willingness to look at the means to achieve social goals in ways that minimize the cost to individuals and to society. The cooperation between industry specialists and government scientists and technical experts embodied in the PNGV program will help increase the understanding of the technical and commercial constraints that determine the potential for improving fuel economy.

Expanding the opportunities for communication is one of the ongoing benefits of the PNGV. Increased informal dialogue at all levels between industry and government fosters a more realistic government assessment of the technical and financial constraints faced by vehicle manufacturers and their customers (including an understanding of the critical tradeoffs between cost and performance that define which vehicles are marketable). Such communication at the same time in-

---

[3] One need only look at the many technical specifications in the Clean Air Act Amendments of 1990 to find a multitude of inconsistencies between these specific requirements and the best scientific and economic evaluations of the alternatives (Harrington et al. 1994). At the top of a list of politically motivated technical specifications would be the requirement that 30 percent of reformulated gasoline contain oxygenates derived from domestic renewable sources—e.g., ethanol.

creases industry's understanding of its important role in meeting national energy conservation and environmental goals. In addition, debate about the relative merits of various technical options reinforces the need for continuous improvement in vehicle efficiency.

Negotiating Partners

One of the most significant barriers to cooperation at all levels is the need for many parties to be involved in the negotiating process. Moving the PNGV from its inception to a working research and development program has been especially hindered by exactly this difficulty. With many organizations from both industry and government involved, closure—much less consensus—becomes difficult. Chrysler, Ford, General Motors, and foreign automakers, as well as the supplier industries, frequently have their own competitive interests at stake. The views of other interested parties, such as environmental organizations and labor, also need to be explicitly considered.

When industry interacts with government, lack of a single negotiator presents a significant challenge. In practice, cooperation with government involves establishing a dialogue with many public entities that often have conflicting objectives and constraints. Congress, the states, and the administration, as well as the specific agencies DOE, EPA, DOT, DOD, and DOC, all have different statutory missions and regulatory agendas. On the regulatory side, each agency has looked at only one aspect of the motor vehicle and its usage and does not have an explicit charter to evaluate the tradeoffs that are inherently generated when multiple policies are designed to meet diverse public goals. Little coordination of policy is achieved in practice, and as a result, inconsistent regulations to meet environmental and fuel economy targets are allowed to persist (NRC 1992). Industry understands that the vehicle is a system and that business success depends on making the system work to meet consumer needs. Likewise, a systems view, if taken by government, could help alleviate conflicting regulations and provide a more balanced set of policy objectives (Crandall et al. 1986).

Specific cooperative efforts that involve government participation must cope with conflict-of-interest regulations and federal contracting regulations that present a significantly less flexible and dynamic environment than exists for private cooperative enterprises. Further, the Freedom of Information Act and the Public Advisory Act potentially provide foreign competitors easy access to new discoveries. The government's unique noncommercial procedures require extensive modification of internal controls by industry, thus diverting resources from research to administration. One USCAR partnership using government funds, the USABC, has taken longer getting research started than other consortia, in part because of these challenges. Developing procedures for streamlining the administration of cooperative ventures and protecting the confidentiality of commercially sensitive information will reduce this time lag in the future.

Resource Issues and Constraints

Finite resources present a problem for all parties. The industry already faces limits on the number of qualified and experienced engineers available to simultaneously address the technical challenges presented by government mandates, emerging cooperative research efforts, and the market imperatives for continuous improvement in vehicle quality and consumer value.

It is anticipated that the PNGV program will require no new federal spending. All public resources are to come from reprogramming existing funds. In principle, such reprogramming is a necessary step to cashing in on the "peace dividend." However, it is likely to be an ongoing problem as the government seeks to reprogram funds from existing projects. In some cases, reprogramming will require abandonment of long-standing research efforts directed to solving defense- or aerospace-related problems. Additionally, existing programs are often supported by entrenched special interests that may be able to delay or even block the reallocation of funds, thus slowing technical progress toward meeting the PNGV goals.

Government budget realities already demand that government agencies seek to minimize government expenditures that may be inconsistent with minimizing social cost (the sum of public and private costs). The limited resources of government agencies along with congressionally mandated timetables often result in regulations and policies that provide very limited flexibility and strenuous reporting requirements, both of which increase private costs but can save on public monitoring expenditures. This dilemma has been particularly evident in the stringent deadlines faced by EPA and the states for meeting Clean Air Act requirements.

In addition, the socially efficient solution sometimes does not minimize government expenditures, as is particularly the case when command and control policies are based on complex modeling exercises rather than on empirical data (Harrington et al. 1994). Performing the basic research and measurement under real-world conditions is more expensive, but it can enable policy development that has real, rather than paper, benefits.

269

Government errors in evaluating the relative merits of particular technical and regulatory solutions are potentially very costly, not only for the industry but also for consumers.[4] These costs are often realized only over time. To the extent that the costs of excessive fuel economy standards fall on the domestic industry, they can directly threaten its competitive position relative to that of foreign manufacturers (NRC 1992).

Given the vast fixed capital stock and increasing vehicle complexity, and the necessary stages of design, development, and production, long lead times are needed to make significant changes in product plans. Furthermore, manufacturers seldom introduce more than one completely new vehicle per year, so changing an entire line of vehicles may take more than a decade.

Financial Constraints on the Automotive Industry

Over the next few years, the auto industry faces a full plate of regulatory requirements. For example, the Clean Air Act Amendments of 1990 generated more than 80 different regulations that affect the vehicle and the vehicle manufacturing process. Many of these regulations compromise fuel economy, and all of them increase the cost of production. Meeting government requirements and competitive challenges requires a high level of investment, which is ultimately financed in the capital market. Between 1989 and 1993, the domestic auto industry was able to raise funds to support $78.7 billion in capital spending by the Big Three, while net income (excluding one-time write-offs) over the same period totaled only $8.6 billion. This high level of investment in the face of low profitability was possible because there was a reasonable expectation by investors that the industry would return to normal profitability. With 1994 financial projections suggesting that the auto industry is in the middle of a cyclical rebound, it may be tempting to think that these profits can fund expensive new regulatory initiatives. However, the profits earned over the next several years are needed to finance existing programs for future vehicles and to prepare for the inevitable next downturn. An open U.S. vehicle market and vigorous competition between internal vehicle manufacturers hold vehicle prices down to the cost of production plus a reasonable rate of return over the business cycle. Innovations in product

---

[4] The California zero-emission vehicle (ZEV) sales mandate could generate price increases on the order of $2,000 for new gasoline-powered cars sold in California once the mandate is in full force (Sierra Research 1994).

or process are quickly initiated if they improve consumer value. In this competitive environment, consumers will ultimately bear the entire cost of regulations.

During periods when there are extensive changes to vehicles because of government regulations, consumers perceive that new vehicles become less affordable. In response, some buyers will choose a smaller or less well equipped vehicle than they otherwise would have purchased. Other consumers may defer purchasing new vehicles because a new vehicle is viewed as a poor value relative to continuing to maintain an older vehicle.

Industry is concerned that potential future regulations, such as higher fuel economy standards, could significantly degrade vehicle affordability. Some recent proposals to the CAFE standard have been estimated to generate increases in vehicle cost that could more than double the regulatory content presently anticipated. Increases in cost of $2,500 per vehicle would effectively eliminate the opportunity for consumers, on average, to continue to upgrade as they purchase new vehicles (SRI 1991; AAMA 1994).

The government's focus is primarily on public benefits. Furthermore, government policies, analyses, and positions are often motivated by the need to generate popular support for government actions. Election cycles frequently create tension between short-term appearances and policies that are sensible for the long term, and it often appears to industry that political decision is overly influenced by the initial incidence of the policy. The most recent proposal to revise the gasoline tax is a case in point. That policies promoting fuel conservation, no matter how good or well intended, have to pass the test of political acceptability is a significant constraint on the range of policy options available to the government.

The Need for Regulatory Flexibility

The Yorktown refinery study provides an interesting case, both for the shortcomings of the existing regulatory approach and for the opportunities presented by industry/government cooperation. A joint study by Amoco and the U.S. Environmental Protection Agency (Amoco/U.S. EPA 1991) of the pollution reduction opportunities at the Amoco refinery in Yorktown, Virginia, succeeded in identifying a number of effective and low-cost emissions control measures that were unrecognized by EPA's refinery emissions models. In some cases, these control options were also unknown to Amoco's environmental engineers. Further, many of the upcoming regulatory requirements were found to be poorly related to improvements in air quality or potential risks to human health when compared with the alternatives identified during the study. Unfortunately, the existing regulatory mechanism lacks the flexibility to accommodate these findings. Thus the more expensive required investments have been made, whereas the more effective alternatives are on hold until they are addressed by specific regulations.

Optimal Policy Approach

One theoretical justification for policy intervention relies on the existence of external costs associated with vehicle usage that are not reflected in the private decisions of individuals. Classic externalities— including air pollution, congestion, global warming, and energy security—have all been mentioned as negative side effects of our present transportation system (Sweeney 1993). These are legitimate grounds for government policies to mitigate the impacts of vehicle usage; indeed, most of the Asilomar conference at which this chapter was originally presented was about these very issues. However, the existence of a negative externality in and of itself is not sufficient justification for a policy response. Government intervention also has costs and can generate unintentional consequences. What has been lacking is (1) sufficient attention to matching the available policy instruments to the externalities and (2) a critical look at the potential for a specific government intervention to increase net social welfare.

Economists advocate two related measures to avoid policy mistakes. The first is the cost/benefit test, which requires that policies produce benefits exceeding the costs. Cost/benefit analysis can help answer the questions, Should this policy be done at all? and When do we stop? The second test is one of cost-effectiveness, which is a measure of the relative costs of achieving a given goal by different means. Cost-effectiveness suggests where society's scarce physical, intellectual, and financial resources can be conserved by substituting a less expensive means of achieving the social goal. Cost-effectiveness can help answer the question, Should this goal be achieved by a different set of policies? Studies of the efficiency of existing regulatory policies to control externalities have consistently found that regulations have been poorly designed, resulting in costs of control that far exceed the estimated cost of efficient policies. Frequently the costs also exceed the estimated benefits by a wide margin (Tietenberg 1988).

How far should environmental considerations be pushed when it comes to increasing fuel economy? The perspective of the vehicle manufacturer is illustrated graphically in Figure 13-4. At any given time and under any given regulatory structure, environmental bene-

Figure 13-4

Cost Curves Faced by Industry in Achieving Environmental Goals

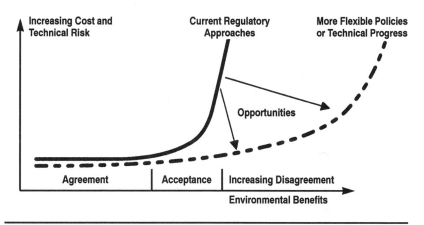

fits can be increased. However, the costs to do so mount at an increasing rate. Additionally, as costs rise for smaller true additional environmental benefits, there is increasing disagreement from industry with the incremental moves to greater environmental control. Over time, however, technical progress will improve these tradeoffs, resulting in lower and flatter cost curves.

There are two main ways in which government and industry cooperation can address the tradeoffs that limit achievement of conservation goals. The first is dynamic government/industry cooperation in research to facilitate the technical advances that lower the future cost of achieving any given level of environmental benefit. An accelerated rate of technical progress means that greater fuel economy is possible while continuing to improve other vehicular characteristics that are valued by consumers. Because there is progress over time, the tradeoffs among vehicle characteristics will always look better in the future. Looking backward, it should be no surprise that both fuel economy and vehicle safety have improved over the last decades. However, this result in no way invalidates the fundamental insight that at any point in time these two vehicle characteristics are traded off. On the margin, improving one must reduce the ability to improve the other.

The second critical area for government/industry cooperation is policy design. Moving to a less costly regulatory structure can essentially shift society to a lower-cost path to achieve the desired level of

273

environmental benefits. Failure to cooperate has an opportunity cost that is real, but not always obvious. Movement to a lower cost curve is the "opportunity" presented by government/industry cooperation when comprehensive market-based policies result; however, such an effect is difficult to achieve in practice. Although industry overall has much to gain from a general move to an efficient policy framework, the reality of the political decision-making process is that often more is to be gained or lost by shifting the burden to some other sector.

Comprehensive market-based policies impact more industries and usually result in costs that are visible to consumers, further increasing political resistance. Because each individual industry and consumer group has an interest in having someone else other than themselves "foot the bill," initiatives such as the Btu tax founder politically. When nearly every interested party is willing to sacrifice efficiency for the opportunity to "opt out," it is no surprise that piecemeal policies result. The tendency to enact narrow legislation presents a significant challenge to a comprehensive approach that could be expected to equate the cost of CO_2 emission reductions at the margin, a necessary condition for economic efficiency. Overcoming this barrier will require more than the usual amount of political leadership.

CAFE Compared with Gasoline Taxes and Other Market-Based Policies

Reliance on fuel economy standards can contribute to overlooking less costly ways to save energy. Options that reduce other externalities at the same time as they reduce automotive fuel use can be particularly attractive. A prime example of a market-based policy that can reduce energy use and vehicle emissions is congestion pricing. The main benefit of congestion pricing arises from the time savings provided by more efficient road use. Such benefits serve to reduce or eliminate the cost of the energy conservation (NRC 1994). Further emphasis on correctly pricing road use and parking is a promising direction for conservation policy. The major challenges will come from overcoming political resistance at the local and state levels.

Consumers will prefer more conservation when fuel is perceived to be valuable. A comprehensive survey of gasoline demand studies finds strong evidence that gasoline consumption is very responsive to prices and income (Dahl and Sterner 1991). The average short-run price elasticity reported in the study is –0.26, rising to –0.86 in the long run. The short-run income elasticity is 0.48, rising to 1.21 in the long run. This has important implications for policy. As income grows, so too will gasoline demand; however, since the long-run price elastici-

Figure 13-5

Real and Nominal Gasoline Taxation in the United States, 1918–1993

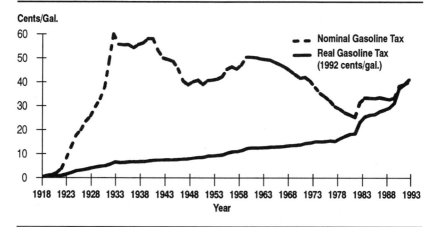

Source: Data from API (1993), Section VI, tables 5 and 15.

ties are also quite high, gasoline taxes could be quite effective in curtailing this demand. In light of the increasing importance placed on gasoline conservation since 1973, it is notable that there have been only very limited increases in the real tax on gasoline since 1982 (Figure 13-5). Indeed, higher fuel taxes are the great underexplored conservation policy in the United States.

Policies that raise the price of fuel use in general will automatically generate cost-effective ways of reducing fuel use in all sectors of the economy. Some studies indicate that if fuel conservation is to be pursued, broad-based programs relying on economic incentives would be much less costly for consumers than significant increases in the CAFE standard. An industry-sponsored study by Charles River Associates (CRA 1991), which evaluated the relative costs of various approaches to reducing petroleum use and greenhouse gas emissions, concludes that higher gasoline taxes, which seek to affect a wide range of choices and activities, are roughly 40 percent less costly than a fuel economy standard that achieves comparable petroleum savings. By allowing individual consumers to select in the marketplace the least costly means of reducing fuel consumption, considerable cost can be avoided. A tax on all petroleum products is less costly still, and a more broadly based carbon tax is even more cost-effective as a way of reducing CO_2 emissions. It should be noted that all of these alternatives will have a negative impact on the auto industry. Indeed, one of the ways that a higher gasoline tax reduces energy consumption is by reducing the stock of vehicles that consumers want to hold. Higher fuel taxes reduce sales, but they bring about a closer correspondence between individual behavior and the social valuation of energy consumption.

Conclusion

Increasing technical cooperation between industry and government promises accelerated development and penetration of commercially feasible technologies to improve fuel economy. These cooperative efforts will continue to be challenged by numerous barriers, primarily related to differences in the operating environment and perspective of industry R&D organizations and government laboratories. Resource constraints also threaten the success of technical cooperation aimed at achieving major increases in fuel economy. In particular, the industry believes that significant near-term increases in the CAFE standard would come at the expense of research into technologies with more promise in the long term. The opportunities presented by successful cooperation provide a strong inducement for both sides to continue working to overcome these barriers.

There is less reason for optimism on the policy side. The adversarial approach continues to amplify differences between the positions of industry and government rather than seeking mutually acceptable compromises. Policymaking through technology-forcing standards continues to create a situation in which policymakers propose unreachable or expensive performance and specific technology standards and then back down to a compromise ruling when industry complaints and political pressure become loud enough. In essence, industry noncooperation is necessary to achieve closure. This process could be greatly improved by a policymaking process that looks at creating consistent incentives for both industry and consumers to take actions that reduce fuel consumption.

More broadly, the key elements for effective and efficient government policy with regard to energy consumption must have the following characteristics: (1) the goals appropriately reflect scientific uncertainty and expected social benefits; (2) the policies are comprehensive and recognize the role of consumer behavior; (3) the regulations and policies are flexible enough to avoid costly mistakes; and (4) the policies recognize the importance of timing issues. Designing and implementing policy with these characteristics is difficult enough given the real uncertainties about the value of reduced energy consumption and the cost of the actions that can reduce energy consumption. Designing and implementing good policy will be impossible in an environment that leaves the industry and its concerns outside of the process of policy development.

References

American Automobile Manufacturers Association (AAMA). 1994. *Economic Indicators: The Year Ahead.* Special edition. Detroit.

American Petroleum Institute (API). 1993. *Basic Petroleum Data Book.* Washington, D.C. May.

Amoco/U.S. EPA. 1991. *Amoco–U.S. EPA Pollution Prevention Project.* Executive summary, revised. Yorktown, Virg. May.

Bohi, Douglas R., and Michael A. Toman. 1993. "Energy Security: Externalities and Policies." *Energy Policy* 21 (November): 1093–1109.

Charles River Associates (CRA). 1991. *Policy Alternatives for Reducing Petroleum Use and Greenhouse Gas Emissions.* Boston.

Crandall, Robert W., Howard K. Gruenspecht, Theodore E. Keeler, and Lester B. Lave. 1986. *Regulating the Automobile.* Washington, D.C.: The Brookings Institution.

Dahl, Carol, and Thomas Sterner. 1991. "Analyzing Gasoline Demand Elasticities: A Survey." *Energy Economics* (July): 203–210.

Greene, David L., and K.G. Duleep. 1992. *Costs and Benefits of Automotive Fuel Economy Improvement: A Partial Analysis.* Oak Ridge National Laboratory ORNL-6704. Oak Ridge, Tenn.: U.S. Department of Energy.

Harrington, Winston, Margaret A. Walls, and Virginia D. McConnell. 1994. *Shifting Gears: New Directions for Cars and Clean Air.* Resources for the Future. Washington, D.C.

Meadows, Donella H., Dennis L. Meadows, Jorgen Randers, and William W. Behrens III. 1972. *The Limits to Growth: A Report for the Club of Rome's Project on the Predicament of Mankind.* New York: Universe Books.

National Research Council (NRC). 1992. *Automotive Fuel Economy: How Far Should We Go?* Washington, D.C.: National Academy Press.

———. 1994. *Curbing Gridlock: Peak-Period Fees to Relieve Traffic Congestion.* Vol. 1. Washington, D.C.: National Academy Press.

Nordhouse, William D. 1992. "Lethal Model 2: The Limits to Growth Revisited." *Brookings Papers on Economic Activity: 2.* Washington, D.C.: The Brookings Institution, pp. 1–59.

Partnership for a New Generation of Vehicles (PNGV). 1994. *Partnership for a New Generation of Vehicles: Program Plan.* Washington, D.C.: U.S. Department of Commerce, PNGV Secretariat.

Sierra Research, Inc. 1994. *The Cost-Effectiveness of Further Regulating Mobile Source Emissions*. Sacramento.

SRI. 1991. *Potential for Improved Fuel Economy in Passenger Cars and Light Trucks*. SRI International. Menlo Park, Calif.

Sweeney, James L. 1993. *Gasoline Taxes: An Economic Assessment*. Stanford Center for Economic Policy Research Working Paper. Stanford University. September.

Tietenberg, Thomas H. 1988. *Environmental and Natural Resource Economics*. Glenview, Ill.: Scott Foresman.

About the Editors

DANIEL SPERLING is professor of environmental studies and transportation engineering at the University of California at Davis and founding director of the campus's Institute of Transportation Studies (ITS–Davis). Dr. Sperling has led the three-year-old institute to international prominence in areas of travel behavior analysis, energy, and environmental aspects of transportation and advanced transportation technology. Prior to obtaining his Ph.D. from the University of California at Berkeley, Dr. Sperling worked for the U.S. Environmental Protection Agency for two years and as an urban planner in the Peace Corps in Honduras for two years. He has an undergraduate degree in engineering from Cornell University.

SUSAN SHAHEEN is a Ph.D. student in ecology focusing on environmental policy analysis at the University of California at Davis. She is also a research assistant at the Institute of Transportation Studies–Davis. Prior to beginning her doctoral work, Ms. Shaheen worked as energy and environmental consultant to the Environmental Protection Agency and the Department of Energy in Washington, D.C. She has a B.A. in English and political science and an M.S. in public policy analysis from the University of Rochester.

About the Authors

STEPHEN BERNOW is a vice-president and cofounder of the Tellus Institute and manager of the Energy Group's Program on Energy and Environment. Dr. Bernow has a Ph.D. in physics from Columbia University.

MICHAEL CAMERON is an economic analyst with the Environmental Defense Fund in Oakland, California, and is currently project director for EDF's Southern California transportation and air quality project. He is author of EDF's 1994 study *Efficiency and Fairness on the Road: Strategies for Unsnarling Traffic in Southern California*, and their 1991 study *Transportation Efficiency: Tackling Southern California's Air Pollution and Congestion*. Mr. Cameron has a master's degree in public policy from the John F. Kennedy School of Government at Harvard University.

RAJU CEERLA is associate transportation planner at the Association of Monterey Bay Area Governments and was a research associate at the University of California at Davis.

JOHN M. DECICCO is a senior associate with the American Council for an Energy-Efficient Economy (ACEEE), where his efforts focus on technologies, programs, and policies for improving vehicle efficiency and reducing travel demand as ways to reduce transportation energy use and its economic and environmental impacts. He received a Ph.D. in mechanical engineering from Princeton University in 1988, where he conducted research at the university's Center for Energy and Environmental Studies.

DEAN A. DRAKE is a manager at General Motors Environmental and Energy Staff in Detroit. He has been active in the environmental area, specializing in California emission regulations, since 1978. Mr. Drake has a master's degree in business administration from Michigan State University and a bachelor's degree in mechanical engineering from GMI.

FREDERICK W. DUCCA is manager of the Travel Model Improvement Program of the Federal Highway Administration. Dr. Ducca has 15 years of professional experience in the areas of travel demand forecasting, land use and transportation interrelationships, and suburban mobility. He holds a B.S. degree in mathematics from St. Peter's College, an M.B.A. from the University of Pennsylvania, and a Ph.D. in city planning from the University of Pennsylvania.

GUNNAR ERIKSSON has been with NORDPLAN, Stockholm, since 1984 and was a guest researcher at Lawrence Berkeley Laboratory between September 1992 and September 1993. He has university degrees in economics and geography and is currently a Ph.D. candidate at the Royal Institute of Technology in Stockholm.

MARK FULMER is a research associate in the Energy Group of the Tellus Institute, a nonprofit energy and environmental research and consulting group in Boston, Massachusetts. Mr. Fulmer has a master's degree in engineering from Princeton University, where he performed research at the Center for Energy and Environmental Studies.

DEBORAH GORDON is director of the Transportation Program at the Union of Concerned Scientists in Berkeley, California. She has worked in the transportation field for ten years and is author of *Steering a New Course: Transportation, Energy, and the Environment.* Ms. Gordon has a B.S. degree in chemical engineering from the University of Colorado and a master's degree in public policy from the University of California at Berkeley.

ROBERT A. JOHNSTON is professor of environmental studies at the University of California at Davis and a researcher at the Institute of

Transportation Studies there. His other research areas include legal methods of regional and statewide habitat protection, impact assessment policy, and land use plan implementation.

MICHAEL F. LAWRENCE is a vice-president at Jack Faucett Associates and has consulted with the Environmental Protection Agency and the Department of Energy on environmental policy and alternative fuels for over 15 years. He holds an M.B.A. degree in finance and applied economics from the University of California at Berkeley.

AMORY B. LOVINS is director of research at Rocky Mountain Institute, which he cofounded with his wife L. Hunter Lovins in 1982 to foster resource efficiency and global security. A physicist, Mr. Lovins has been an energy consultant for over 20 years, advising international organization, governments, and corporations. He has taught at Stanford and Dartmouth Universities and has authored over a dozen books, including the groundbreaking *Soft Energy Paths*.

PAUL MCCARTHY is a research economist at Ford Motor Company, where he is responsible for policy analysis, including energy and environmental policy, and industry studies related to employment, industry structure, and vehicle demand. He has worked for the Congressional Budget Office, Natural Resources and Commerce Division, on industrial policy and national gas price decontrol. Dr. McCarthy has a Ph.D. in economics from the University of Michigan.

LAURIE MICHAELIS is in the Environment Directorate of the OECD, working on policy issues relating to climate change and energy use, especially the electricity and transportation sectors. He previously worked in the International Energy Agency and has done research in the U.K. and in an international setting on the technical, economic, and policy aspects of energy production from biomass, alternative transportation fuels, and transportation technologies.

LAURENCE O'ROURKE is a research assistant at Jack Faucett Associates, where he has been working on environmental quality and transportation planning issues. He has a B.A. degree in political science from Johns Hopkins University.

LEE SCHIPPER is a staff senior scientist at the Lawrence Berkeley Laboratory (LBL), University of California at Berkeley, and co-leader of the International Energy Studies group. He is also associated with the Stockholm Environment Institute, formerly the Beijer Institute. Dr. Schipper has a B.A. degree in music and an M.A. and Ph.D. in physics from the University of California at Berkeley.

KENNETH M. VAUGHN is a Ph.D. candidate in civil and environmental engineering and a postgraduate research engineer at the Institute of Transportation Studies, University of California at Davis, where he is researching the effects of advanced information systems on driver behavior.

MICHAEL QUANLU WANG is a staff researcher in the Center for Transportation Research, Argonne National Laboratory. He has worked on air pollutant, energy, and economic impacts of alternative-fuel vehicles for the last five years and has published several major papers on the topic. Dr. Wang has a Ph.D. in environmental policy analysis from the University of California at Davis.

Index